Telling Tales

Living the Effects of Public Policy

Sheila Neysmith
Kate Bezanson
Anne O'Connell

Fernwood Publishing • Halifax

Editing: Eileen Young
Printed and bound in Canada by: Hignell Printing Limited

A publication of:
Fernwood Publishing
Site 2A, Box 5 32 Oceanvista Lane
Black Point, Nova Scotia, B0J 1B0
and 324 Clare Avenue
Winnipeg, Manitoba, R3L 1S3
www.fernwoodbooks.ca

Fernwood Publishing Company Limited gratefully acknowledges
the financial support of the Department of Canadian Heritage,
the Nova Scotia Department of Tourism and Culture
and the Canada Council for the Arts for our publishing program.

Library and Archives Canada Cataloguing in Publication

Neysmith, Sheila
Telling tales : living the effects of public policy /
by Sheila Neysmith, Kate Bezanson, Anne O'Connell.

Includes bibliographical references.
ISBN 1-55266-161-X

1. Canada--Social conditions--1991-. 2. Canada--Social policy.
3. Canada--Economic conditions--1991-. 4. Canada--Economic policy--1991-.
5. Social problems--Canada. I. Bezanson, Kate II. O'Connell, Anne
III. Title.

HN103.5.N49 2005   361.1'0971   C2005-901430-X

Contents

Acknowledgements

Conventional terms of acknowledgment cannot begin to reflect the contributions that a number of persons and several organizations made to this book. Undoubtedly the biggest debt of gratitude is to the members of the forty households who, over a three-year period, willingly partook in sharing with us their experiences and interpretations of what was happening to them between 1997 and 2000. It was these ongoing conversations that made the analyses presented in the chapters in this book a possibility. Words are not sufficient to express our appreciation for allowing us to share your understandings as we tried to interpret the meaning and consequences of events to people differentially located in Canadian society.

The "Speaking Out" project would not have been feasible without the generous financial support of the Atkinson Foundation. This foundation has funded numerous initiatives within the tradition of progressive social policy. We thank you for once again taking a chance on an innovative approach to social policy research. The Caledon Institute of Social Policy sponsored the research project and made available its resources and experience in profiling policy issues. The Periodic Reports issued throughout the project were made possible through the use of the Caledon Institute's publishing resources. We thank Ken Battle, Director of the Caledon, for his ongoing support.

The research team had seven members. It was only over the years of the project that it became increasingly obvious what an unusual group had come together. As one of the principal investigators of the "Speaking Out" project, Sheila Neysmith wants to thank Michael Mendelson, co-principal investigator on the project, and a senior policy analyst with the Caledon Institute, for pursuing, with the Atkinson Foundation, the idea of gathering stories as a grounded route to documenting the policy experience. The research team was lucky enough to convince Susan McMurray to join us as project manager. As all members of the team know, Susan was the linchpin who helped us and the analysis stay on course month after month, year after year. The team was comprised of four research associates, two of whom were Kate Bezanson, now Assistant Professor, Department of Sociology, Brock University, and Anne O'Connell, Ph.D. candidate in Sociology and Equity Studies, OISE/UT. Both are co-authors of this book. The chapter analyses reflect the insights gleaned as they interviewed household members over time. They brought to the writing of this book the same critical strengths and energy that I remember so well during the life of the "Speaking Out" project. Fraser Valentine and Mary Louise Noce were also research associates during the three years of the project. Although current commitments meant that they could not participate in writing this book, their analytic selves are present in all the chapters. Indeed, as we debated how to present the data, we often called on ideas or positions that we knew they would argue were they physically present. This project would never have been transformed into a book if it were not for the efforts of Fernwood Publishing, in particular Errol Sharpe, publisher, the cogent point raised by an anonymous reviewer and the skilled editing of Eileen Young. We thank you for the vision and support that bringing a book into being entails.

To all participants, household members, research team members, the Caledon Institute and the Atkinson foundation, we offer this book as a concrete token of the contributions you have made toward pushing the goals of social justice.

Sheila Neysmith
Kate Bezanson
Anne O'Connell

Chapter One

Experiencing Social Policy
Focusing on People, Not Policy Arenas

> Speaking out is not a simple gesture of freedom in a culture of
> domination. (hooks 1989: 16)

Introduction

Capturing and articulating the effects of changing social policies on
people's lives is important in countries like Canada that have a welfare-state tradition.[1] Relating the quality of life of citizens to the existence
of certain types of policies is seldom contested in the field of policy
analysis. Rather, the challenge lies, both conceptually and methodologi-
cally, in illuminating the dimensions of this complex relationship. This
book takes up that challenge. It strives to capture how social policies daily
affect people as individuals, as members of households, as participants in
communities of various sorts, as employees and as citizens in a country
where many enjoy a relatively high standard of living. Drawing on interviews with members of forty households conducted between 1997–2000,
this book presents some of the outcomes of neoliberal economic restructuring in Ontario and poses stark questions about mainstream policy
analysis and research. Chapter Nine details our methodology in depth.

In an international context of rising wealth disparities and economic
and social crises in many nations, increasing attention is being paid to how
to build social well-being in order to buffer societies against social disen-
gagement (World Bank 2000). As the uneven effects of market economies
become more global, policy discourse about citizenship has moved from a
focus on social security and universal entitlements to discussions of social
exclusion/inclusion, social cohesion and the role of social capital. The
research presented in this book captures some of the complex local effects
of neoliberalism operating under the aegis of globalization.[2] Household
stories document how aspects of globalization reached into people's lives;
they also reveal the limited theoretical understanding of these effects.
Each chapter presented here documents not only the microeffects of
neoliberalism but also its larger implications for policy analysis.

Our approach to understanding the experiences of individuals confronted by social policy change, which itself has resulted from neoliberal
globalization, is embedded in critical theory. In the social sciences, the
term critical theory has become a shorthand reference for a variety of
attempts to break with the theoretical moulds presented by the dominant
strands of liberalism/neoliberalism. Originating with theoretical work

emerging from the Frankfurt School, it now encompasses reformulations of Marxist theory, the spectrum of feminist challenges and poststructuralist inquiries. Critical race theory also informs our approach. We consider how race is formed, fashioned and operates in relation to and through other systems of exclusion, marginalization, abuse and oppression (Goldberg and Essed 2002: 3). Discourse analysis, which emphasizes speech as performance and "talk" as action, grounds our interpretation of popular and household-derived discourses about welfare recipients, immigrants, youth and taxpayer. In this book, a central concept in sampling and analysis was social location. Social location is defined by the inter-sectionality of dimensions of privilege and oppression.[3] Starting with the lens of social location, this book insists on approaching social policy by considering its differential effects, based on individual and household location within the Canadian social landscape. In the chapters that follow, household stories reveal how social policies and programs played out in ways that reinforced social inequalities arising from differences in class, gender, race, region, ability and sexuality.

The approach employed in this book deviates from mainstream single-issue policy stances. Issues deemed important from the perspective of those who live with the effects of policies do not map neatly onto pre-set categories. Although policies are developed and implemented as discrete entities, they are not experienced in isolation from one another. Engaging in policy debates from a different entry point, the book is grounded in the experiences of participants in forty households who were interviewed repeatedly over three years. During each of four rounds of interviews, the primary focus rested on the concerns and priorities that were central to household members; questions about policy issues that were in the news were secondary. The narratives of the households interviewed for this study demonstrate how welfare state restructuring affects quality of life. Key themes that emerged were the scope and speed with which economic and social policy changes affect people's lives; the surveillance, violence and policing that mark the lives of many; the multidimensional effects of income insecurity; the harm resulting from dominant expectations of a work career; the mechanisms that maintain social exclusion; how the myths of family and community deny access to social services; and how social policies affect people's subjectivity, critical capacities and ultimately their identities. By linking these accounts to conceptual and methodological debates about definitions of household, income, paid and unpaid work, support networks and research design, we suggest that the way policy analysis is commonly understood and practised must be rethought. Set within the context of the political economy of social policy in the 1990s, this chapter places the themes emerging from household stories alongside several important conceptual and methodological debates amongst policy analysts. It reviews our approach to researching social policy and discusses

8

the use of narrative as a source of policy data.

This chapter proceeds in four stages. First, we set the context in which ①
the household case studies took place. We consider the 1990s as a decade
of economic restructuring, intensified globalization and neoliberal ascend-
ancy in political discourse and practice. In such a context, citizenship is
redefined. Individual experiences of changes in social and taxation policy
are thus framed by new definitions of "who counts" as a citizen in a
shrinking welfare state. Second, we consider the potential and limitations ②
of social policy analysis in a neoliberal era. Third, we argue that taking the ③
experiences of members of households seriously matters. Finally, we pro- ④
vide a map of the layout of the book.

The Nineties—A Decade of Growing Disparities

As in most regions of North America, the province of Ontario, Canada,
was undergoing significant economic and social change during the 1980s
and 1990s. Many of these changes are commonly attributed to the globalization of markets since the 1970s, the effects of which reoriented the
Canadian economic and political landscape. The size and nature of the
relationship between globalization and social change is the subject of
ongoing dispute. For the purposes of this book, globalization is important
because it became the rationale for economic restructuring and an ideo-
logical reorientation regarding state provisioning and social citizenship. In
1995, a provincial election in Ontario saw the return to power of a conservative government (under the leadership of Mike Harris) with an economic and social vision closely aligned with that of the former Thatcher
Conservatives in the U.K. and the Reagan-Bush Republican right in the
U.S. Provincial initiatives introduced during the three years of the research
confirmed this assessment.[4] For example, at the provincial level, employment equity legislation was revoked; labour legislation was weakened;
social assistance payments were cut by almost one quarter; and education,
public service and health care sectors underwent massive restructuring,
with cuts to their labour forces (for an overview of the speed and scope of
some of these policy changes, see Bezanson and Valentine 1998). Significantly, that election also marked a turning point in what was considered
legitimate public policy discourse.

Policy changes reinforced conditions for setting groups against each
other. A decrease in federal transfers and a focus on tax cuts at the
provincial level of government pitted upper-income groups, who were
presumed to require few public goods, against lower-income households,
who required more; the repeal of the Employment Equity Act and cuts to
programs aimed at immigrants and refugees reversed the anti-racist gains
that community groups had fought so long and hard to achieve (Trickey
1997). These events, and the divisions they generated, were not unique to

Move towards Reaganomics and diminishing of welfare state

Ontario.[5] Furthermore, interviews for this study were taking place at a time when rapid local changes were also occurring as cities were amalgamated into administrative regions. Thus, the whole public sphere was destabilized, making quite visible the tension between local identity and global pressures.

Restructuring has become a household word in recent years as governments grapple with changes stemming from the globalization of markets. Restructuring and globalization have become code for summarizing a number of trends: (1) the emergence of an economy based on the activities of transnational corporations; (2) the rapid introduction of new information technologies that are revolutionizing communications and the international dissemination of culture; (3) the formation of regional trading blocs such as the North American Free Trade Agreement (NAFTA), the Free Trade Area of the Americas (FTAA) and the European Common Market (EC); and (4) the development of supranational institutions such as the World Trade Organization and the World Court (Castles and Davidson 2000: 4). The powers of nation states seem to be increasingly circumscribed by the forces of globalization (Beiner 1995). At the micro-level, based on data from this study, the changes brought about by restructuring resulted in a pervasive insecurity around employment and the disappearing social safety net at a time when the economy was booming (see Bezanson and McMurray 2000). Chapter Three takes up the theme of income insecurity in the lives of members of households, while Chapter Seven reveals the ways in which the depletion of social infrastructure affects personal relationships and choices available to people.

What Does it Mean to be a Citizen?

In the context of globalization and restructuring, citizenship emerges as a central concept. Most accounts of citizenship in western countries are informed by T.S. Marshall's theory (1965), which assumes the existence of a nation wherein a welfare state operates to redistribute, through taxes and social benefits, some of the resources that accrue disproportionately to different sectors of the population. The existence of the welfare state suggests a recognition of the contradictions that exist between the ideals of democracy and equality on one hand, and the operation of a market-based economy on the other. Marshall, and others, also argued that civil rights can progress to social rights such as rights to education, housing, employment and health. In countries like Canada, citizenship rights have been tied to participation in the market economy. This results in the de facto exclusion of many people who do not, and cannot, participate in the paid labour force. Furthermore, such citizenship models render invisible the mechanisms by which segments of the population historically and currently are disenfranchised. The stories of Aboriginal households, people with disabilities and many women reveal how rights are negated and claims invalidated. Juxtaposed to the above welfare-state tradition has been the movement by a wide variety of groups over the last decade to expand the arena of citizenship claims and to challenge long-standing exclusions by broadening the definition of democracy (Lewis, Gewirtz and Clarke 2000; Vandenberg 2000). These efforts expose some of the limitations in Marshall's assumptions, not the least of which is that the nation-state is the deciding factor in determining the quality of life of its citizens. The nation-state's role is no longer fixed in an era of international flows of capital and continent-wide agreements such as the FTAA. Furthermore, a global market economy gives rise to inequalities not only within nations (where there may or may not be the political will and capacity to address these) but also between countries (Jordan 1998). This debate shapes the changing international context within which federal and provincial policy is formulated.

Household stories might be thought of as the experiential dimension of a changing dialogue on citizenship. For instance, Canada is a nation which has an official policy of multiculturalism, a policy that, some argue, aims to offer the basis for building a society where difference does not result in social exclusion. This claim has been challenged repeatedly by the very groups it seeks to encompass:

> Official multiculturalism represents its polity in cultural terms, setting apart the so-called immigrants of colour from Francophones and the Aboriginal peoples. This organization brings into clearer focus the primary national imagery of Canada.... It rests on posing "Canadian culture" against "multiculturalism." An element of whiteness quietly enters into cultural definitions marking the difference between a core cultural group and other groups who are represented as cultural fragments. The larger function of this multiculturalism not only takes care of legitimation of the Canadian state, but helps in managing an emerging crisis in legitimation produced by a complex political conjunction evolving through the years after the second world war. (Bannerji 2000: 10)

I think I disagree here.

Policies need a concept of citizenship that does not reduce groups to cultural fragments outside of a cultural core. Important debates are occurring as the claims and meanings of citizenship are redefined and the boundaries and authority of nation-states are questioned (Beiner 1995; Castles and Davidson 2000; Drover 2000). In Canada, challenges take the form of Aboriginal claims (Henderson 2002), demands for sovereignty by Quebec and the protests by many—particularly people of colour—of the stonewalling they encounter as they try to influence the direction of important social institutions. Similarly, refugee claims are transformed

Which people of colours?

when they are considered within a framework of international obligations wherein the privileges enjoyed by people living in countries like Canada are part of an economic and political structure that results in poverty and violence in refugees' countries of origin.

Western countries are increasingly focused on global security issues. Since September 11, 2001, the very word security has taken on new and contradictory policy meanings. Discussions of social security formerly linked to welfare-state citizenship are now displaced by referents to securing borders against (usually racially profiled) "outsiders" who are seen as threatening "Canadian citizens." Abu-Laban (2002) shows how a renewed popularity of arguments positing a "clash of civilizations" (Huntington 1993), as well as renewed ethnic profiling, exists in spite of Canada's liberal democratic and multicultural tradition. In the arena of social policy, borders are policed through immigration policy, while federal and provincial social programs have regulations that include and exclude people, based on ideas of who qualifies as a full member of the Canadian nation state. These practices that separate and differentiate reinforce oppressive discourses of who is a real citizen (Castles and Davidson 2000). Household stories in Chapter Six reveal how this happens.

The dimensions of household stories presented in the following chapters reveal some of the experiential dimensions of a changing dialogue on citizenship. The experiences of participants in this study suggest that the priorities of post-World-War-Two welfare states are being reordered toward more restrictive definitions of equality, merit and need. Equality of opportunity, rather than outcome, and rights, rather than social benefits, are emphasized. These concepts, rooted in modernist ideas of individualism, do not challenge economic and political processes that reproduce social inequities and the resulting policy orientation, referred to as neoliberalism. "Merit" becomes not only the basis for economic and social rewards, but inequalities structured by race and gender are sanctioned as they get folded into ideas of merit. Meanwhile, a narrowing definition of what constitutes "genuine need" becomes the only basis upon which to claim state support, and, even then, support is provided under increasingly strict tests for eligibility (Gilbert 2001; Jordan 1998).

The meaning of work comes up repeatedly in household stories. It is quite apparent that paid employment covered a small fraction of the work in which participants engaged. Yet people's lives were regulated by the hegemony of paid labour as the only legitimate form of work. Scholars examining the paid work assumptions underlying prevailing definitions of citizenship have noted repeatedly how they exclude women, people with disabilities and racialized sectors of the population (see, for example, Morris 1993; O'Connor, Orloff et al. 1999; Williams 2000). Neoliberal conceptions of citizenship prize self-sufficiency and independence, disparage need and dependence, and thus sanction receding state intervention and greater privatization of, for example, caring responsibilities. A "normal citizen" is first and foremost constructed as an individual participant in the labour market. This individual is also expected to translate his/her needs into market-oriented behaviour, for instance, conceiving of self as a care consumer in the market of caring services (Aronson and Neysmith 2001; Sevenhuijsen 1997: 57). Ongoing attempts to define and measure unpaid work (Glazer 1993; Luxton and Vosko 1998; Neysmith and Reitsma-Steet 2000; Perrons 2000; Statistics Canada 1995; Waring 1988), which culminated in Statistics Canada counting the hours spent on housework and child and elder care in the 1996 census, highlight the amount and types of unpaid work being done, particularly by women. These studies have also noted that the offloading, for example, of health care into the informal realm of family-based care is increasing. The cumulative effects of decreasing social provisions on the options available to households persuaded us that it was important to document people's personal experiences in order to more fully understand the dynamics of these policy changes for citizenship within and across households.

The entrenched oppositions in dominant political discourse between independence and dependence, taxpayer and service user, "us" and "them" along with the withering of many universal social programs increase the likelihood of what Tronto calls "privileged irresponsibility": she describes this as a situation in which "those who are relatively privileged are granted by that privilege the opportunity simply to ignore certain forms of hardship that they do not face" (1993: 120–21). Plus, the social programs they do access, along with benefits such as increased tax breaks, elide their own dependence on the state. The way dependency is constructed, however, suggests that relatively advantaged groups, i.e., those who are "included" will not support more inclusive types of policies. Thus, any analysis of responsibilities that citizens have in the spheres of family, paid work and community needs to take into account the differing social locations of people. Where individuals and households are located in Canadian society will promote or impede their capacity to engage and to make claims as citizens. Chapters Four and Six in particular take up this discussion.

Alternative Ingredients for Policy Analysis?

Policy analysis has, typically, concerned itself with the assessment of policy formation, implementation and particular effects. Many assessments start with a statement of what a particular policy is intended to do. The analysis then proceeds to consider the resources and measures associated with implementing the policy; that is, the actors, institutions and instruments involved, the nature of the public good anticipated and the populations affected (see, for example, Howlett and Ramesh 1995). These models are concerned with understanding the dynamics and results of a policy program. In contrast, research coming out of the policy sciences often focuses on how and why a particular policy came into being in the first place; that is, the policy itself, not its effects, is treated as the dependent variable (Dobuzinskis, Howlett et al. 1996). In this book we move outside both these traditions to examine how policies play out in the lives of citizens from the perspective of those who experience them—those for whom, ostensibly, they are designed.

Tapping into citizens' experiences and knowledge of the effects of social policies in their lives is a complex undertaking. People do not usually position themselves as assessors of how social policies are affecting their daily activities. Few household members who took part in this research used policy language to describe the barriers they faced or the help they received to meet, for example, their needs for transportation, for shelter or for assistance with a child with an attention deficit disorder. Nevertheless, in the chapters that follow, the complex routine impact of policies in people's lives are vividly illuminated. This book introduces that complexity into mainstream policy analysis and into what are often ideologically rigidified debates about public policy. Policies are simultaneously personal and political; they affect sectors of society differentially—the same policy can promote the welfare of some while adding to the insecurity of others. Understanding the unequal and compounding effects over time of policies across the population is critical if meaningful engagement of citizens in local and national debates is to occur. People take action based on their interpretation of events around them; however this often occurs in ways other than those anticipated by analysts when they talk about the feedback that influences agenda setting, problem definition and ultimately the shape and content of programs (see, for example, Dery 2000).

Doubuzinskis (1996: 112) poses the question, "Does policy research really compel us to rethink policy problems in creative ways, or does it merely add a veneer of pseudo-scientific legitimacy to the claims and counter claims of competing interests?" Building better theory often means moving outside the confines of disciplinary boundaries—in this case, looking beyond the usual administrative, judicial and policy communities which are concerned with the development and implementation of policies. Normal policy making is not about change that shifts power relationships in the society. Transformative possibilities can often only be envisioned when alternative information and perspectives are used. The extensive use of household voices in this text is based on the premise that there is no reason to assume that the needs of various communities reflect the particular policy priorities and forms that policy makers articulate. We do not question the utility of this focus from the policy-making side of the equation. Indeed, assessing if policies are delivering their claimed benefits is an important thread in the critical policy literature. However, we have positioned ourselves quite differently. Stories told by participants differed from what might be called powerful organizational stories, that is, those told by health care professionals, Ministers of Education or welfare officials. In the discussion sections of each chapter we deliberately juxtapose these household stories to the dominant organizational forms that silence alternatives.

During the three years of the study, reports were regularly issued by the research team on topical policy issues such as employment, education, health and income security (see "Speaking Out" Reports at www.caledoninst.org). Each report was based on an analysis of interviews with household members about their experiences in the preceding eight months. Key concerns identified during the first round of interviews became the basis for a more in-depth exploration in subsequent interviews. Thus, the guide used in each round of interviewing had many similar questions but there was also a changing substantive section that anchored each of the preceding reports. As discussed in Chapter Nine, secondary data available from other studies were used to elaborate and generalize from the particulars of what an individual household might experience.[6] Now, with over three years of household stories, the cumulative impact of policy changes from participants' perspectives is examined. The analysis in the ensuing chapters comes out of a re-examination of household interviews with the purpose of building theory and suggesting alternative analytic approaches to policy analysis.

Conceptual Strengths in Using Household Stories as Data

The use of people's experiences for understanding social phenomena and for developing alternative explanations of why and how practices take the form they do has a long history. There has been a resurgence in the use of qualitative methods in the social sciences as the limitations of positivist research paradigms and existent forms of quantitative data analysis for understanding social phenomena became increasingly evident. The development of new concepts and theorizing is usually the result of pushing from the margins. For instance, by the late 1960s, feminist activists were engaged in exploring why so many of their experiences were not reflected in prevailing theories of work and family life. One of the key ideas emerging from thirty years of feminist research is that "the personal is political" and that "policy is personal" (Ungerson 1987). Analyzing what was happening to women and then trying to name it led to the emergence of concepts such as invisible work, the double day, "his" and "her" marriages and the glass ceiling. Similarly, critical examinations of these concepts revealed their white middle-class roots about images of the nuclear family. Low-income women and women of colour have straddled the separate spheres in quite different locations from those which feminist theorists of the time were experiencing (Dua 1999: 241). The specifics of participants' stories in this book may be personal but the shape they took in the late nineties reflected the social structures of the society within which they lived. This book documents some of the complex relationships between private troubles and public issues.

The household stories in the chapters that follow are particularly rich because they were gathered continuously over several years by the same interviewer/research associate returning four times to each household. Thus, interviewer and household members developed a rapport over time which allowed for a deeper understanding of the complexity that characterizes the interaction of public policy and private lives. Because interviewers were also research associates, this understanding was carried into the analysis of the longitudinal data. In each chapter, the tone is set by household voices. We draw on their narratives as the means for documenting the effects of public policy. The importance of documenting the experiences of individuals as a way of understanding social change was articulated by Berthoud and Gershuny as they reflected on their seven-year panel study of British families:

> The micro-dynamics of life, the processes through which individuals and household circumstances are maintained or transformed from year to year—what might be thought of as life chances—may simply be the best, the most informative and the most powerful way to describe the current workings of the society.... Events experienced by individuals do not necessarily create trends in society as a whole. On the other hand, the major trends that have occurred during the past generation are made up of altered life experiences for individuals, and it is only by studying those personal experiences, and the influences on them, that it is possible to understand the trends fully. (Berthoud and Gershuny 2000: 215–16)

These authors also comment on how presenting their findings in chapters that focused on policy areas such as health and housing disguised the interactive and cumulative effects of people's experiences. We attempt to capture this important dynamic by organizing the chapters in this book in terms of analytical themes emerging from three years of data rather than around policy arenas.

The definition of household was a broad one. We loosely defined it as comprising one or more people sharing living space on a regular basis, where adult members share some or all resources and some degree of commitment to the relationship. Households may consist of a mix of men, women and children of different ages, in different jobs, involved in different aspects of community life (McMurray 1997: 2).[7] This sampling strategy proved invaluable in tracing the iterative effects of policy change. Thus, throughout the book we sometimes use the term "participants" and at other times refer to "households." This fluid use of two terms captures a component of how policy works; namely, it usually focuses on individuals but it is experienced by citizens within multiple sets of social relationships, some of the most central being those with others who are part of an individual's household. Thus, the lack of affordable housing, for example, was experienced quite differently by James, one of our participants who was an unattached young person living on the streets, than by Ashley and Rosa, a three-generational household who lived together not by choice but by the necessity of combining resources to get adequate accommodations.

It was only over time that the static demographic characteristics of the sampling strategy became greater than the sum of their parts. For instance, in designing the study, the sample was built to ensure the presence of households with different levels of income. However, the experiences of participants cannot be considered as some kind of objective or essential statement of class reality. Likewise, we were not looking for correlates of any single social relation. Although class, like race and gender, is a highly relevant lens for social analysis, how it is experienced will vary across time, location and social structures. Thus, if experience, in part, is thought of in terms of relationships of power that are reinforced and reproduced through social policies, it can be found today embedded in policies such as tuition for education, the minimum wage level and welfare regulations. Social location, then, is much more complex and fluid than income level or class. It captures the multiple and intersecting vectors of difference based on gender, ability, immigration status and so on that result in privilege and oppression. Over the life of the project the research team began to think in terms of a social map of Ontario—a multidimensional space made up of personal, economic, social and political axes within which participants occupied differing social locations. Particular social policies, at their best, consider one or two of these dimensions for different sectors of the population, but participants experience them interactively. In summary, social location and social map are useful concepts because they facilitate the examination of the intersectionality of social policies.

Many events marked the lives of household members and the communities in which they lived during the life of the project. What might be termed social mobility during a booming economic period was, however, absent for most (for national data, see Statistics Canada 2003). Sources of income often changed, as did household composition. Individual members might fare well at one point in time but then fall back at another. The overall picture for most participants seemed to be one of trying to hold on as the economic and policy terrain shifted under foot (see Charts 1, 2 and 3 in Appendix). Although we tracked households for only three years, the persistence of precariousness for those with low incomes and the increas-

3 Years
Really?

.ing insecurity of others experientially captured what other analysts were showing statistically, namely, that the gap in wealth in Canadian society is not only widening but becoming entrenched (Yalnizyan 2000). The use of panel data (interviewing the same people repeatedly) enabled us to document underlying patterns of privilege that reproduce class, gender and ethno-racial disparities.

Discussions of using experience as data emphasize how the former needs to be put in context and understood in terms of "the historical processes that through discourse, position subjects and produce their experiences" (Scott 1992: 26; see also Clandinin and Connelly 1994; Mulinari and Sandell 1999). In this book participants' experiences are seen as a source of understanding stemming from their social location. These accounts became the fulcrum which enabled the research team to turn in several directions at once as the meaning of participants' experiences were explored, putting their stories alongside other accounts of what was happening in social and economic policy. Such an approach reveals how the design of a policy may be non-discriminatory in intent but it can be disenfranchising in its effects for many households.

To capture the complexity of the socio-political context, we worked with a notion of experience that was empirically grounded; that is, in our gathering of data we focused on individually lived experiences but saw these as tied to collective identities and structures of domination. Identity implies both a sense of self and a sense of belonging. It offers a means of understanding how struggles for self-realization are linked to struggles by groups. However, the term is also problematic. It can obscure the hierarchical positioning of groups in the larger society, as well as disparities within groups. As Williams points out,

Identity Drama
Victor Turner
Essay

> It is common in contemporary politics to invoke a network of solidarity and duty which moves effortlessly from the individual to family, community and nation. Without reference to identities these may be insufficient as the basis of inclusion, solidarity, and support. The multiple identities, which create forms of belonging, solidarity, resistance and support for groups (some of which may be excluded from family or community or nation) may cut across, indeed, reconstitute the very meanings of family, community and nation. (2000: 347–48)

Our methodology emphasizes a particular notion of experience which analytically links lived worlds to social structures. However, the relationships between social location and experience are not always obvious. We have underlined these ties by including within each chapter a selection of households which occupy differing positions on the social map of Ontario. A close examination of the actions they took in meeting an array of daily responsibilities suggests that, depending upon their social location, policies helped or hindered individual and joint efforts of household members to find security and build for their futures.

A Word of Caution When Interpreting Experiences

Arrangements within households are usually considered to be private matters. Even though it is acknowledged that policies affect how private decisions are made, and how lives are lived, the ways and means of taking them into account are ambiguous and seldom studied as part of assessing policy impacts. In this study what was considered "relevant data," both in terms of substantive areas and pertinent issues, were determined by participants. On the one hand, using these experiences makes a major contribution to the literature on policy analysis. On the other hand, despite the use of a reflective methodology that helped us to see how we were constructing what participants said, certain dimensions of their experiences will have been ignored for various reasons: we may not have heard them; we may have effectively silenced them because our attention was elsewhere; or participants may have chosen not to share them with us. Thus, these stories have been shaped by us as authors. This occurred as a result of the responses we pursued further in the interviews; as a result of the leads we followed or ignored in our conversations with household members; and as a result of our interests as policy analysts. This interactive factor points to an important tension in building critical theory.

As individuals we must deal with an ongoing series of changes that intersect with the lives of others, particularly those with whom we live on a daily basis. The many events that make up "normal" household life are subject to myriad personal, relational and social, political and economic influences. The interactive effect of these means that attempts to separate the private from the public domains in people's lived experience can result in false dichotomies that conceal more than they reveal. We know that people experience policy at the personal level. However, personal stories are not a simple retelling of details. They are continually constructed and may be reconstructed by individuals depending on the context; such stories are, however, far more than fantasies and idiosyncratic narratives even given that they do change over time. The interpretation of personal experience is always embedded in the larger stories, myths and normative structures that permeate Canadian society. It is important to bear in mind, however, that how participants describe individual and combined experiences is limited by the language and dominant discourses available to them (Torgerson 1996). Thus, participants in this study, like policy makers and analysts, had a finite box of conceptual tools available to them for capturing and relating multiple policy impacts. In Chapter Eight we lay out some of the forms these interpretations took and the processes participants,

Turner

who lived in very differing places on the social map of Ontario, used to understand what is happening around them. Not surprisingly, some participants accepted racist, anti-immigrant explanations of labour-market instability; others supported the demonization of sole-support mothers receiving social assistance, setting them in contrast to the image of the hard-working but overburdened tax payer. All grappled to understand and respond to the impact that the changing nature of employment and the shrinking of the public sector, its programs and its services were having on every dimension of their lives.

Finally, this book has many stories about survival but it is also witness to the many costs of surviving in an affluent society in the final years of the twentieth century. Power relationships shaped the experiences of household members, as well as the social institutions with which they interacted, as they dealt with daily concerns. Because the interviews were ongoing over three years and the focus allowed considerable leeway for household members to determine which issues were salient to them, we were able to capture some of the dynamics of making choices, coping with difficulties and infusing meaning into the multidimensional aspects of household life.

Participants showed tremendous resilience and optimism in the face of what often seemed to us to be a constant onslaught of change that disrupted hopes and plans for the future. Because households in this study came disproportionately from lower-middle and low-income strata, policy changes were often seen as a threat to already precarious circumstances. Household members took action, frequently turning to each other and those in their social network at such moments. These networks, however, were made up of people who often were going through similar types of difficulties. Chapter Seven shows what can happen when social policies assume that family can substitute for a social safety net. If circumstances force one to rely on family and friends, the outcome can be very costly to all concerned.

Organization of the Book

Each household has its own story in which the specifics of social policies intertwine with the specific circumstances of people's lives. The significance of this becomes apparent as household experiences unfold over time. Nevertheless, chapters must have a sequencing. The order presented here is based on what we saw as major issues that participants were dealing with during the three-year period of the project. Our selection of organizing themes means that other possibilities were left out. We have included all forty households, although the presence of some will be more visible than others to the reader. In order to keep within the confines of a book, all household stories are necessarily only skeletons of what was conveyed to us. Indeed, most participants experienced aspects of each chapter theme: it was through an examination of all forty households that the themes were derived. The strategy of placing households within one chapter was adopted because it was confusing to present slices of forty household stories in each chapter. Some households are in a chapter because their experiences were particularly dramatic in illustrating a theme. Our concern about the differential impact of social policy depending upon social location meant that it was important to include a range of household types in each chapter. We are persuaded that the chapters, as a whole, capture critical components of people's lived experiences of the social and economic policies that characterized North American society in the late 1990s.

The core of each chapter concentrates on understanding how household members, as individuals and members of collectivities, interpreted and responded to the changes that they were confronting. However, limiting the analysis to understanding the meaning of events to participants could obscure the complexity of power relations that reproduce privilege and oppression in Canadian society. Thus, the last section of each chapter moves beyond considering how people experience policies, to critiquing policies, given the wider context reflected in the themes that organize each chapter. Neglected issues come to the foreground as household narratives inform policy debates via "participatory expertise" (Fischer 1990).

Chapters Two through Eight use the voices of participants to convey several thematic analyses. These are preceded by an introduction that sets the analytical stage. The discussion section at the end of each chapter starts with several questions intended to highlight how the impact of policies are uneven, contradictory and can be contested.

This book can be taken up in a variety of ways. Readers most interested in how policy debates are framed will want to further consider the points raised in this chapter. Those primarily interested in research design or policy methodology issues will find food for thought in Chapter Nine. Readers interested in particular substantive areas such as income security, social exclusion or family policy, might turn immediately to Chapters Three, Six or Seven respectively. Educators looking for case materials can dip into any chapter to select cases that meet their teaching needs. Those with a particular interest in how discourses about difference, diversity or privilege are taken up will examine Chapter Eight. Finally, we hope that many will read the book as a map of the social landscape that exists for citizens that are differentially located in Canada.

Notes

1.   The term social policy is ambiguous (Lewis, Gewirtz and Clarke 2000). Traditionally, it has been used to refer to a range of state programs, legislation and regulations focused on the well-being of citizens. In North America and Europe in the twentieth century, programs and certain laws were captured under

the umbrella of "the welfare state." Health, education, culture and income assistance or security initiatives have formed the substantive program arenas for most discussions of social policy. Economic policies are included in this list by some analysts (Bakker 1996; Elson 1998).

2. Neoliberalism is a social and political philosophy which assumes: (1) that markets are the best and most efficient allocators of resources in production and distribution; (2) that societies are composed of autonomous individuals motivated chiefly by material and economic considerations; (3) that competition is the major vehicle for innovation (Coburn 2000: 138). Globalization refers to a specific form of internationalization that responds to specific financial and economic interests that are articulated in the class relations of society (Navarro 1999: 220).

3. Social location was initially operationalized in terms of such household characteristics. Households were selected for their diversity in terms of income levels, sources of income, household structure and geographical location, as well as differences related to race, ability, language, sexual orientation and Aboriginal status (see sampling template, Tables 1, 2 and 3, in the Appendix).

4. At the same time as the provincial government was reducing social spending, the federal government was actively reshaping the federal welfare state. It cut transfer payments to the provinces for social programs and eliminated national standards in key areas.

5. They had parallels in other jurisdictions (e.g., in other provinces, in many U.S. states, in the U.K. and in New Zealand). In fact, while writing this book the Liberal provincial government elected in British Columbia replicated the policy agenda of the Ontario Tories.

6. Nud*ist 4.0 was the software package used to organize the panel data. This allowed us to readily cull earlier rounds of interviewing on the selected topic.

7. The template used to select households included the following: low-, medium- and high-income; geographic diversity; various household structures (two-parent families, single-parent families, single people, singles living with roommates or friends, couples, three-generational households); different sources of income (people receiving social assistance, people with various types of jobs, retired people and those with other sources of income such as federal Employment Insurance, workers' compensation and rental income); characteristics such as race and ethnicity, physical disability, sexual orientation, housing status, age and gender (McMurray 1997: 3–4). Chart 4 in the Appendix organizes some of the attributes of those who made up the forty households in the sample.

Chapter Two

The Compounding Effects
of Policy Change

Policy makers and analysts usually discuss policies in terms of discrete areas such as child care, housing, education, employment training or pensions. Yet, within households, various social policies interact. The effects of policies are seldom examined from an interactive perspective. Often, a single-policy focus results from framing issues in a manner that reflects the areas of expertise of those who formulate policy. Organizations and government departments tend to be concerned with the effects of individual policies; these policies are examined from the perspective of efficient service delivery and cost (Howlett and Ramesh 1995: 170). When new policies are being formulated or older ones revamped, groups identified as stakeholders, such as business organizations or labour unions, are sometimes invited to participate in the policy formulation or evaluation process. Individuals who are not formally attached to such constituencies but who are greatly affected by policy initiatives are often left out of these processes. Furthermore, in such consultations, a set of questions related to a specific policy usually defines the parameters of discussion, excluding consideration of the ways in which one policy might intersect with others. When other issues are raised, they are generally deemed to be outside of the purview of the consultation and are not recorded. Knowledge that is not documented appears not to exist. Taking account of the interactive and cumulative effects of social policy changes, then, is a challenge for policy makers and analysts.

In Ontario in the mid to late 1990s, a dramatic overhaul of the province's welfare state infrastructure and protective social legislation took place. The massive restructuring of health care, education, social assistance and municipal funding was widely discussed in media and public fora (see for example *Toronto Star* 2002).[1] Far-reaching changes to multiple areas of social policy were implemented quickly, with little public consultation and with long-term consequences for the fabric of the social safety net as well as for the supports available to citizens. Less reported changes occurred at the level of regulations and eligibility criteria, particularly in social assistance, which made getting access to or keeping a service or support more difficult. These kinds of policy and regulatory changes interacted in the lives of individuals: less money, fewer resources and supports, cuts in jobs or changes in working conditions, extensive waiting lists for social housing and long-term care along with fewer educational supports at all levels translated into increased struggles for the members of many households. The changes did not take effect all at once; rather, participants managed changes over time: the combination of changes in several areas of policy pushed some of the households profiled here to their coping limits. As services and programs became less universal in their coverage, those who fared better in managing these changes were those with financial resources to pay for private supports or those with personal time and connections to make up for the loss of public assistance.

In this chapter, the multiple, cumulative and interactive effects of social policies on the lives of participants from a number of households are mapped. Household stories suggest ways to think about and conceptualize policy effects that cut across traditional policy boundaries (see Chapter Nine for details on how this methodology informs policy research). The stories of interviewed household members profiled in this chapter highlight how policy changes in a number of areas affect individuals differently depending on household structure, social location and the stability of resources available to various members. While health care emerges as a common theme in many stories, it is one among many: education, housing, social assistance, transportation, food bank use and public sector restructuring intermingled. The household experiences highlighted here suggest that social policy analysis must engage in debate about how to understand and redress social imbalances and inequalities arising from cumulative multi-policy effects. The methodology employed in this study captures the dynamics of policy changes over time and permits the identification of interactive and compounding outcomes of such changes.

Victoria was divorced and the mother of two daughters. Over the three-year course of this study, Victoria's job became insecure due to changes in provincial funding and policy, her own health deteriorated and so did the health of her parents. In her paid work and in her role as patient and primary caregiver, health care and labour policies enacted by the Conservative provincial government intertwined in their efforts. *Teresa* was a woman in her early thirties who had a severe disability. Although she was well-educated, her health status prevented her from continuing to work in the area in which she was trained. She depended heavily on a range of health care services and supports. Her provincial disability assistance did not cover her basic costs; changes to this policy caused her enormous anxiety. Teresa had a personal support network, but the financial situations of members of this network were similar to her own; she could not rely on them for economic assistance. Her access to adequate income, health care services and other supports became more insecure as new policy changes took effect. *Josie* was a woman in her fifties who had raised her own four children and found herself at the time of the study raising three grandchildren while their mother was being treated for addiction related problems. She constantly struggled to make ends meet. In her job as a health care aide, she witnessed care for seniors deteriorate. Josie attempted to balance a series of changes in the areas of labour, health care, social assistance and housing policy. *Janet and Christopher* constituted a blended family with seven children. Their income security diminished during the last half of the nineties; the demands of managing family needs left them with little leisure time. These experiences, while profoundly unsettling, were understood by Janet and Christopher as examples of an increased vulnerability that many Canadians experienced as a result of what they describe as mean-spirited social policy decisions. *Cheryl and Paul* were a middle-income couple who owned their own home. Paul's position as an administrator in the public school system, along with his experience parenting two boys attending primary and secondary school, resulted in his being very attuned to the depth and breadth of changes to education in the province. Over the course of the interviews, Paul's father had a stroke while Cheryl's mother became ill and died. Although buffered from the worst effects by race and class privilege, this couple invested a huge amount of energy in navigating the education and the long-term care systems, both of which were undergoing massive restructuring. These are their stories.

Victoria

Victoria, a white woman in her early fifties, lived in a mid-sized city in the eastern part of the province with her youngest daughter. Victoria held a graduate degree and worked full-time in an urban hospital. She had a stable income, owned her house (which was mortgage-free) and car, made regular Retirement Savings Plan contributions and had sufficient spending money. Although Victoria seemed to be financially stable, since 1996 she had experienced major changes in her job related to shifts in provincial health care policies and changes in labour legislation. In addition, because Victoria, her daughter and her parents had significant and ongoing health problems, she also managed health policy changes as a patient and caregiver.

In the first interview in 1997, Victoria foresaw the collision of a variety of elements in her life. In 1996, she lost her job as a direct result of provincial funding cuts to hospitals; imminent hospital restructuring also meant that her new job was insecure. Her elderly parents were living in their own house, but both were in their mid-eighties and had failing health. Victoria anticipated that, as her parents' health worsened, their living situation would have to change. Finally, Victoria's own health required ongoing attention and care and had the potential to rapidly deteriorate. A year later, Victoria's predictions were realized. Her chronic condition had resulted in two hospitalizations, her parents had moved into separate custodial care facilities, and her job security and morale decreased as the provincial hospital restructuring process moved forward.

All of these elements affected Victoria's ability to cope on a daily basis:

I come home at the end of the day and I just have anxiety because I have to figure out how to do everything that needs to get done. I have my own treatments that I can't ignore. So that means that I simply cannot sit beside my mother's bed for hours. Sometimes when I come home from visiting my mom, I get teary-eyed because I just think that she has to be okay. I can't juggle one more thing. I just do it because I have no choice. I know that my house is paid for so I won't be on the street, and I cope by pretending and focusing on my job.

Victoria was passionate about her work. She cared about helping people and wanted her work to make a lasting difference in their lives. After 1996, however, Victoria's commitment to her employer declined. In 1996, the Ontario government imposed a six-percent cut to hospitals across the province. Each hospital had to independently determine how to absorb the decrease in operating funds. Victoria said:

Hospitals were given a free hand to decide where to cut from their budgets. There was a doctor at our site who had a lot of research money from a pharmaceutical corporation which he decided to take to another hospital. That loss of revenue for the hospital meant that our unit was a sitting duck to get cut because we didn't have a research arm that brought in external dollars. We were expensive because we were an in-patient service which requires a lot of diagnostic testing. The money for this testing comes out of the hospital's budget, not OHIP [Ontario Health Insurance Plan] money. So, our unit was an easy target for hospital administrators to cut and save money. That's exactly what happened.

At the time of the layoffs there was no union in place. Thus, despite ten years' seniority at the hospital, Victoria had no guarantee of moving into a comparable position elsewhere in the hospital. In time, she was able to secure a new position but her professional community was fractured, and she lost daily contact with many of her colleagues. Not long after Victoria had secured her new position, the Ontario government initiated the hospital restructuring process. In 1996, it appointed an arms-length body called the Health Services Restructuring Commission to restructure Ontario's health care system (Bezanson and Noce 1999). Less than a year after finding a new job, Victoria felt that she was in danger of losing it.

For Victoria, however, this experience had two significant differences from her layoff in 1996. First, in 1998, the hospital service workers held a successful union drive. Not only did Victoria notice an immediate positive difference in working conditions and benefits, but she also felt that she had more job security. Second, in the same year, Victoria and fifty of her colleagues successfully negotiated a pay equity settlement with the hospital, after an eight-year battle. The experience of getting this settlement gave Victoria a lot of confidence.

Throughout this time, Victoria's health status had been poor. In October 1997 and February 1998, she underwent what she described as "significant health crises" requiring hospitalization. Her recovery was slow and her health status remained tenuous throughout the remainder of the study. She was unable to work on a full-time basis for four months. Her health insurance was vital to her financial stability. In 1998, for instance, she spent $8,000 on prescription drugs. Her newly negotiated labour contract ensured that eighty percent of these costs were covered by extended medical benefits. Victoria also received a provincial Assistive Devices Program grant for medical supplies. While she retained the grant throughout our study, she found it more difficult to qualify for support under the program as the provincial government introduced new regulatory frameworks and narrowed eligibility requirements in an attempt to reduce the program's size and scope.

The only doctor with the specialized knowledge required to appropriately treat her condition was located in Toronto. During her recovery, she was unable to drive the considerable distance alone, and she did not have family upon whom she could rely for this kind of help. She said:

> I was really frightened. I had to get to Toronto ten days after I was released from the hospital. I thought, "Well, how am I going to get there?" At first when I was at the hospital they talked about transferring me by ambulance, but once you leave the hospital you aren't their responsibility. Well, I had to go on the bus. I was worried that I might have to do the procedure on the bus, and start to bleed.

Compounding Victoria's concerns about health restructuring at work and her own health care was the failing health of her father and mother. In the spring of 1997 her eighty-five-year-old father caught pneumonia and fell, injuring his hip. Her father was briefly hospitalized and then received home care support for six months. At the time, Victoria described home care as "marvellous." By 1998, however, the situation was very different. Her father's health deteriorated and her mother was no longer able to manage, even with home-care support. Victoria described the difficulty her mother experienced caring for her father and the inadequacy of home care coverage:

> The home care case manager said: "Yes, I'm hearing loud and clear from the treatment team that what he needs is more services, and we just cut your hours by 33 percent because of budget cuts. We know it's terrible and so you should go to the private sector and pay." So we did that, and we had twenty-four-hour nursing care for him because about a week after the care conference, he got shingles, he couldn't feed himself and he became incontinent, bowel and bladder both. We needed something. My mother—this little old lady with her

diabetes who is exhausted—had been up for twenty-six hours because my father was calling out. A hospital-in-a-home is a great concept, but it doesn't work. My mother had been doing laundry, because my father wouldn't wear a diaper. The nurse was doing the care, supposedly freeing up my mother to be resting. That's a great concept. But my mom was doing all the laundry. Finally, we all agreed that this wasn't working, so the nurse came with us to the hospital and told them that my father was no longer a home care case. He was hospitalized, and we waited for a bed in a facility. He never went home again.

While growing up, Victoria described her parents as frugal, saving considerable money and investing for their retirement years. As our study proceeded, Victoria's father did encounter considerable expenses for his care. While in the hospital for two months waiting for a bed at a long-term care facility, for instance, he was forced to pay a daily fee. Victoria said:

Anyone who is waiting for some kind of residential placement is what the hospital calls "alternate level of care." While he was waiting to get into a facility, the hospital charged us $42.16 a day, which is the portion of the cost not covered by OHIP.

Victoria felt that the facility to which her father was admitted was not adequate. In December 1998, he was fortieth on a waiting list for a better facility. In October 1999, he had not moved up the waiting list. It was an expected two-year wait, and Victoria said: "He'll be dead before he gets into a better facility." During this period, Victoria and her siblings decided to sell the family home and move her mother into a residential facility. It was expensive and, after more than thirty years of marriage, Victoria's parents were separated from each other.

The compounding stress associated with her insecure job, unstable health and elderly parents began to take a toll on Victoria. In 1998, Victoria recounted one experience when she was sitting in the hospital emergency waiting room with her mother from 7 p.m. until 1 a.m. Her mother had the flu and was dehydrated. Victoria found herself getting frustrated and angry at her mother:

I had to tell myself to calm down. My mother is eighty-seven years old, she is frightened, and I can't be that testy. But, I notice it in my work as well. I am usually a person with infinite patience, but I'm not that person anymore. So, I guess that's the difference. I'm not patient anymore. I get angry now. I guess I'm not coping.

Meanwhile, Victoria's youngest daughter finished high school and planned to attend university. Reductions to the operating budgets of Ontario universities meant that tuition was rising by as much as 20 percent a year across the province. Her daughter was able to afford the approximately $10,000 a year required to attend university through a combination of the money her grandparents invested, an entrance scholarship, prize money from winning a national writing contest, full-time work through the summer and part-time work during the school year.

During the last interview with Victoria, she reflected on her life:

I'm privileged you know. There are lots of people who are better off than I am, but I have a company pension, and some savings, and I own my house, so I'll be okay. I don't need much.

Teresa

Teresa was a single white woman in her thirties, with a disability, living in Toronto. She suffered from a host of chronic and often debilitating health conditions. During the time of the study, Teresa's main source of income was social assistance for people with long-term disabilities.[2] After waiting four years for subsidized housing, Teresa was finally able to move into a residence specifically designed for adults with disabilities. The residence offered specialized services such as attendant care and homemaking services, and it was close to health care facilities, shopping and transportation. Teresa had a diploma in veterinary science. Her health kept her from maintaining steady employment in this field but she devoted much of her time to caring for animals. She shared her apartment with her cat and dog, volunteered for a local humane society and trained seeing eye dogs for the Canadian National Institute for the Blind.

Teresa was eager to train for another occupation. With the assistance of the now defunct Vocational Rehabilitation Service (VRS), a provincially funded agency that assisted people with disabilities with job training and educational upgrading, she was counselled to go into an administrative field. Upon their recommendation, Teresa enrolled in a medical secretary program offered through a community college. She was working towards completing her diploma when changes introduced by the provincial government to VRS made it impossible for her to complete her program. Because VRS was covering the cost of Teresa's tuition, its collapse meant that no funding existed other than the Ontario Student Assistance Plan (OSAP). In order for Teresa to continue her post-secondary studies, she would have to take out a student loan to cover the cost of tuition. She was reluctant to do this because it would disqualify her from receiving social assistance and having access to the provincial drug plan that provided drug coverage. Given her frequent hospitalizations, she feared that she would have difficulty paying off the debt she would have incurred. With no alternative, Teresa withdrew from college. She continued to keep busy taking general interest courses that were offered free through the district school board. As the study began, Teresa had given up hope of re-entering the labour market.

Teresa struggled to balance the necessities of life such as nutritious food, clothing, rent and transportation with the financial cost of her ongoing health condition. She found herself facing impossible choices. She said, "I needed new shoes this month. Do I get new shoes or do I get groceries? I got new shoes, so I'm going to be relying on the food bank this month because I had to get new shoes." Her request for a dietary supplement provided by social assistance was declined. Over the course of four rounds of interviews, it became clear that Teresa was cutting back on food as a strategy to control costs. This cost consciousness came at a price to her health:

> If you look in my cupboards you'll see that they are absolutely bare, I don't have anything right now because I ran out of funds. (INT: So how are you getting by?) I don't eat, or I have just one meal a day. That's not good for me, but that's all I can do, that's all I can afford, so that's what I do.

She attributed her worsening finances to out-of-pocket health-related expenses. Even with a drug card, she did not have comprehensive coverage. Drugs that were not covered under the provincial plan had to be paid for out-of-pocket. Whether it was paying for an epinephrine pen or having to incur higher living costs because of the necessity of living close to health services, these health-related expenses played havoc with her budget.

Teresa's limited income had repercussions for her social life. At the time of the first interview, Teresa was involved in a number of activities, but had not established meaningful connections with others:

> Like the choir and everything, it keeps me active and it keeps my mind going and I feel like I'm not vegetating. But I have no friendships from any of these things that I do because I can't go out and socialize afterwards because it takes money to be able to do those things.

Her ability to participate in these activities had ended by the final round of interviews. She cited the user fees that her recreation centre was now charging and the loss of her wheelchair transportation eligibility as reasons she could no longer participate. Her social world shrunk as a result.

Teresa's small friendship network did permit her to be resourceful and to stretch her limited finances:

> My friend and I both look out for special buys for each other. We save coupons for each other. We know what each other needs. We look out for stuff for each other. Sometimes we buy something that's too big for ourselves, so we split it in half, and we split the price in half.

Teresa was quick to add that people in her support network were no better off than she was, and friends offered limited instrumental support. She said, "I have a friend and we just talk and stuff, but that's about it. She's kind of in the same boat I am."

Financial pressures weren't Teresa's only concern. She talked about how her support network of doctors, hospitals, therapists and social workers was being dismantled. She worried about what this would mean to the delivery of her care:

> FBA and health care are my biggest concerns because they affect my medical equipment and my medication. I'm always terrified when I get a news clip. Is this medication going to be covered or is this going to come out of my pocket? The next thing [I worry about] would be other programs that I'm involved in, [like] therapy. Without it I can't even survive so there's no point in giving me FBA because I'm not going to be around. And they [support programs] keep getting cut and I don't know if they're going to be around.

She felt ill-equipped to manage all of the changes that were occurring to the delivery of health services and was fearful about what these changes would mean to the continuity of her care. She was distressed about the closing of three hospitals she frequented. As a lesbian, she was anxious about how accessible amalgamated services would be. She feared losing relationships with nurses and doctors whom she trusted, and she worried about where her medical files would go when one of the hospitals she used was closed. She remarked that all her supports were being dismantled and she felt powerless to effect any change.

Teresa's other contact with the health care system, attendant care, was also undergoing change:

> Everybody is squawking that their funding has been cut back. And so staff hours have been cut back. And it's really been hectic because staff are complaining that they have too much to do, with too little staff. And so my bookings are late, or people don't show up or stuff like that happens. There's nobody to call if there's an emergency at this point. You can call the emergency beeper, but there's no guarantee that someone will come, because they're busy with someone else at the time. If you need something sudden[ly], and you're not booked at that time, you can't call over and say, could someone come and help me because I did this or that, and I need some help, because everybody is back-to-back bookings right now.

Compounding these changes to health care were changes that were occurring to social assistance. At the time of the first interview, the provincial government had yet to announce the eligibility requirements under the newly created Ontario Disability Support Plan. Teresa worried that she would fall outside the new criteria:

> FBA, [Family Benefits Act] whatever it's called now, that weighs on my mind. I'm afraid that it will be decreased or taken away completely, or given a welfare status instead of a FBA status because I can't work, and I'm afraid that somehow I'll end up doing workfare, which is something I can't do. I'm also worried about ADP, which is the Assisted Devices Program. They helped me get my machinery that I needed. My assistive devices need to be replaced every four or five years.... I've had to struggle with Social Services to pay.

Under Family Benefits, Teresa was classified as unemployable. While she dismissed this label, she felt secure in the knowledge that social assistance would not put unrealistic demands on her. In addition, under FBA she received money through the Vocational Rehabilitation Service (VRS) for meaningful employment training; with the introduction of new social assistance legislation, she was forced to forgo this. The introduction of Ontario Works and the mantra of "work for welfare" alarmed her as she anxiously waited to hear whether she would be deemed "disabled enough" to continue to receive benefits. Teresa feared this onslaught of changes and responded by not watching the news and refusing to read the newspaper. It seemed as though everywhere she turned she was bombarded by a host of changes that were directly affecting her daily life. She commented, "I live in fear of getting a letter in the mail. I'm like, 'Oh no, here we go, social services has sent me a letter.' It's like you live in fear waiting to see what's going to happen."

A constant state of uncertainty undermined Teresa's ability to handle the day-to-day pressures of finances and her well-being. Her health and morale deteriorated. She hoped that the pace of change in the province would slow down so she could once again attain some stability in a life that had been turned upside down.

Josie

Josie was a white Francophone woman in her fifties living in a co-op. She had raised her own four children, but found herself once again raising a young family. Prior to this undertaking, Josie was living on her own and was able to go out to a movie or dinner when she felt like it. In response to her youngest daughter's serious difficulties, and, with her daughter's agreement, Josie applied for custody of her three grandchildren the year before the study started. At the beginning of the interviews, her daughter was in a drug treatment program and planned to move in with her mother in the hope that she would get healthy and regain custody of her children. The agreement between them was that she had to "be clean" for three years.

In 1996, Josie had to leave work to care for and settle the young children (girls aged five, four, and two years). She did not qualify for Employment Insurance parental leave since, at that time, she was not yet the legal parent; this meant that she had to rely on social assistance. Because she did not fit into the proper category of "family," she received less support than her daughter had gotten when she was considered their legal guardian. Josie appealed her case, eventually winning a meagre top-up that covered about $250 of child care a month once she returned to work. When her daughter moved in with Josie, she was cut off from the child-care supplement. The government then claimed that Josie owed them $4,000 for past child-care costs, even though she, and not her daughter, had become the legal parent. She was eligible to appeal her case; however, there was a $200 charge for every $1,000 dollars of the claim. For Josie, it was just not worth the cost. Josie's own work as a health care aide paid her $18.00 per hour and provided a decent benefits package. Two of the children qualified for a small social assistance allowance, and Josie received $229 per month from the Child Tax Benefit. Her own daughter received $190 per month from social assistance, but a housing allowance was not included because she lived with her mother.

Changes in social assistance, employment insurance, health care, education and housing during the three years of the study fundamentally altered this family's daily life and coping strategies. With changes to co-op by-laws in 1996, residents had to reapply yearly for a subsidy; they were then put on a waiting list. Before these changes, a person's rent would be adjusted monthly as their income levels fluctuated. Now, if Josie's daughter took any form of employment, the household rent would go to market level, threatening future subsidies. By the second interview, her daughter did get a part-time job at a bagel store, which increased their rent. However, the store went bankrupt three months later. During the same time period, the daughter's boyfriend moved in, increasing the rent even more; however, he moved out shortly thereafter. Since calculations for rental rates were done on an annual basis, Josie had to wait to reapply for a subsidy; she had no guarantee she would receive one. By the second interview, for the first time in her life, Josie turned to a food bank.

Josie constantly juggled monthly costs, was perpetually in debt and had no funds for herself or any emergency. She worried about the costs of cold medicine, late car payments, dental bills (that she paid over numerous months) and furniture that was purchased on credit. She also had fears about her daughter's and grandchildren's safety from a past abusive boyfriend. Josie said,

> Money is the biggest concern for me. From pay to pay there's always a gap, I don't have enough… but my concern is about the three granddaughters, that they will come through these ordeals with not too many scars, and that my daughter makes it.

In the first two interviews, Josie's work, which she loved, was primarily in union negotiating. Her job status was part-time as a unit officer, although she worked full-time hours and had high seniority. However, in the first interview, she noted that the provincial mandate to merge municipal services was leading to less job security. She knew that, if a full-time permanent position became available, she would have to take it and leave her union work behind. She was concerned that her union might lose its collective agreement as a consequence of the amalgamation, because they would be merged with other long-term care facilities. This could mean a drop in wages. Already part-time workers' shifts were moving from eight to six, five, four and even two hours.

By 1998, Josie had moved to a full-time permanent position in a nursing home. Returning to the nursing home full-time meant that Josie would be doing heavy lifting of residents from wheelchairs to bed every night, bathing them and assisting them with walking. She needed a large back brace in order to do this work. At the time of the second interview, she was on a two-week sick leave, stressed out by her schedule, which involved getting the children off to school by 8 a.m., doing a couple hours of work in her new position as co-op president and then doing a daily shift from 3 p.m. until 11:30 p.m., returning home by 1:00 a.m. What bothered her most at the time, however, was seeing the number of residents who did not get weekly baths and proper food.

As a health care aide for twenty years, Josie had witnessed the ups and down of care for seniors, the increased demands made on families and health care workers and the resulting conflicts and stresses that placed these groups at odds with one another. She noted, "Cutting costs means there no longer are the same kind of inspectors that come to see if the level of care is up to par." Although conditions had improved drastically since the late 1960s, Josie described how poor conditions were re-emerging. She said, "I found there's much more bed sores for the residents. I see residents sitting there all day, nobody talking to them. Before, at least you had a couple of minutes to go talk to them, you can't do it anymore." When families visit, she explained that:

> They come in and they want their parents to be looked after. There are not enough bodies there, so they have to look for a nursing assistant or a nurse, and they can't find anyone so they get frustrated and then whoever they see first gets it. I find a lot of people are being reprimanded by management because they have lost it with a visitor.

Instability at the work place was accompanied by instability in the education sector, where, for two years in a row, Josie's granddaughters had to wait until the end of August to find out if junior kindergarten would be offered. Josie noted that her granddaughter's class size in junior kindergarten was twenty-three. Teachers were extremely overextended: the children did not receive the attention and support that Josie felt was appropriate. Josie also worried about policies like workfare: she said that it would certainly drive down wages, threatening her salary as well as the role of unions in the work place.

By the third interview, Josie's daughter had married. With a fourth baby on the way, the demands on Josie were exacerbated by the father's departure and a difficult pregnancy. Her daughter, who had taken over caring for the children and running the household, could do less and less as her pregnancy progressed. At her work place, the workload continued to increase:

> Residents fall and break their hips, because we don't have time to go and check on them, to find them. We found a resident on the floor the other night. She had no injury but her knees were already bruised by the time we found her. So how long was she there? She said she was there for about four hours.

According to Josie, there was no investigation of why the fall happened in the first place. The floors of the residence were filthy, equipment regularly broke down, and, because of a new centralized placement system, residents were sent to nursing homes by staff who knew little about what each home really provided. By this time, Josie's health also had deteriorated. She was diagnosed with arthritis throughout her body.

Josie had begun thinking about early retirement. Her benefits plan would continue to give her drug and dental coverage until she was sixty-five, but her pension would only be $400 per month. She said, "So I'm actually thinking about looking down east at the job situation. But at fifty, do I want to start over again?" With all of the changes around her and, in an environment of cutbacks, Josie recalled that she used to be better off:

> Five years ago I was alone and I was better off. I looked after me. Now I have all these people, so money-wise I'm not better off but in some ways I like it better now than I did five years ago. But I cannot see my life alone any more.

Soon after our last interview, Josie moved back to her home province with family in tow.

Janet and Christopher

Janet and Christopher are a white blended family of five (two parents and three children, plus two others on weekends and two who live away) who resided in a beautifully restored nineteenth-century home in a medium-sized south-eastern Ontario city. They were a low- to middle-income household; they had a sizeable mortgage, cars that were "about to die" and one son in university, but they managed to make the most of what disposable income they had. Christopher worked two part-time jobs at two hospitals as a nurse. His work became increasingly unstable with the restructuring of hospitals and health care. Janet was self-employed. She ran a cleaning business, which was starting to do well the year before the study started. Janet received Mother's Allowance in the early 1990s after her marriage fell apart. She put herself through college and started her business in the middle of the decade. Janet and Christopher said that they were unable to plan for their futures as they had so many expenses to meet. Christopher's parents ran a farm and Janet and Christopher said that the farm produce—beef, chicken, vegetables, canned goods, dairy—made all of the difference in their ability to get by with such a large family. Janet grew flowers and sold them in the summer to make a bit of extra money. Janet and Christopher were actively involved in assisting Christopher's parents.

All of their children, with the exception of Janet's eldest and Christopher's eldest, were in public, Catholic or post-secondary educational institutions. Janet said that the cuts to education at the secondary school level were very visible: kids had fewer trips, music classes had been eliminated and she had to provide most of the children's school supplies. Janet's son had Attention Deficit Disorder and she thought that teachers did not have the time or facilities to give him the kind of attention that he needed. She saw this as symptomatic of a more troubling consequence of education restructuring in Ontario:

> The kids that are needing extra help, the onus is on the parent to educate the kid at home, and the parents are so stressed out, trying to make ends meet, they don't have the time at home to make the kid excel and do their homework and all that stuff. And it just sort of widens the gap in the social spectrum of things.

In a later interview she noted,

> Education should teach you, prepare you for life and the crises in life and how to cope with them, without going crazy.... We're not coping with our lifestyles, we're not coping with technology, we're not coping with the rich getting richer, and the poor getting poorer. There aren't supports out there for people that need help. Our education system is not preparing us for that, for what the real world is.

The status of their employment was a constant source of struggle for this household. In 1998, Janet injured her back at work and experienced some of the problems in the health care system first hand. This was made worse by the fact that, because she was self-employed, she spent the whole recovery time thinking about lost wages:

> The whole time I was thinking I'm not making any money, and Christopher wasn't working. I don't have any insured earnings because I'm self-employed. By the following Wednesday I was back to work. But, I'm telling you, I have never felt pain like that in my life! However, I strapped on my back brace and I went back to work.

In 1999, the local paper ran a story about Janet, the work that she did and the kinds of supports that she provided for clients. This increased her business substantially, and she was able to hire two full-time staff. The timing of this increase was fortuitous because, around that time, Christopher's father had to be hospitalized and his mother had a stroke. Janet and Christopher provided care for them and also took over some duties at the farm.

Janet's and Christopher's jobs and incomes were cited as major concerns in all rounds of interviews. Both of their jobs had been affected by changes in provincial policies—his because he was a nurse working in restructured hospitals, and hers because downsizing meant that she lost office cleaning contracts, as offices closed. When we first met, Christopher had just been laid off by the hospital at which he was working. Because he had seniority, he was not dismissed, but he ended up working in the kitchen at the hospital. Janet explained:

> Now they [the hospital administration] have introduced this new job description called the multi-skilled worker. The trend is that they've gone from having health care aides to having personal support workers, which is an eight-month training position. What's happening is they are phasing out the Registered Nurses (RNs), and the Registered Practical Nurses (RPNs) are taking the RNs' work. The health care aides are taking the RPNs' work. They are doing vitals and catheter care with eight month's training!

In 1998, Christopher was hired on contract at the local hospital, but the provincial government withdrew funding after he was hired. Christopher looked for other work in the area. Janet described what happened:

> He did get a three-month contract at a local hospital. Now this is a joke. He goes for the interview on a Tuesday. The following Wednesday, they hired him and three other people. That Thursday the government withdrew funding and they didn't open the unit that they had hired these four people for. They had all signed their contracts, they were all on board for three months. So the latest we heard is the funding is going to go through, and they will be hiring people back again for this ward. His three-month contract ended the first of February. He was then a casual worker and he did get shifts. He had to resubmit a

résumé to be on hold or to be ready for hiring for this next job.

Christopher took a job working part-time in a nursing home as a nursing assistant in order to increase the household income. He said that this nursing home was a frightening place to work and that he could not wait to get back to hospitals. Janet said,

> The nursing home has got 254 beds in five different wings. They have one nurse on duty for 254 patients. So he's doing everything that the RNs do in hospitals, as a RPN, and getting paid as a RPN. And his pay as a RPN is about $3 less an hour than the pay as a RPN in a hospital. He's dealing with life and death situations. Everybody that he has worked with so far has said, "Don't work as a RPN on that ward; you'll lose your licence because it's impossible to do a good job." The chances of a drug error are pretty high.

In late 1998, Christopher was hired permanent part-time at two different hospitals. Christopher explained that the restructuring of hospitals and cuts in funding and staff meant that those in the nursing profession were tired and overworked:

> What I find in the nursing profession is that we're frustrated. We're frustrated with not being able to do what we want to do. And if I'm at the end of a twelve-hour shift and somebody wants me to do something that I know I can't do, I'm totally frustrated. I wouldn't take it out on that patient. But there's abuse, more so onto the nurse than there is onto the patient. There's no forum for nurses' frustration. They don't want to hear it in hospital administration. You take the shit from the patients, from the doctors, from the family. But families are frustrated too.

Returning to a hospital setting, Christopher was keenly aware of the corners being cut, which were saving money in the short term but making things worse in the long term. Christopher remained stressed and concerned about the quality of care he was able to provide and about the quality of his own working conditions. He maintained optimism though and had a strong sense of humour and solidarity. Working in a unionized environment was very important to Christopher, but he felt that his union had taken a beating from the provincial government. Labour legislation had been eroded and the general bargaining power of those in the health care sector had decreased. He also noted that, as a part-time worker, he was part of a pool of far less radicalized workers; because no part-time workers received benefits, and they had less invested in the work place.

Janet and Christopher linked problems in health care to a focus on deficit reduction and tax cuts at the expense of public services. Christopher said:

I think the bottom line for me is pretty simple: Mike Harris [premier of Ontario] is into power, and one of his promises was I will not touch health care, and he has. Please don't bother giving me that tax break, if you have to cut a whole bunch of jobs out of hospitals and cut back on the services that you can offer in the community. If you've got to close hospitals that people obviously need, don't give me a tax cut. I don't want it.

One of the central themes in Janet's life was managing. She said that she had been through a good deal of hardship—mostly alone—and had come out at the other end. After her divorce, Janet raised four children by herself and went to college. She began her home cleaning business, and supported her children with only minimal child support from their biological father. In early 1998, she explained how she managed the demands on her:

Maybe it's just that you get a little older and you get a little wiser. You realize that it's not going to be like this forever. As long as I try to look after my own mental health as best I can, it will pass. Spring is coming and the garden is going to be wonderful. I was thinking, I've got today and tomorrow off. I'm going to get the plant stand out, and plant my seeds and start all over. It's a cycle. You just do it over and over again, and you get through the winter.

Janet and Christopher saw the changes implemented in Ontario as undermining democratic institutions and processes:

We've been brainwashed to believe that we live in a democracy. Social programs are gone and people are starving, and people are stealing from each other, and living out of dumpsters. And it's because there is somebody who is power-hungry in government and doesn't give a shit about any other human being. Harris is trying to break everybody down so that we can't fight, and it's working really well. If you take away people's food and livelihood and houses, and warmth in the winter, and kids, what do you have left? Nothing. You don't care about anything anymore. We've lost our humanity.

Cheryl and Paul

Cheryl and Paul lived with their two sons in a medium-sized southwestern Ontario city in a home that they owned and had lovingly restored over the years. When they were first interviewed in early 1997, Cheryl described their household as "a pretty close-knit, happy, traditional family." A high middle-income white household, Paul held a senior teaching and administrative position at a high school. Cheryl's job history was peppered with short-term contracts in a number of fields, and at the time of the last interview, she was considering returning to school. Both Cheryl and Paul were university-educated. Their children, both teenagers, attended a local high school.

Cheryl and Paul realized that they were cushioned from the worst effects of the many changes in public spending and in priorities in education, health care, community life and the labour market. Their most significant concern over the four rounds of interviews was understanding the implications for themselves and others of the deteriorating quality of life they observed around them. Paul said,

> It's not just our lifestyle that is at stake. We have children going through the school system. We have parents who need the hospitals, who need resources. So it's not just how it impacts on us in terms of our disposable income, or lack thereof. It's the whole pattern of life.

Because Paul was a teacher and their children attended public school, dramatic changes in provincial policies governing spending, structure, curriculum and staffing in primary and secondary education profoundly affected the household. Cheryl and Paul were also concerned about the increasing cost of post-secondary education; they worried about how they would fund their children's schooling. In the first interview, Paul mused,

> My kids don't have textbooks at school. The libraries have been cut back. The *Fewer School Boards Act* will mean job losses.... I think it is a sort of new industrial revolution. So I fully expect that there will be a strike in the next three years. I hope to be proven wrong.

Paul's most pressing concern was his inability to plan because of the lack of information provided by the province about funding and curriculum:

> The [secondary] education system is just chaos. We can't prepare for next year because we don't know how many teachers are going to be there. We don't know how much money there is. I now am acting head of the department and am trying to forecast a department for next year. We don't know how big the classes are going to be. On top of that we have the curriculum changes coming which are also a future concern.

Their children's schools were overcrowded and lacked resources. Cheryl explained,

> It's just bare. When our son was having trouble with math, we had an interview with the teacher and asked to see the textbook, and she said that she was just giving out Xeroxed material as she did not have a textbook.

40

While changes to education remained a central worry for Cheryl and Paul throughout the study, the health of their parents overtook most other concerns for a while. In 1997, Cheryl's and Paul's parents all lived nearby and were reasonably healthy and self-sufficient. In 1998, Cheryl's mother was hospitalized and later sent home with some home care support. Meanwhile, Paul's father had a stroke and was diagnosed with Alzheimer's disease. Paul recounts his father's experience at a hospital:

> My dad had a stroke, and he went to the hospital. He was there in emergency for five hours before they saw him. When finally somebody did see him, she said he had better stay overnight. There was no bed for him, so he spent the night in emergency. I went to see him, I guess it would have been about eighteen hours after he had been at the hospital, and he was still in emergency. They finally got a bed for him up in the maternity ward and that's where he ended up staying for a couple of days.

Paul's parents decided to move closer to Paul's sister and brother in another part of the province. Paul was upset that they were so far away, but Cheryl felt it was a blessing as her mother's health rapidly deteriorated, and she began to take on most of the responsibility for caring for her mother and her father. Cheryl said she could not have cared for Paul's parents as well. Cheryl's mother entered a nursing home in 1998. She was on a waiting list for several months and was in hospital during that time. Cheryl had to fight to get care, including rehabilitation services, for her mother. Until her mother's death in 1999, Cheryl visited her mother almost every day and also provided some care for her father, who lived on his own. She described her stress and fatigue levels as extremely high. "Last week I told Paul that I'd had enough," she explained. "I said I just can't take care of you, my mother and my father, the cat and the kids." She wanted better care for her mother:

> I can't tell if I'm being fair or not. She's my mother. But I go there and she's not dressed properly and they've lost her clothes.... I'm trying to be reasonable, but sometimes I just don't know what to think. I went to visit her one night, and she had to go to the bathroom, and they just put her to bed. I said, "It's seven o'clock at night, and I'm visiting. I know it's convenient for you to put her to bed now, because she's been to the bathroom, but couldn't you wait?" And they say to me that she likes to go to bed now, and I think, "Oh yeah, I just bet." Another time I went there at four o'clock, and she had to go to the bathroom, so they put her to bed. I said, "Well, you know, she only had her dinner at ten to four, it seems a little early to me." I understand that she's tired at night, but, what the hell is going on here, lady, what are you talking about putting her to bed, this is the summer and it's four o'clock. This is supposed to be such a great place? They did a real P.R. job of me, saying, "I know it's

upsetting for you." Well you know, the reason it's upsetting for me is how she is being treated.

After her mother's death, Cheryl not only felt her loss; she also felt she needed to have a directed plan for her life. Cheryl had worked in a number of sectors. She took a part-time job at a retail store and was considering returning to university but did not want to start again at the bottom. She had been out of the labour market on a full-time basis for a number of years while she raised her children and cared for her parents. She felt this was a barrier to her re-entry. In addition, Paul's experience as a public sector employee had been such a strenuous one that Cheryl wondered if the working conditions for those doing human service types of work would be so compromised as to be unbearable. Cheryl's mother left her some money when she died, so the household was less concerned with finding the personal money to finance things like educational pursuits.

As the interviews progressed, Cheryl and Paul expressed grave concerns about community life. They linked the provincial government's tax cuts with increased costs in other areas, like user fees and municipal taxes, and fewer public health and welfare services for those who needed them. They noted that the air quality in their community in the summer was often worse than in Toronto and that water quality was a grave concern. Over the last few years, the downtown core of the city to which they had moved began to deteriorate, and strip malls appeared on the outskirts of town. Michael, their eldest son, claimed that the downtown was dying. Cheryl and Paul claimed that their local taxes had increased dramatically, while public services had decreased. They saw this change as a strategy to gut the inner city. Paul said, "If you live in the downtown core in any city your taxes are going up, if you live in the suburbs your taxes go down, because they want to drive everybody out of the inner-city." Cheryl: "Well, there are taxes in the suburbs that are about equal to ours, but they have always been paying them, so their taxes haven't really gone up." Paul: "Yeah, but they have brand new streets, brand new plumbing, brand new sewer systems, and you know, they've all been put in recently and they haven't been paying for 125 years. It's going to adversely affect those living in older homes." Cheryl explained, "I think that there has got to be a minimum standard of living for everybody. We need environmental policy that protects the food that people eat, the air that we breathe, the water we drink." Paul feared that whatever the provincial government touched was destroyed:

Virtually every area this government puts its hand to is of concern. Whenever the government says they're going to fix anything, I think, "Oh, no!" Because I know that what it means is slash and burn. They're dismantling a whole infrastructure that has been built up in this province. It's like [the government] is a junk bond company selling off all of the assets of the province.

Discussion

Examining the interaction of policies gives rise to questions such as:

- How do policies act together for people, as individuals and as members of households, who are situated very differently across the social map of a province such as Ontario?
- What are the invisible, as well as visible, costs and benefits of these policy interactions to different segments of the population, both as individuals and members of households?
- How do policies come together to support, or hinder, people's efforts to manage the various aspects of their lives?

As the stories in this chapter document, at any given moment, members of households experience the separate and interactive effects of several social policies. The period from 1995 to 2000 saw a huge and far-reaching restructuring of Ontario's welfare state. Massive changes occurred on multiple fronts, especially in social assistance, health care, education, municipal structure, labour legislation and housing. Household stories suggest that, at this time, the caregiving work—for children in education, for the sick in health care and for the elderly in long-term care—was usually shifted to women to provide via their unpaid work. Indeed, long-term caregiving work appears in many of the stories in this chapter. Taking on this work is intensely difficult; it is rendered more challenging in a context of restructured services and supports and changes in job protections and security. Yet the effects of policy changes differ widely depending upon the social location of participants, as individuals and as members of household units. As household stories attest, social location involves much more than social class. It incorporates dimensions such as gender, household composition, age, social networks, race and ability. Social location shapes the options available to people.

Policy areas interacted in ways that made Teresa's life more difficult. Changes in education and training policies affected the overall quality of her life. Health care policy—central for someone with a serious illness—was gutted and restructured, decreasing her sense of health security. Changes in one area, if the others had remained constant, might have been accommodated by Teresa; the interaction of health care changes with social assistance and education restructuring in this case had devastating effects. Teresa feared not only what was happening at the time of each interview; she also dreaded what might happen. Due to her social location, Teresa lacked the financial and support resources to buffer her against the effects of multiple policy changes.

Cheryl and Paul experienced changes in health and education policies in quite a different way from Teresa. Education policy changes affected Paul intensely in his roles as teacher, administrator and parent. Although

Women's invisible labour

Cheryl lived in the same household as Paul and was very aware of the changes happening in education, health care policies had a stronger direct impact on her life, not because she personally used these services, but rather because of how they affected her aging parents. These changes escalated the amount of caring work that fell on Cheryl's shoulders. The amount and costs to women, who do most of this unpaid labour, does not appear in public health care accounts (Baines, Evans and Neysmith 1998) but they do appear in the lives of women such as Cheryl and Victoria. The costs also appear in the private market, as a system of private services expands to fill the gaps caused by the crisis in public provisioning. Cheryl's and Victoria's parents had savings, which meant that their children did not have to cover the costs associated with their care. Access to disposable income to cover these significant costs becomes a determinant of quality care; social inequality is thus a significant factor in assessing the effects of policy changes on the well-being of different segments of the population.

Although social policy changes in employment standards affected all workers in Ontario, workers in the public and para-public sectors were particularly affected. Despite the positive gains of unionization and a pay equity settlement in Victoria's work place, Victoria's and Christopher's stories portray the dramatic effects of budget decisions by the Ministry of Health concerning hospital financing on their health and work. When hospital budgets were cut, hospitals were given leeway to decide where and how savings were to occur; workers were not consulted in this process (Drache and Sullivan 1999; Gustafson 2000; Evans, McGrail et al. 2001). As a result, health care workers often lost their commitment to health care: they began to see themselves as workers producing a health product within a competitive market, where protecting oneself from exploitation and trying to maintain steady employment overshadowed the goals of health care provision.

Unpaid Reg.

Josie's reflections on what was happening in one long-term care insti-tution echo Cheryl's and Victoria's experiences with their parents as well as Christopher's experience in his employment and his parents' care. Josie, like Victoria, found that union activity gave her some room for dealing with the onslaught of changes that were occurring in her job, but munici-pal restructuring imposed by the province and new labour legislation increased Josie's job insecurity. Furthermore, Josie, unlike Victoria, did not own a house, and she was the major source of support for others in her family. Although she earned a decent wage, Josie had to use a food bank. When she needed help, Josie was frustrated by social assistance policies that failed to support her assumption of important family responsibilities.

The focus in this book on participants' experiences documents how policies affect people's ability to cope with the demands of daily living. The ethos of individualism in western societies reinforces a tendency to see problems as personal troubles rather than public issues. In a democratic system, engagement in issues in the public realm is crucial (Lewis, Gewirtz and Clarke 2000). However, this kind of public engagement was difficult for many people living in Ontario in the late 1990s. As people disengaged, they also felt disentitled to social goods. Since entitlement is central to the concept of citizenship, the speed, scope, style and cumulative nature of policy change eroded that concept. Cheryl and Paul were very conscious of what was happening in the small city in which they had hoped to spend many years. These two articulate and relatively privileged persons often felt powerless to influence what was happening around them. They could retreat when necessary because their social position afforded them some protection. Josie was very committed to the well-being of her extended family, neighbours, fellow workers and elderly patients. She worked hard for her union and co-op. She was engaged and obviously derived considerable satisfaction from her many arenas of work, but it was often a strenuous experience. Exit was one of the few options available to her. She chose to exercise it.

Policies intersect with people's lives in multiple ways, but such interactions are not the stuff of most policy assessments. Analysis is limited to examining a narrow range of specific effects. Furthermore, even in an era when policy changes were rapid and visible (almost daily making front page news), people did not necessarily link their individual experiences with how policies were formulated and implemented. Several participants explained that they were able to manage because they saw themselves as privileged. If the privileged are those who manage, what happens to everyone else in a society where disparities are increasing?

Notes

1. See Bezanson and Valentine (1998) for a detailed account of the speed and scope of policy change in the province. See also Ontario Federation of Labour (1998).
2. Social assistance, sometimes referred to as welfare, is a policy area that was overhauled during the mid- to late 1990s. The *Family Benefits Act* (FBA) and the *General Welfare Act* were replaced by the *Ontario Works Act* (OWA) and the *Ontario Disability Support Program* (ODSP). Teresa received FBA at the beginning of the study and later received ODSP. She was extremely concerned about the introduction of the new policies, as the new eligibility criteria for the programs were strict.

Chapter Three

The Outcomes
of Income Insecurity

Security comes in different forms.[1] In Canada, it has often been associated with a good education, holding down a job over time, an income that places one within the broad category of "middle class," the presence of social contacts and personal supports, good health and access to benefits if crises arise. However, a key factor in this security, paid employment, is being threatened at the same time as access and entitlement to public social provisioning are decreasing (Vosko 2000). Under such conditions, areas like housing become better indicators of security than do jobs. Participants in this study lived in households that obtained their income from varying mixes of employment, a relationship with someone who was employed, public programs and other sources. Likewise, people covered their expenses in different ways. The options available to particular households to meet the high costs of housing were especially crucial. For many, housing subsidies from informal networks of family and/or friends were pivotal factors that kept them out of poverty. The stories in this chapter suggest that a focus on jobs as the solution to income insecurity is misplaced; cobbling together multiple sources of income while relying on the assets of family and friends was the shield that protected many from crisis.

Because households rely on incomes from multiple sources and because government legislation and regulations significantly affect what income and expenses people have (as well as the structure of the labour market) social policy in a range of areas plays a role in creating or undermining income security. Non-standard employment—jobs that deviate from the full-year, full-time with benefits model—is increasingly the norm for a significant portion of the Ontario labour market (Fudge, Tucket and Vosko 2002). Managing the lack of advancement opportunities, low pay, poor hours and/or the lack of predictability in such jobs limits the choices and control available to individuals. If income from paid work is unpredictable and income from other sources, such as government transfers, is smaller and harder to get, planning for the future is difficult. Educational pursuits, which might assist a household in moving out of the low income category, are deferred; an unexpected cost, such as medicine, is a source of fear and anxiety. Level of income, then, does not wholly capture income security.

Among the households followed in this study, some faced new and higher expenditures for health care, transportation and education over the course of the late 1990s. Others took on substantial debt, paying day-to-day bills through the use of credit cards or accumulating large student loans. Income could become unpredictable because of a move from permanent to contract work, or because the income of one household member rose while that of another fell. In many cases, income was not distributed equally within households. These variations usually followed gender, race and age discrimination patterns existent within the broader society. For example, participants who were women, people of colour or older workers were over-represented in nonstandard jobs. Access to assets, often in the form of housing supports, was central to managing small incomes. These housing assets were usually gifts or loans provided by family members who had received the benefits associated with the post-World War Two standard employment norm. These assets were rarely available to first-generation Canadians. The quality of participants' lives was dependent on their primary source of income, but resources and supports available to them from a variety of sources were equally important. A change in one of these, such as an adult child moving out of or into the house, a marriage dissolving, a change in the type of job held by a household member or a sudden health crisis had varied and unpredictable effects. A theme that emerged over time from the experiences of many households was that apparent income security was often a thin patina that covered a fragile structure of formal and informal supports. Contrary to claims that jobs are the best route out of low-income insecurity, household experiences suggest that social networks that offer access to things like housing are more important to income security.

In this chapter, we start with the story of *Sara* and *Anand*. They both had good jobs, high incomes, good health and supportive families; they owned their home. Their story was one of security and increasing prosperity. It is juxtaposed against other stories where the assumption of regular, secure income did not hold. In fact, what is often thought of as traditional income security (full-time, full-year predictable work and income) existed for few participants. Even for those whose income improved over the three years of the study, few experienced the level of security enjoyed by Sara and Anand. *Randy* and *Monica*, and their three children, managed because they could rent the main floor of her mother's house. This household had some room to manoeuvre because Monica ran a home day care and could increase the numbers of children she took in by extending her work week, while Randy did seasonal work. *Jerry* was a young sole support father who enjoyed freedom from economic insecurity because his housing costs, some bills and food were covered by his parents. *Melanie, Heather* and *Ron* also managed because they operated as a three-member multi-generational household with one member having a good, if not exactly fulfilling, paid job. *Sabrina*, a single woman, had lived through a deteriorating job situation in the two years before the study started. A good friend subsidized Sabrina's income. These three households had some income security because of key relationships in their lives, not because of secure employment or public social transfer arrangements. *Barbara* described herself as relatively well-off at the time of the study compared to her own poverty in the past and that of those around her. Nevertheless, she felt the effects of living in a northern community which was not doing well in a period of economic boom. *Rosie* and *Bob*, a retired couple, lived on a pension that needed to be supplemented while health issues associated with aging limited their employment options.

Sara and Anand

Sara and Anand were a high-income South-Asian couple in their late thirties. They and their children, nine-year-old Adam and six-year-old Lily, lived in a large home in a quiet, spacious neighbourhood. Sara's parents lived close by. Both sets of grandparents vied to spend time with the grandchildren. Although having children, moving to a new home and getting permanent jobs were all significant and important changes, Sara and Anand's lives were stable and secure. Throughout the interviews they felt confident about their futures. Anand explained their sense of control: "Our jobs are secure. We're pretty well-buffered against problems like money issues, finding affordable housing, worrying about nutrition, getting transportation or suffering from poor health."

Sara and Anand were not concerned about their income security, but they experienced significant changes in their work lives and in the lives of those with whom they worked as a result of changes in provincial policy, particularly in the areas of education and health. They were acutely aware that their own sense of having choices, control and security was in part the result of their social location: their children's school was well-equipped because parents were well-off and they could entertain the idea of private school—hence they could exercise the option of exit—if they felt the public system was failing. Both parents volunteered at their children's school. Anand, for instance, signed up for a weekend fund-raising event: "I'm going to call bingo on Saturday," he said. Sara noted that, in their children's school, "parents raise something like $20,000 over the course of the year. The money is spent on 'frills' such as computer software, extra library books, the gym equipment and resurfacing of the gym floor." Anand added, "The school's got a very nice computer lab and CD-ROM centre which was essentially donated by the Parent Teachers' Association. In a school whose community lacked those kinds of resources, those things may not be in place." In the final year of the project, Adam returned to the local school to attend Grade Three and Lily started Grade One. However, Sara said,

We've got the kids in the public school but we're keeping a close eye on it. If current trends continue, I anticipate that we will probably have to send the kids to a private school. We'd like to support the public system but we want to think about what's best for our kids as well.

Anand had been affected by changes in post-secondary education through his job. His field of research was growing, and he was promoted to head his department, so he considered his job secure. However, he saw reductions in many areas. For example, because there were fewer support staff, he did more of his own administrative tasks. He noticed the most significant changes with respect to his students:

With the cutbacks in the library and other services like that, there's less available for the students. And tuition is increasing substantially. Students can no longer get subsidized day care if they're receiving OSAP [Ontario Student Assistance Plan]. I find that I've been dealing with more and more students having trouble making ends meet. The effect of this is that they have to work more for pay, so their studies suffer. Then worry affects their concentration. It takes them longer to complete their studies and more students never complete.

Anand mused about the impact of changes to the post-secondary system more broadly, saying, "I think the changes underway will affect the way in which we teach and the way students interact, as well as the mission of what post-secondary institutions focus on."

Sara's work dealt with home care, the health-related care provided to people after they leave hospital or when they live independently at home. She pointed to a number of changes that affected the well-being of patients. Her initial concerns were about difficulties in coordinating care, because the central body that allocated home-care services had been dissolved (replaced by Community Care Access Centres or CCACs), and for-profit services in homes were being greatly expanded. As health policies and funding changed, and hospitals began to feel the effects of restructuring, additional concerns emerged about the reduction and rationing of services. Patients were limited to a maximum of one bath a week, and there were changes to the information about patients collected by service providers because of new contractual obligations. This last change, Sara worried, threatened the whole notion of home care:

If somebody wants to remain in the community you have to know what their activities of daily living are after they leave the hospital. Can they bathe, can they dress, can they eat? Are they back to the level where they can function and stay independent in the community? That sort of stuff is not being collected, so how are they going to evaluate the companies providing the services when all we know are numbers of visits—that's not helpful.

Sara also observed that:

> More acute patients are being sent out from the hospitals, and now you have daughters quitting work to take care of their parents. If the Community Care Access Centres know you have family, your chance of getting any home-care service is much slimmer. And, we don't know what is appropriate care because patients are leaving the hospital earlier.

About their own health, Sara and Anand were less concerned because, as Anand indicated, "I think we're pretty well buffered against most of the stuff that makes people unhealthy. Income is the biggest determinant of health."

Randy and Monica

Randy and Monica were a white couple in their early thirties who lived in a medium-sized community with their three children. At the time of the first interview, their ages were fourteen, seven and five (the eldest, April, was Monica's child from a previous relationship). They lived in the home of Monica's mother, who had an apartment in the basement. Monica ran a home day-care business. This housing arrangement was central to their ability to manage on their modest household income.

When we first met, Randy had returned to school to finish Grade Twelve and was receiving Workers' Compensation for a back injury that had left him with a permanent disability. Money was their biggest concern throughout the four rounds of interviews.

The crisis of Randy's injury, and his subsequent depression, in the mid 1990s was a huge point of transition in the lives of the members of this household. Randy had worked doing physical labour. After his accident, he did not work for pay for three years. Their children were very small at that time. Randy had applied for Workers' Compensation Benefits (WCB) shortly after his injury, but the processing of his claim took some time. Monica explained that they applied for social assistance in the intervening period:

> We were waiting for his compensation to come in. We kept calling and calling Compensation and asking "When is the cheque going to be sent?" We finally got this one lady that talked to us very nicely, and didn't say, "It's in the mail." She said, "I don't know." I said, "Look, we have no money, we have three kids, we've got to do something here," and she said, "If you call your social services, there is an emergency welfare thing that they do." So I called and they said, "Oh yeah, no problem." A lady came down and talked to us, and she said, "That's what it's there for."

Randy's recovery period dramatically changed this couple's relation-

Male
Role

ship. Randy noted that up until his injury, his expectation was that his wife would do most of the work of maintaining the home and raising their children. He was working long hours and was "money-focused." "I always saw myself as the breadwinner," he said. "I support my family and if I can't, that makes me feel bad... me not being able to has made us closer than we were before I hurt my back." After his accident, during his convalescence, he spent most of his time caring for his kids. He felt that this was a major life shift for him; later he tried to organize his paid work around spending time with his family. He explained the change in the household division of labour after his accident, noting that he had to adjust to Monica being the primary wage earner:

> It's sort of changed over the last three years since I've been off. I've always encouraged Monica to be home to raise our kids. Because she had in-home day care, we saw the kids take their first steps, say their first words and I didn't want us to miss that for our kids. When I hurt my back, Monica ended up going to take a job in a factory and I did the cooking and cleaning, the laundry, the housework, whatever. Well, our son Shawn did a large part of it because whatever I couldn't bend down and get, he picked up.

Randy decided to use the time he had while receiving WCB to return to school. At the time of our first interview in 1997, he was completing his Grade Twelve equivalency. He spent a lot of time doing homework with his kids and, despite the fact that he felt limited and frustrated by his disability, he saw it as something of a blessing because it put him on a new path with his family and his life.

Monica's perspective on the situation was somewhat different. Having a full house, with Randy around when he was not working, was stressful for Monica. She explained that Randy was much easier to be around when he was doing some paid work:

> He's the happiest person on the earth when he's working, and he's okay for the first day or two when he's not working. But after that he gets cranky. He nit-picks at everything. He's yelling at the kids. Nothing is done right. I think, "Just go away! This house has been like this for years, and like now all of a sudden it's not right and the house is a pig-sty." He goes on and on. It's because he's getting frustrated, so he takes it out on everybody else, which isn't fair to the kids.

Although his attitude was positive about his accident, money was a significant concern. In 1997, Randy received about $14,000 from WCB, while Monica made between $6,000 and $8,000 per year from her home day-care business. Since his accident, Randy had tried to get Compensation to help him with career training in fields that would not be too demanding physically. His struggles with Workers' Compensation focused on them wanting to find him work in the sector in which he had worked prior to his injury; he wanted work in another field. Randy's benefits were terminated in 1998; later that year he received a settlement. Randy would have preferred to receive substantial training to get work that would not hurt him physically. He drew on racialized stereotypes to explain his position, asserting that services and supports were hard to access for white men like himself:

I'm not receiving any benefits. They give you six months after your training to find a job, and then your benefits are done. My main concern is they didn't give me any training. I went back to school and got my Grade Twelve. And so did everybody! I'm competing with these people. I can't do excessive bending, lifting, sitting, twisting, so everything that I enjoy doing I can't do. That's why I've accepted this job at a call centre. I tried to get free training through compensation, they basically told me if I didn't speak English and I worked in a factory my whole life then they would be willing to put me through university for four years. They told me that to my face.

Randy decided to appeal the decision:

Well we got a letter the other day saying there's new rules in effect and you can appeal it. So we are going to appeal it because I wasn't trained to do anything. Their idea of training me was to put me in a call centre.

Randy had a great deal of difficulty at the call-centre job because of his back, as he could not sit for long periods of time. Also, the hours were such that he did not see his kids very often. In 1998, he quit the call-centre job and began doing summer work in landscape design. He also worked part-time in a small business to earn some additional money.

The biggest challenge for Monica in providing home day care was not cooking, programming or cleaning up after the children; it was getting the parents of the children who pay her privately to pay her on time, or at all. During the time of the study she began getting clients placed with her through a regional service, so the pay and number of children permitted per home were regulated. This also provided more predictability in terms of how many hours each child would be with her and hence, how much income she could count on:

I can only have five kids from the region. I've got four now again, so the region is trying to find me another one to fill that spot. That makes it easier. I don't even have to look but I do an interview. She [a representative from the regional placement centre] just calls me and says, "Okay, I found someone in your area." I had one problem with one father. I only had that kid for about two weeks, and I called the region and I said I'm not doing it anymore. The father had a temper-tantrum in the house. I said, "I don't take that crap from nobody." My job is pretty secure as long as there's people out there wanting to work and needing child care.

Although there was slightly more predictability in her work, because she was considered self-employed, Monica did not have a great deal of security: "If I got sick for a long time [like Randy], I would lose all my [day-care] kids."

Monica found it challenging to draw a line between her paid work and her home life. Her hours were very long and the schedule was hectic. She and Randy explained:

[Monica:] I provide care [for my kids and the day-care kids] about eighty hours a week. Like this morning, I've been up since 6:30 a.m. and I'm babysitting till 9:30 p.m. tonight.
[Randy:] She has two more girls that come at 1:00 p.m. Their mother finishes at 9:00 p.m. and she usually gets here by 9:30 p.m. Another girl comes at 7:30 a.m. One boy comes at 8:00 a.m. One comes at 9:00 a.m. Then she's doing homework with our kids, Nicholas and Shawn. She's helping our daughter April. Because I'm doing landscaping in the day time and working at the garage at night to make that extra income, I'm not here. By 9:30 p.m. Monica's pretty much beat so she'll go and lay in bed and because she's so tired she can't sleep.

Living in the same home as Monica's mother was a source of both support and tension. Though Monica and Randy maintained a separation in their lives between themselves and her mother, the proximity of living quarters meant manoeuvring so as not to get in each other's way. Despite a certain lack of privacy, both Randy and Monica acknowledged that they could not have managed without this kind of housing arrangement. They paid for upkeep, utilities and property taxes (about $500 a month). In addition, Monica ran her business from the home, which had a large yard and lots of room. Because the big-ticket item of housing was covered, their biggest expense was food, including food for the day-care children.

Monica and Randy did not consider themselves to be "political." Monica did not vote in either the 1995 or 1999 provincial elections. Randy said that he supported the Harris government, particularly for the harsh stand they took against those receiving social assistance, despite their own reliance on it and other public supports. At the same time, he was angry about the kinds of reforms that were implemented without consultation. For instance, he thought that workfare would now replace paid jobs. Also, their property taxes increased, and hence their housing costs went up. In 1999, this couple earned about $37,000. They were both reluctant to talk about unreported income, although Randy suggested that he took some jobs on a cash basis. In the final interview Monica and Randy stated that, although they are not prospering, they were feeling more secure financially. Randy explained their situation: "Monica's getting a couple of extra kids in her day care. My business is increasing a little. We're getting by. We're the working poor again."

Jerry

Jerry was raised in a white upper-middle-class family. Both his parents worked in management positions. Although his parents divorced ten years ago, while growing up Jerry enjoyed the benefits of a family cottage and regular vacations. His parents' high disposable income meant that Jerry was able to participate in a range of sports. Throughout the three years of this study, he noted that leisure activities were a personal priority because they helped him to cope with the stresses of his daily life. Jerry lived rent-free in a separate apartment in his mother's and stepfather's house, which was located in an upscale neighbourhood.

Jerry always had low-paying jobs, high debt and significant expenses, including child care. He kept a detailed monthly budget, but was often unable to cover his bills, especially legal fees associated with an ongoing custody battle over his daughter. Although Jerry and his former wife Melissa shared custody of their daughter, Erin lived with Jerry full-time and saw her biological mother two evenings a week. At the time of the first interview, Jerry was working full-time in the hospitality industry, but he was earning only $16,000 a year. He came to this position after a series of low-paying, non-standard jobs and two failed attempts at post-secondary education. While searching for stable employment, Jerry dreamed of a career as a professional ski instructor, working at the best resorts in the world. The birth of his daughter and his failed marriage, however, radically changed the direction of his life. He said:

My daughter has helped me out in so many different ways and has changed me as a person. I'm much better now than I was before I had Erin in my life. But at the same time I look back and can't help but think "What if?" I was getting to a point in my life when I was about to hit the fast track of a career and it was just going to skyrocket. But, I know that I can't ever go back to that, not with Erin in my life.

When we asked Jerry if he thought his job in the hospitality industry was stable and secure, Jerry said, "Judging by today's labour market, I'd say it's pretty stable. But judging by standards of people in the last generation, it's probably as unstable as unstable can get!" This sense of stability led Jerry to talk about a future in the industry. He saw potential for growth and opportunity but had concerns:

> The one concern I do have is lack of health benefits because all of those expenses come out of my pocket. I'm not a student and I don't have company benefits. I get my paycheque every two weeks and that's the end of it. If my daughter gets sick and she needs a prescription, then that expense comes right off my paycheque and it really takes a chunk out of my monthly budget.

In May 1998, Jerry's employer was forced to reduce expenditures, so Jerry's hours were cut back to fifteen from forty hours per week. During this period, he was unable to make ends meet and used credit cards to pay the bills. He had to find a new job. Through family connections, Jerry found a job as an administrative assistant for a large corporate multinational consulting firm. He told us that, while he didn't like his new job, it offered stability, regular hours, extended medical and dental benefits, life insurance options and a flexible working environment. Rather than a career opportunity, Jerry described this job as "a way to pay my bills, get my debts cleared, have medical benefits and get some experience in an office environment." The new job paid $23,000 a year. While still a low-income position, it was a $7,000 annual increase from his previous position. When asked about the impact of higher paying employment, Jerry said:

> I've noticed a big difference. I don't have any extra cash in my pocket, but the expenses that do come up I can handle better. I'm happy that I've got full-time gainful employment that's giving me a steady income. Although my income is low, it's a steady income and I can budget with it. I'm also on better terms with my bank now. Having a full-time job that is socially recognized as a "career job" has helped out a lot. It's that added stability that banks are looking for, so if I need to extend my personal line of credit so I can fix my car, the bank will do it. They don't see me as a risk like they did before.

During each interview, Jerry revealed the various ways in which his mother and stepfather were providing him and Erin with support. Aside from living rent-free for a number of years, some of his household-related expenses were offset by his parents. They provided financial support in other ways as well. When Jerry's car needed a new engine at a cost of $4,300, which he could not afford, his parents provided him with an interest-free loan. In the summer of 1998, when Jerry's hours were cut back while working in the hospitality industry, his parents stepped in to help. He said:

> There were a few months in the summer where things were really tight, and my parents actually helped supplement a lot of meals and stuff. Erin and I would just go downstairs into their part of the house and we would have supper with

them. That really helped out with my expenses and I was able to get back on my feet.

Making enough money to support his family has been an ongoing struggle for Jerry. He said quite simply: "It just sort of digs you deeper into the hole." Nevertheless, over the course of the three years that we followed Jerry's household, he was consistently optimistic about his future. Although he was an effective self-advocate, with the skills and confidence to obtain the supports and services he needed, his family were essential to Jerry's survival. Without their financial and in-kind support, Jerry would have required a range of additional supports, such as subsidized child care and probably subsidized housing and social assistance. When asked to reflect on his life, Jerry stoically said,

> As much as things didn't work out with my ex-wife, I would do the same thing over again. I've learned a lot from my experiences. I've learned a lot more about myself, especially being a parent. It really gives you a lot; it thrust me into growing up a lot quicker and thrust a lot of responsibility onto my shoulders. It ended up working out well. I'm very happy with my position in life right now. I'm happy about having my daughter and glad it's just the two of us. It gives me a close bond with her, and I know we're going to have that for a long time.

Melanie, Heather and Ron

Melanie, Heather and Ron made up a household consisting of a white mother, daughter and son-in-law. They lived in a three-storey red brick house on a tree-lined street in a modest Toronto neighbourhood. Melanie, a fifty-three-year-old single woman who worked as an instructor of English as a Second Language (ESL), was Heather's biological mother. Heather and Ron (Heather's common law partner of seven years) were both in their late twenties and lived in a separate apartment on the top floor of the house, while Melanie lived on the main floor and basement. Although they lived in two separate living units, Melanie, Heather and Ron considered themselves part of the same household, providing each other with ongoing financial and emotional support.

Melanie had been legally separated from her husband for fourteen years. The couple decided not to seek a divorce because of financial constraints. Once separated, Heather lived with her father, and only saw her mother on the occasional weekend. As an adult, however, Heather decided that she wanted to rebuild her relationship with her mother. In 1996, she suggested that they buy a house and live together. Although Melanie jumped at the idea of living with her daughter, she had very little income and could not afford the down payment on a house. Fortunately, financial support from her father made it possible for Melanie to purchase a modest home. Heather and Ron paid Melanie $550 per month for their apartment, which Melanie reinvested in the house. Heather and Ron felt very fortunate to be living in an affordable, safe, comfortable and stable housing situation. Melanie supported their low monthly rental rate. She said,

> They have high debts and student loans. I know that eventually they may both want to further their education, and I fully support that goal. It's very crucial for their futures that they get more and different education. If you are going to pursue an education, then you need a cheap and decent place to live. Their rent isn't totally based on altruism; it also has to do with the cost of running the house and our expenses.

The three shared household-related costs and often had Saturday and Sunday meals with each other. Given their tenuous attachment to the labour market, this living arrangement gave each of them a sense of security and an ongoing support network, as well as an independent life-style. Heather said,

> Ron and I wanted to live independently. We were students when we met, and now that I'm finished school I would like to make a living as a performer. But I know that it takes a long time to establish yourself in a career like that. And we wanted to live in a decent place that was clean, quiet and stress free. We knew that on our incomes we would not find a place like that, that we could afford.... This situation just seemed to fit. I like the idea of doing this with my mom because I wanted to pay her rent, rather than to a landlord. It feels good to be able to contribute to my mom. She had never owned property before, and this situation means that she can have her own house. Ron was all for it, so we just went for it. We really see this living arrangement as a team effort. Even though my mom technically owns the house, we really see all of us working together to have this place. We all get stability and flexibility with this arrangement.

While pleased with the opportunity to live with her daughter, given the significant financial support provided by her father, Melanie continued to feel that the house was not really "hers." Melanie had set a long-term goal to repay the loan provided by her father. She said,

> We have a wonderful home, and it's really coming together. But, I would feel differently if I could repay my parents and live in this house free and clear of any debts. Then I would feel that it is truly mine. We are living here because I was able to obtain this house through an act of family generosity and family welfare. There is no question about that.

Melanie had been an ESL teacher for more than twenty years She had been with the same employer, a small agency that ran a program for recently-arrived immigrants and refugees, for over thirteen years. She taught language skills, job search skills and life skills. Melanie was committed to her work because she felt it made a difference in the lives of her students. Melanie was confident that, after taking a series of training courses, her students were better prepared to enter the labour market and begin their new life in Canada. Despite her commitment to teaching, however, Melanie never had any job security. She said,

> Nothing is stable in Continuing Education and English as a Second Language. It's remarkable that it has lasted this long—it's really a testament to its importance and success. But, you know, I've been living with unemployment and job insecurity for more years than I'd like to remember. When I first started in the field, I'd be looking for a new job every twelve months. It was very, very hard. I could handle the stress when I was thirty years old, but I didn't think I'd be doing the same thing in my fifties. I have no idea what the next three years will bring. We're battening down for a storm. I don't know—I just cope. You have no choice, you just have to keep going.

In 1997 Melanie's gross annual income was $34,000. This was lower than previous years because she had faced a 14 percent decrease in her salary in 1995.[2] Melanie explained,

> They cut my pay by cutting my hours. It was because the federal government and the provincial government were putting less money into post-secondary education and continuing education programs. The school boards had to cut costs because of the new Canada Health and Social transfer Act. So there was less money, so less hours, and that meant that they cut my hours. I was in a union, but our bargaining unit was very, very weak, so we had a weak collective agreement. They were just basically allowed to cut my hours back.

Having her own house meant that her housing situation was stable, and she was confident that she would live in her home for many years to come. Nevertheless, throughout the interviews, she expressed deep concern about her future. In the first interview, Melanie said,

> Well, at the moment I'm getting along okay financially. But, I'm really concerned about my retirement. I'm just getting to the point where I can retire, but I'm worried I won't have a job for much longer. I'm good at my job, and it's what I like to do for a living. However, I would never recommend my way of earning a living to a younger person. It's a wonderful job, and fun—but very, very unstable. So, I have two concerns—first, about earning a living until I retire, and second, just retiring with dignity. You get very worried about your

job when you are fifty because it's harder to apply for one and get re-employed somewhere else.

In the summer of 1998, as a cost-saving measure her employer laid her off for two weeks. Up until 1998, the agency had never experienced any problems receiving referrals from government social workers. However, Melanie described how the problems in one policy area can have an effect in another—in this case, the education system. Fewer students were able to access adult education training because of the confusion created by the provincial overhaul of social assistance. Melanie said,

> The intake procedures have all collapsed. All of the teachers in my program have been laid off. The welfare workers are unable to make referrals because the rules have not been given to them. In the past, they would refer people to various agencies but, when Ontario Works came in, the entire system broke down.

By November 1999, Melanie's hours had been reduced to twenty-five per week. Given her reduced income, she was finding her options and ability to plan curtailed. It was difficult to make ends meet and for the first time in twenty years, Melanie considered a career change:

> My employer insists on laying me off in the summer. They insist on closing classes so that they can save money. I am now living on a smaller paycheque, and I have to absorb the costs of being laid off. I don't take holidays anymore, because I just use my holiday time when I get laid off. I'm struggling to pay all the bills. I can't afford to do any home renovations anymore. I'm not suffering yet, but I have to be very careful. I'm also thinking seriously about a career change. I need to think about different ways of making a living. I'm trying to figure out how to plan for the future and have a secure retirement. It's always on my mind.

Melanie was laid off for three months in 1999.

Compounding Melanie's job insecurity was her daughter Heather's unemployed status. In 1997, Heather she had just been laid off as the general manager of a local theatre company. It was a position she held for a little over a year and work that she enjoyed very much. The theatre company received almost all of its funding from government sources, and as governments reduced support to the arts, many organizations were forced to close their doors. She said,

> Our funding was just suddenly yanked by the government. We were just cut—like we lost more than 25 percent of our funding. It began to be a real burden on all of the people involved in the company. We weren't growing, but instead

were just struggling. We were just holding on by our fingernails. The Board refused to operate in a deficit, so we just closed our doors.

Heather was unemployed and ineligible for unemployment insurance benefits. She had no source of income. Fortunately, her common-law partner, Ron, was employed.

In January 1997, Ron was hired on a two-month contract by a multinational corporation to provide in-house computer support. His contract was extended, and in May he was offered a permanent position with extended medical and dental benefits. Ron's $30,000 gross annual salary covered their expenses, including a joint $18,000 student-loan debt. Heather and Ron were surviving, and their stable housing situation meant that they were able to afford a quality of life that otherwise would not have been possible. Nevertheless, Ron had concerns about the future. He said,

> We are worried about the future. We don't think we will ever be able to afford to buy a house or have enough money and stability to have children. It's a real worry. I mean right now we are just living hand-to-mouth. We are not able to save anything, and, when we try to save, it just backfires because some unexpected expense comes along.

The following year Ron's salary increased because he worked a considerable amount of overtime. His gross annual income was close to $40,000. However, Ron was not happy at work. His employer had promised Ron the opportunity for additional training and job opportunities—none of which ever materialized. He said,

> I'm making more money, but things have gotten progressively worse with management. They are hiring more and more people who don't seem to be qualified to do their jobs, and there is a lot of friction between lower levels and upper management. A lot of people are stressed out and the desire to leave is high. I'm certainly thinking about leaving.

By the summer of 1998, Heather's frustration with being unemployed led her to give up on a career in the arts. She was simply looking for a job to help pay the bills. In October 1998, Heather secured a temporary full-time contract position working for a community-based agency doing clerical work. She enjoyed the work environment and the opportunity to participate in the labour force. She said,

> It felt really good to be working again. I had been out of the work force for a long time, so it was valuable to be back in the work force and regain some confidence that I am capable of keeping down a job and being a valuable contributor to an organization.

A year later, in September 1999, Heather's contract position ended, and she was once again unemployed. She did not qualify for unemployment insurance benefits and thus did not have any source of income. With few employment prospects in the arts, Heather decided to return to school and upgrade her skills. In the meantime, she was looking for a job to "help pay off her student loan, get out of debt and buy a couch." Heather's tenuous employment situation meant that Ron's income was paying all the bills. Despite wanting to pursue other career opportunities, Ron continued to work for the same large corporation. They needed his income to make ends meet. However in September 1999, they were unable to pay rent to Melanie. They simply did not have enough money and decided that their student loans and personal debts were a higher priority than rent. Because they paid rent to Melanie, the couple had some financial flexibility. Despite their constant battle to find secure employment, this household flourished in a loving, supportive environment. Heather said,

> The three of us are a team. I really feel like the three of us are trying to make something happen here. And, I know that it will happen—for all of us. We just have to keep supporting each other.

Sabrina and Elizabeth

Sabrina was a white woman in her early thirties who lived in Toronto with no dependants. She had completed some post-secondary education in the social services field. She was passionate about social justice issues and the arts. She sang with a band and was an avid music fan. She and her long-time friend, Elizabeth, rented a house with two other room-mates in a trendy downtown area. They both felt connected to their community, which they described as vibrant and politically active. However, they were aware of changes in their community that seemed to be eroding its fabric. Garbage pickup wasn't very regular, user fees had been introduced for some community activities, and their local hospital had closed. Both worried about local and provincial changes and wondered what else was in store. Sabrina commented,

> I think that part of [the provincial government's] strategy is to keep us feeling overwhelmed so we feel like we can't do anything about it because then you give up and you don't protest, you don't write letters, you don't make telephone calls, because you feel like it's a done deal.

Both Sabrina and Elizabeth kept abreast of local and provincial politics. They described the changes they saw in the province as cost-saving measures rather than those designed to enhance services.

Everything's financial now. That's all anything is decided on. Nobody has any beliefs or philosophies or values or they don't shoot for anything. It's just, "Can you afford it?" That's what we've been reduced to. It's not even civilized.

Sabrina attributed the loss of her job as a service manager to an emphasis on the "bottom line": as a result of funding cuts to the social service agency where she worked and the subsequent internal restructuring of the organization, her employment was terminated. This was a devastating blow. Ever since leaving university, Sabrina had worked in the social service sector, specifically with people with disabilities. It came as a surprise that she was laid off given her breadth of experience and her commitment to the client base she diligently served. She talked about how insecure employment had become in her field:

About three months before I got laid off, [I was] saying, "Well I'll always have a job. There'll always be developmentally delayed people in need of support, I don't have to worry"—and then, boom! I don't think anything's that secure now. My client could lose his funding like that. These people are really vulnerable, which makes me really vulnerable because I support them for a living.

Sabrina was unable to find another full-time job in her field at her former pay scale. She was unemployed for a number of months and, despite an extensive network of contacts (both she and Elizabeth were involved in a job club), she was only able to find part-time employment. Sabrina managed to piece together a full-time work week consisting of three part-time jobs. Ironically, one of those jobs was babysitting for a former co-worker who had taken over her caseload. The income she received did not, however, come close to approximating what she earned while working full-time, nor did she receive any benefits. Sabrina felt betrayed by a booming labour market that only seemed to churn out non-standard employment opportunities. She felt desperate as she entered her thirties, underemployed and with few job prospects. Her perspective on work and welfare changed as she joined the ranks of the working poor.

The drop in income and the loss of benefits was so drastic that Sabrina applied for social assistance. She qualified for a financial top-up and although this only amounted to $100, social assistance provided Sabrina with a drug card that covered the cost of her medication. An asthma sufferer, Sabrina's drug costs consumed a significant share of her income. Without the support from social assistance, she would have had to go without the needed medication because she simply could not afford to fill prescriptions. She described the experience of applying for social assistance as surreal. A service worker by profession, she had become a client in need of the services that she used to provide. Although the experience was humbling, she commented that her experience allowed her to navigate through bureaucratic hoops more easily than the average person in need of assistance. She knew the "right" answers and used her knowledge to manipulate the system:

> Lying to welfare, getting out of them what I can get out. It's so funny. Before, there would have been no way. I would have been working my ass off looking for a job. [With this government], the second I was unemployed I just felt like [saying], "You're ready to fuck me at any moment. I don't really care. I am going to [work in the] underground economy"—which is something I've totally been against my entire life. My whole mentality and ethics have changed. I don't like it but, at the same time, I feel like, look, I've never resented paying taxes—never, never, never. I've even been willing to pay more, but now I just feel like you're going to get what you can out of me or I'm going to get what I can out of you. So it's too bad. I feel kind of bitter but you've got to do what you've got to do.

By the second round of interviews, Sabrina was no longer in receipt of social assistance. She continued to work at a number of part-time jobs as a personal support worker. Although her income remained low, one of the part-time positions was salaried with benefits. The health and dental coverage enabled her to leave welfare. Her employment as a personal support worker paid wages that were below what she had been making ten years earlier when she entered the labour market, and her working conditions were far from ideal. Not only were her hours unpredictable, with calls at all hours from families in crisis, but also, when some of her clients physically assaulted her, there were no occupational or safety provisions that protected her. The boundary between work and home was not respected and was difficult to enforce. She acknowledged that the families with whom she worked were in crisis: often they saw her as their only source of support. However, as a result, Sabrina's work week exceeded the hours she was contracted to work. She felt she had little choice but to put up with the conditions of her employment. If she spoke out, she did so at her own peril since it was the parents who paid her wages. She feared that her job hinged on how well she got along with the client's family members and not how well she did her job. She found that it was increasingly difficult to work with high-needs families because of their limited resources and the amount of stress they experienced:

> My job is to connect people with services that don't exist anymore and that is really depressing. You go to people's houses and meet them. They have real dire needs and there is nothing out there for them. You can't just expose yourself to that every single day—it's too depressing. You feel bad because you know they need support but at a certain point you can't do it anymore.

She felt that the work she did was tremendously undervalued. Indeed, the families that employed her often felt resentful that she got paid for the caring work that they often did for free.

Sabrina's drop in income also meant that she could no longer maintain the lifestyle to which she was accustomed. Although she had not lived lavishly, Sabrina had enjoyed an active social life which included entertaining, going to concerts and having discretionary spending money. After her initial termination, as she struggled to cover necessities such as groceries and rent, she was not able to afford many of her leisure pursuits. Elizabeth, her long-time friend and room-mate, decided to increase her own contribution to rent and utilities to offset the amount of income Sabrina had lost. In addition to Elizabeth, Sabrina was able to turn to her parents for assistance. Her retired parents, who were not well-off, but were nonetheless financially secure, agreed to take on her student loan. "Elizabeth doesn't share her finances with me but she shares her car," Sabrina explained. "She buys me meals out. I still get these fun things that keep your spirits up that other people can't have or don't get. So I still feel really lucky." This support did not come without a cost for Sabrina. Her siblings, who were all financially independent, couldn't understand how their sister could have fallen on such hard times; they were upset that their parents were paying for her outstanding debts. In order to assist their daughter with her finances, her parents had to forego a cruise they had been planning as a celebration of their wedding anniversary. Sabrina felt guilty and talked of feeling that she was burdening those she loved the most.

Sabrina and Elizabeth felt that their quality of life had declined over the last five years, and they blamed the provincial government as much as the changes in the economy. Sabrina explained,

I think as Ontarians we were having a better quality of life and it has just been chopped and now we have to claw our way back to that standard that we had four or five years ago, which wasn't even that great. Like let's face it, we have a long way to go. I don't feel super-hopeful, but I don't feel quite as depressed as I felt when [Mike Harris] first got in power. Maybe I'm getting used to it, the subtle things, like the dirty streets, the little grinding things.

Barbara and Adam

Barbara was a thirty-nine-year-old Ojibwa woman living in northern Ontario with two teenage daughters. At the time of our first interview she had just moved into a new home built and owned by her boyfriend. For years she had raised her daughters alone and was unsure how this new arrangement would work out. While Adam was her partner, it was quite clear that, for Barbara, "family" meant her and her daughters: all financial arrangements were split that way. She was in charge and responsible for everything related to her girls. She had a full benefits package at her job, paid half the rent and all the food, while he covered the utilities. Barbara planned the meals and did the shopping; she paid for the girls' phones, her student loan and her credit card bills. Everyone was responsible for his or her own dishes and laundry; both of the girls could cook. A lot of the purchases she made were second-hand ones. She commented, "I'm very frugal and I stretch everything to the maximum." In the past, if any emergency came up in Barbara's life she had been able to rely on her parents for small loans until she could pay them back. After her father died in 1995, her mother bought her a car, which "was a blessing because there's no way I could have bought myself a car like this. I never refuse anybody a ride, I just feel so fortunate."

After Barbara left her husband in 1985, she raised her children alone. Over the years, Barbara had worked as a bus driver, as a salesperson for Avon products and as a hairdresser: in this last occupation, she eventually built a clientele of forty customers who dropped in regularly for hair cuts: She realized, however, that "the person who made the money was the person who owned the shop and I'm never going to get more ahead than I am now." After years of receiving Mother's Allowance, Barbara decided to attend university, encouraged by a friend who trumpeted her talents. Although she studied social work in the 1980s,

I didn't really like it because I lived the system for so long. All those problems, you know, your cheque is late and the rent is late, and there's not enough money for groceries. I was disgusted with the education I was getting in social work. What they were teaching me in school had nothing to do with the way you're treated or what you have to go through when you're on welfare or Mother's Allowance.

Barbara's education was made financially possible by Ontario student loans. Although she did not finish her degree, attending university represented a turning point in her life, in that it helped build her confidence.[3] As her daughters started looking at future careers, she stressed the importance of education and how it connects to the level of income you bring in. She noted, "I try to stress that because I was always living in poverty, they had to live it too. I felt bad about that; I could never get to that higher income." Barbara was making about $30,000 per year as an office manager in a small service agency at the time of the study.

In 1992 Barbara had a serious illness and was hospitalized. Friends and family pitched in, and her young daughters took on a lot of responsibility for the running of the household. Barbara was crippled with arthritis and was often unable to get off the couch. She was told by doctors she would be sick and on medication for the rest of her life. Since that time, she has immersed herself in the beliefs of Native spirituality. She reported,

You're supposed to be sick with that for the rest of your life, but I worked on myself with vitamins and prayer and I go to sweats, I go to support meetings, and that kind of support just can't compare to anything. It's very, very powerful.

Cuts to social programs affected those around Barbara:

[I have] to help my friends, because I'm lucky to have the job that I have. Even in my circle of friends people are struggling. I share whatever I can—that includes buying food, taking friends shopping or I'll take my girlfriend $40, which isn't a lot, but I'll shop with her in the way I know how to shop and try to help her stretch that $40. Or I'll buy medication or drive her to a doctor. If it [the appointment] falls within my workday then I'll take my break at that time.

Barbara was well aware of how cuts to social assistance "are a lot worse than what I've suffered, but it still affects me." She counted about ten women with whom she remained close over the years: all were raising their children on their own and depended on one another to survive.

At her own work place, Barbara reported that posting notices for full-time jobs would bring in many applicants; in one case 130 people applied for one receptionist job. "For every single job posting, and this is chronic, half of the people are overqualified for the positions that we post. People are desperate for work," she said. With an insecure job market, Barbara was unsure of how to advise her children about t heir search for employment: "You could get a contract job for a year, and then they'll have to keep looking for a job, be a professional job searcher," she said. The lack of jobs, the general atmosphere of cutbacks and the impact this had on friends and on her community, meant that

All the work that people have done in the past hundred years, you know, to gain equality, to gain security, that's all being flushed down the toilet. And those fights have to be taken up again, you know. Those fights take a lot of energy, a lot of understanding. Being very political [is important. It is about] not just having a heart for it but being informed enough to recognize… if they're offering you something that's nothing with a lot of dressing on it or they're offering you something that's really going to help everybody, not just one group of people. There's no need for Canada to have people living on the streets. This government wants the poor and middle class to be a gardener, maid or service provider for the rich.

By the third interview, financial problems at the community centre led to every staff person taking one day out of seven without pay. For Barbara, this meant a loss of $300 per paycheque. Because her schedule was so demanding, she worked on the "no-work" day and donated the money back to the organization for a charitable receipt. With changes in management and work style, Barbara's world was turned upside down for a while. Her work had been the mainstay of her life up to this point but "now it seems like a lot of days I don't even want to go to the office." To get through tough times Barbara adopted a philosophical outlook: "You're not in control of the world, you live in the world. You always have to remember to just let things go and trust that the creator will take care of things." She also found some solace in her partner Adam, who was calm and had most aspects of his life well-ordered. Barbara found that, with less money and, with the increased expenses her daughters had, the budget was very tight. She commented, "Now it's three adults, and they need everything that I need. They need transportation, access to a vehicle. Car insurance is going up, gas use is up, and I still have my student loan."

In the final interview, Barbara reported that her eldest daughter had decided to do her Grade Thirteen instead of going to college. Her daughter had also crashed Barbara's car, "so my insurance went up major!" There were talks of layoffs at Adam's plant, "so we're not really doing any planning." Barbara's own work was going much more smoothly. While things stabilized at her work, Barbara commented, "If I wasn't living here and I had to pay rent, I would be poorer than I have ever been." Her position of being "slightly better off" was always tempered by her past experience of poverty: "I'm financially free to be able to do the things that I want to do. If I want to buy my godchild a little present when I'm shopping I can buy it now, for the first time in my life I can."

Rosie and Bob

Rosie and Bob were a white couple, aged fifty-nine and sixty-six, living in downtown Toronto, who had just celebrated their fortieth wedding anniversary the weekend before the first interview. Bob had retired a number of years before and lived on Old Age Security (OAS), Canada Pension Plan (CPP) and Workers' Compensation (WCB). Since Rosie was too young to collect OAS, and Bob's income was too high for her to be eligible for a Spousal Allowance, she had no income of her own. Just as the study began, Rosie sent in her application for a Spousal Allowance, but she said, "I'm nervous about it, because they asked for his Social Insurance Number (SIN) number. When it is for me why do they want his number? I don't want them taking any money off him." Not having her own source of income greatly worried Rosie: she hoped to find some kind of work that would bring some money of her own.

Rosie and Bob lived in an unrenovated Victorian house on a street that has been gentrified. Inherited from Rosie's mother, a seamstress who bought the house with her life's savings, their lodgings were mortgage-free.

Their son lived downstairs in his own separate apartment and paid a nominal amount of rent; another apartment in the basement was rented out for $500 per month. This household fell into a medium-income bracket, just marginally above the low-income cut-off. The house was their most significant asset. Bob said, "When we got the house we were both lucky there."

Rosie and Bob finished each other's sentences and spent most of their time together. While they joked around a lot, they were deeply worried about their future. No longer in optimum health or able to have the flexibility of earlier days, they were feeling very vulnerable. All of their income was pooled; bills and personal expenses were paid by both of them. Running the household finances was Bob's duty. The house was registered in Rosie's name, while the car was in both their names. Their Registered Retirement Savings Plan (RRSP) had been spent on renovations designed to clean up the downstairs and legally separate the apartments. Although Bob did the manual work around the house, Rosie had input into the decisions. Bob explained:

> We get together and I say, "Rosie, we need this, we got to get this," so she can't say, "Where did all that money go?" I didn't buy the car without her coming down to see it, to try it out. Of course she tells me later that she doesn't like it, but that's beside the point.

Since they were living on a fixed income, the rate of change to social policy in the province was quite frightening for this couple. They were particularly worried about their health costs and the instability of the health care system. They did not have the option of increasing their income with pay raises, promotions or transfers to better-paid jobs. The fear that they would be hit with a new property tax bill or a new health cost that they could not manage produced anxiety. Bob's work as a crane operator for twenty-three years had provided him with little security. He used a hearing aid due to the loss of hearing he had suffered at the work place. Rosie worked at a number of jobs over the years; the last one was in the service sector where she was paid minimum wage. She hurt her back on the job, but explained, "I couldn't prove it. You can hurt your back anywhere and, at that time, everybody was being investigated for back troubles. So I didn't get compensation." During the time of the study, Rosie did try to get some work. She sent a letter to an agency that advertised "make money at home." However, she learned that, in order to make money stuffing envelopes, she would have to pay $35 up front!

The annual cost of Rosie's medications and medical aids was over $2,000. She had a number of health conditions, including diabetes, high blood pressure, asthma, deteriorating discs, a bowel disorder and depression. Her mobility difficulties required a motorized scooter and safety bars in the bathroom. Because she did not have her own income, she felt that she was not pulling her weight:

> Financially really I'm a big burden. I cost a lot of money, and I don't want to go to the doctor because I'm afraid that every time I go the doctor will write me a prescription. It costs too much money.

Bob and Rosie's other main concern was their property tax. They had not had their property assessed in some time, and they feared their tax would jump by thousands of dollars. Bob explained, "That's our biggest concern. I'm worried about our taxes, whether or not we'll be able to meet them. If we're not, then we're in a predicament. We will have to sell the house and then what are we going to do?" He said, "We can't plan anymore... because you don't know what's going to happen." The property tax assessment was raised the next year to $1100 annually.

In 1998, Rosie attempted to offset her sense of financial insecurity with a part-time job as a crossing guard. It paid $10 an hour and she worked twenty hours a week. Rosie's new job involved labour on both their parts. As Rosie explained,

> He dresses me up very warm and sends me off to work.
> [Bob:] I drive over and then drop her off, in about an hour I pick her up. At noon I take her over for two hours and then pick her up. I got a stool for her so it's not too bad.
> [Rosie:] I sit in the TTC booth if it's really windy and cold; you've got to have a good coat; I worked through that last storm and everything. Bob needs to do something. He's staying home all day and I'm out working. It gives him something to look forward to. [Bob:] Rosie really enjoys the work, seeing the children every day. [Rosie:] I get very depressed and I don't get depressed when I go out like this. And knowing that I'm making extra money that I put it into an account [is important]. If we need it, we'll dip into it. They put my paycheque right into the account.

At the time of the third interview in 1999, on doctor's orders, Bob had quit drinking completely. According to Bob, the doctor said, "You can stop drinking or you can have a heart attack and end up in the hospital." Upon hearing this news, both of them felt afraid of losing one another. Rosie felt more vulnerable about her own situation. She worried about "being left alone and not knowing what to do or where to go." Bob shared her concerns:

> I guess it's along the same line. How is she going to cope without me, if I go first? And if she goes first, I'd be the same as her, left without her. It's just something you don't want to look at. I'm not worried about dying, that doesn't scare me. But being left alone does.

By the final interview, Rosie was working as a contingent staff. She was told by her boss that she was unreliable. She was also being placed at a number of different locations despite the fact that she liked the crossing walk near her house. The small spousal allowance of $185 per month that she had begun receiving eight months previously was discontinued because her job made her ineligible to receive it. In spite of their adherence to the post-World-War-Two employment model (full-time, full-year male employment with pension contributions) along with home ownership, Rosie and Bob were not financially secure enough to enjoy retirement together.

Discussion

- What constitutes income security?
- How can social policy increase or decrease people's experience of income security?
- How is income security affected by factors such as household composition and differences arising from age, ability, ethno-racial membership or gender?
- What happens when the family must substitute for social programs in areas such as housing and health care?

The dominant theme running through these stories is that income security is essential to household coping and survival. Multiple sources of income (like Sabrina's top-up from social assistance) and in-kind contributions (such as housing provided by parents) characterized almost all households. More often than not, these combinations of resources were required to meet basic expenses. The households profiled in this chapter illustrate that income security is about a lot more than employment. Many households had to combine income sources in order to get by. Furthermore, whether the income source was employment, social transfers or family and friends, income was generally not secure: it required significant effort to sustain it. The experiences of household members suggest that income security today is something enjoyed by a privileged few. The incomes of Jerry, Monica, Randy, Melanie, Heather, Barbara and Sabrina were anything but secure. All would be facing major crises if they did not have parents who could help with loans and provide assistance with housing.

Social policy can exacerbate or ameliorate income insecurity. As Chapter Five illustrates in detail, labour-market policy affects how people get jobs and what kinds of jobs they have. In Ontario, many factors, including the freezing of the minimum wage at pre-1995 levels, decreases in protections for workers in the province, the cutting and contracting out of jobs in the public and para-public sectors and a significant growth in temporary and contingent work made access to employment income precarious for many participants. At the same time, social policy related to the provision of affordable housing affected the choices available to households, particularly to those with low incomes. Housing emerges in policy discussions mainly in relation to homelessness or crisis, but it is at the centre of household security. Policy decisions which increase user fees, decrease taxes, eliminate mechanisms for controlling rents or restructure services, which then have to be paid for privately, also affect the income security of households. Heather, Melanie and Sabrina's experiences show how policy decisions also cut jobs and change working conditions in the broader public sector. The changes in their service-level jobs also show that the lives of their clients were made more vulnerable. As the stories in this chapter highlight, the benefit of having a consistent income level can be undermined significantly by the cost of medications that are no longer covered under the provincial plan or by new fees that result from social service restructuring.

How else would this work

Amongst the households in this chapter, Sara and Anand were the exception. They were the only participants who could be said to have had any substantive sense of choice or security of income. Yet the financial security of a standard employment situation, with advancement opportunities and benefits, is presumed to be the norm. The policy discourse of tax cuts, which was so dominant at the time these data were collected, assumed that most people lived in two income households where adults had permanent jobs, discretionary money and family supports and resources. As well people were expected to possess sufficient skills and information to make them knowledgeable consumers and negotiators of the educational, employment and health care systems.

The experiences of participant households indicate that provincial and federal government policy was exacerbating the effects of an insecure labour market. For example, Randy and Monica were attempting to run a home business while, at the same time, pleading for emergency welfare, to tide them over until Workers' Compensation replied to Randy's application. Sabrina, who once worked in social services, had to obtain a welfare supplement to top up the income she received from three part-time jobs. Confronted by an insecure labour market and dwindling public supports, she turned to the "informal" economy as a survival strategy. At the same time as wages stagnated, labour-market protections were weakened. For many households, this meant a drop in real income and increased income insecurity. For instance, changes to the funding of ESL and government downloading of services resulted in a steady drop in Melanie's income over the last decade. Her situation as a member of a female-dominated profession also illuminates the gendered nature of these changes.

There is much income insecurity that is hidden. Randy and Monica's story illustrates that access to an asset like housing provided by a parent is a determining factor in managing insecure and small incomes. Without parental assistance this couple would not have been able to afford to rent a space adequate for Monica to set up a home day care. In addition, the household would have had enormous difficulty weathering the financial turmoil of Randy's compensation claim if they had not had access to low-cost housing. In Jerry's case, access to housing, child care and loans from his parents made it possible for his family to manage on a small income, even though they had large debts. Although turning to family and friends to deal with these difficulties, as will be discussed further in Chapter Seven, was a strategy used by most participants, it can also put a strain on key relationships in people's lives.

Melanie's home ownership, possible only because of a loan from her father, cushioned Heather and Ron from the rent imperatives that ruled the monthly expenditures of other households.[4] Ron's job, although not very fulfilling, did provide an income anchor. This household not only functioned as a team as they claimed, but their apparent security was underpinned, once again, by the older generation, which had the resources to provide the down payment on a house. Researchers examining intergenerational transfers have argued that, rather than constituting a burden, an aging population often makes possible the flow of resources from elderly parents to adult children and grandchildren (for a recent review see Henretta, Grundy et al. 2002). This is more than the traditional bequeathing of wealth from one generation to the next. For people like Rosie and Bob, these resources are now available because of post-World-War-Two social policies that allowed people to build equity in the form of home ownership and pensions. Such options are dwindling today for "middle-class" households. So, while Melanie's father could provide funds for a down payment on her house, as a fifty-year-old woman whose work is underpaid and undervalued, Melanie will not be able to pass on that kind of support to Heather. Sabrina's parents paying off her student loan is yet another example of support provided by those who have retired from the labour market. Other housing subsidies flowing from those who enjoyed post-World-War-Two social benefits can be found in the stories of Jerry and Barbara. These options, however, are not available to those without family or to recent immigrants to Canada, who are far more likely to work in precarious jobs.

Income security, then, encompasses more than merely employment stability. It is influenced by job type and tenure; by levels of labour-market protections; by labour-market legislation, such as the level of the minimum wage; by access to private benefits and public supports (such as Employment Insurance, social assistance or health care); by access to assets in the form of credit or relationships with people who have assets; and by kin and friendship relationships that give access to in-kind or direct moneys. In examining the experiences of these households, the fragility of income security is striking even in those cases where participants could marshal resources from several sources. Indeed, income insecurity was the norm. In this chapter, we have limited our discussion to that of income insecurity. However, we recognize that the terrain of human security is much greater and deserves more attention in Canadian social policy.

Notes

1. The word security is being limited here to considerations of resources available to people. The word is used on the world stage to cover issues of national and human security. This concept is emerging as central in Canadian debates as international market economies with their resultant inequalities within and between countries spread. Participants in this study, however, were centrally concerned with security of income (Hudson 1998).
2. As the federal government attempted to reduce expenditures, they decreased transfers for post-secondary education, including continuing education programs. The Ontario government responded to lower levels of federal transfers by reducing its support of ESL programs. The cutbacks to adult education began with a $60 million reduction in November 1995. In June 1996, the provincial government made junior kindergarten optional and reduced funding levels to adult education. School boards were put in control of adult education funding, and, given their other funding priorities, many boards were unable to offer an increase in supports; this had a direct impact on both teachers and students.
3. This avenue for women to raise children on their own while pursuing their education has been eliminated. Receiving OSAP means women are automatically cut off assistance. Going back to school often means less financial support, in addition to the pressure of paying back a loan in an economic environment where a great deal of work is precarious or part-time.
4. The influence of the cost of housing on household expenditures varied considerably. It seemed greatest for middle-income households (depending on whether or not they had access to *de facto* housing subsidies from family) but was most dramatic for low income households who had to rely on market housing (see Bezanson and McMurray 2000: 35).

Chapter Four

Policing Motherhood
The Gender and Racial Effects of Poverty

This chapter explores some of the issues confronting five female-headed households in the study. Sole-support mothers are frequently depicted as either victims of the system or as abusers of it. This entrenched polemic ignores the strategies women employ to counter policies that put them and their children at serious risk. In this chapter, the women reveal how the reduction of public provisions was matched by rigorous efforts to criminalize them and to increase the surveillance of their daily activities. These policies and their effects are structured by the intersection of race, sexuality, class and gender. Over the course of this study, these women conveyed how a range of policy changes had significant, damaging and long-term effects on them and their households. While neoliberal policies are generally viewed, in the literature on globalization, as bringing about a reduction of state power, the experiences of these mothers suggest otherwise. What is most startling here is how the nation-state operates in concert with corporate global practices to insert itself, through new methods of surveillance, into the micro routines of these households. This process is neither benign nor indifferent: this chapter shows how the state (with assistance from the private sector) aggressively discounts the citizenship claims of these women who, for many reasons, are the primary caregivers of their families.

The cut to social assistance payments in 1995 and the further restructuring of the welfare system in 1997 (the *Social Assistance Reform Act*) were followed by a series of cutbacks to the social programs on which women and children rely. Many incomes were well below the poverty line. The lack of child care, affordable and safe housing, stable employment and meaningful training opportunities, along with shrinking health coverage and restructuring in the education sector (*Fewer School Boards Act; Education Quality Improvement Act*), interfered with their attempts at sustaining the physical safety and security of their households. The presence of small children, frequently with at least one health problem, often made steady employment for their overextended mothers untenable. The diagnostic rate of Attention Deficit Disorder (ADD) and Attention Deficit Hyperactivity Disorder (ADHD) has skyrocketed in the last decade. For sole-support mothers this diagnosis became a considerable burden. Notably, the increased incidence of medicating children has occurred alongside the reduction of social supports, resulting in what many have argued are pharmacological solutions to social inequities.[1] When these women took jobs, they often conflicted with prior child-care arrangements; often the wages they were paid were not sufficient to cover their monthly expenses. Other activities designed to meet the needs of their families were thwarted by personal and income-related circumstances and brought about a significant increase, on the part of state officials, in the surveillance of their daily activities.

During the years of the study, the reduction of a host of social programs was matched by an increase in punitive programs, invasive of personal privacy: the enforcement of the Consolidated Verification Process (CVP),[2] an increase in charges related to welfare fraud,[3] the "spouse in the house" rule,[4] and supervision by the Children's Aid Society. In order to maintain eligibility for Ontario Works, the women in this study had to produce an endless paper trail that in the end helped facilitate the charges against them. They encountered great difficulties with a welfare system subject to constantly changing regulations. Case workers were often as confused as clients. For most people on limited incomes, balancing the household budget was managed in spite of the variations in the amount of their monthly cheque. Budgeting decisions were reduced to a choice of which utility would be cut off or what food item or school program would be put on hold. Requests by the government that women receiving social assistance recoup money from ex-partners through the *Family Responsibility Support Arrears Enforcement Act* left them with less money and made them the target of the violent behaviour they had already escaped.

Although the ingenuity and perseverance of these participants over the three years of our study was remarkable, the struggle to get by required constant attention and energy. The first two households presented in this chapter, *Veronica* and *Angie*, were headed by women who seemed able to pull reserves of energy from nowhere. The stories of *Jenny*, *Sadan* and *Anne*, however, illustrate the consequences for women who begin to lose ground as they are forced to dip ever more deeply into material, physical and emotional reserves. The degree of systemic violence in all their stories was palpable.

Veronica

Veronica, a sole-support mother of two children, Harry (aged three) and Sally (aged six), undertook a range of approaches to providing for her children. Increasingly, however, just getting by was harder to do:

Lack of money is my number one concern. I never know from one month to the next if the hydro's going to be on, or the water, for that matter. And it's not even a matter of, you know, "Hey, Mike Harris, give me some more money on welfare." If there was more reliable day care, if there were more places in the work force that tolerated children, you know, that had day care. It's not as accessible as it once was. Any of those things [would help].

Veronica and her children, who identified themselves as a white family with no ethnic association, were born in Ontario. Both children had significant health problems. Added stresses resulted from living with Veronica's abusive ex-partner. These factors convinced her that she should remain at home with the children. However, after the Ontario government cut social assistance payments by 22 percent in October 1995, Veronica could no longer afford to do so. She picked up odd jobs, such as cleaning houses or delivering the community paper. In 1998, she found steady part-time employment as a school bus driver. The pay was so low, however, that she qualified for a social assistance top-up that supplemented her earnings and provided her and the children with drug and dental benefits. Despite her paid employment, daily survival remained difficult.

Veronica and her children lived modestly on the top floor of a house furnished mostly with borrowed and second-hand items. When her social assistance payments were reduced in 1995, she was informed by her worker that she would have to move because her rent exceeded the allotted rental allowance. Veronica refused. She liked her neighbourhood. She was in close proximity to her support network, and she felt her daughter had moved too many times in her short life. Even if she had wanted to move, she was unsure where she would go, given the lack of decent, affordable housing in the metropolitan area. Shortly after asking her to move to cheaper accommodations, the social services department accused her of being in violation of the "spouse in the house" rule. This rule assumes that if a male and female are residing in the same household, they must be sharing household expenses and are, therefore, in a spousal relationship. The accusation was made because Veronica's downstairs tenant, with whom she had no relationship, forwarded his share of the monthly rent to Veronica; she, in turn, wrote out one cheque for the full amount of the rent to their landlord each month.

Veronica's relationship with her social assistance worker became increasingly antagonistic over time. In one interview she described how the social services agency was pressuring her to go after her ex-partners to formalize child support payments. While Veronica received some child support from the children's fathers, the support tended to be unreliable and sporadic. She noted, "Sally's father is $20,000 in arrears, while Harry's father pays what and when he can." This arrangement did little to provide stability in the children's lives. However, Veronica feared formalizing Harry's father's support payments. He told her that, if she pursued formalized payments, he would harm her physically and that he would work only for cash, so his wages could not be garnisheed. Veronica reasoned that, although payments were sporadic, she was still in receipt of some support and the terms between them were congenial. Had support payments been formalized, Veronica would not have had more income: because Social Assistance deducts support dollar-for-dollar, they would ultimately deduct the payments from her income until she would no longer be in receipt of social assistance. Veronica was angry at a social assistance system and at a provincial government that refused to shift the responsibility for collection away from the mother:

The government can say 'til they're blue in the face we've got the Family Support Plan, we'll garnishee their wages. Well then, get off your butts and do it. Like, seriously, how many years do you have to wait? My first husband was giving me money until [social services] forced my hand. Then it was a two-year court battle. But it was three abductions later, three kidnapping incidents, two years of hell and what do I have to show for it? A piece of paper that says yes, he's supposed to give me this much money every month. Am I getting it? Am I likely to get it? No. Now I know that they're going to do the same thing [with Harry's father]. They're going to say "No, no you've got to go through custody and support," and I know what's going to happen. It's going to turn what was a pretty regular $100 a month into a nothing. You get nothing and then they're putting me in a position of stoking his anger. Look, "Why don't you guys get him drunk, stand us face to face and get him to hit me, or put his hands around my neck again. Like that's what you're doing to me. You're setting me up!"

Veronica found it difficult to budget, not only because of sporadic child support payments, but because the amount of her assistance varied from month to month depending on the hours she worked. The cut to welfare benefits was accompanied by the assurance that recipients would be able to make up the shortfall through earned wages. As Veronica explained, her cheques did not necessarily reflect this policy in practice:

I realize that they say all these wonderful changes happened so that people who are on social assistance can make a go of it. I basically see things exactly opposite. They hand it to you with one hand and take it away with the other.

Veronica described how she coped with the paid and unpaid work demands in her life in a typical day:

I'm up at 5:30 a.m. and I get Harry's and Sally's breakfast together and packed. I get Sally up at 6:00 and get her well on the way. Harry gets up at 6:15. I get him dressed and ready to go. We're out the door at twenty to seven. Over to the school bus and they sit in the car where it's warm and I do the circle check and get the bus started. Then they come on the bus with me; I drop Sally off at my friend's, that's usually about five after seven. Then I go off and I do my school run. My girlfriend gets Sally her breakfast that I've packed. Sally does any kind of late homework she didn't get done, and my girlfriend gets her off to school. I do my two schools and I'm usually home about twenty after nine. Then at 11:00 a.m. I'm out the door again to do my lunch run. My girlfriend provides the lunches; I prepare them: as she's walking out the door to get the kids, I'm making lunch so when she comes back it's already on the table for them. I see Sally and we talk about the morning. When my friend takes them [the children] back to school, I tidy up. When she gets back from dropping the girls off, Harry and I usually come home and we'll spend some time together. I get his snack ready and off we go, so about quarter after two we're gone to the bus again. Then I do my afternoon route; meanwhile my friend has picked up Sally at school with the other kids. I'm clear at 4:00 p.m., so I'm usually at my friend's house by twenty-five after four, in my car. I've already parked and secured my bus and then we come home. When Sally comes home we usually do her spelling test—if the teacher has decided to send it home this week! She'll sit in the kitchen and talk to me while I'm getting dinner prepared, and Harry just usually vegges out in the living room and does whatever. By that point he's tired! Sally helps me set the table; any homework is done by then.

Veronica was required to submit pay stubs to social assistance; this turned into an administrative nightmare. She talked of overpayments and confusion that took months for the social services department to resolve. In the meantime, she often turned to her mother and friends for financial and practical help. She was guarded about revealing this support to social assistance, even if it was payment for the children's skating and dance lessons, because any assistance her family provided would have been construed as monetary support and therefore deemed as income. Veronica resented that she had to hide the support from grandparents and close family friends. She felt her children were deprived of enough already and that, by having to disclose gifts, social assistance was unfairly targeting the familial and friendship relationships of low-income people. She counted her small circle of friends and family as an important source of support.

In addition to informal supports, Veronica sought out formal counselling for herself and her children in order to work through issues of domestic violence, only to be put on long waiting lists. She argued, "It's all [because of] budget cuts. What importance does government put on women and children?"

Over the period of the study, as she attempted to deal with the social assistance income assessment juggernaut, Veronica felt increasingly alone and isolated. Especially stressful was social assistance's constant focus on fraud. After accusing her of cohabiting with her neighbour, her welfare worker questioned her about her numerous absences from work. Veronica's son had been hospitalized for several weeks, so she had reduced her hours in order to spend time with him at the hospital. The social assistance department interpreted her absence as a refusal to work and demanded an accounting of the drop in hours:

> [My welfare worker] wanted a letter of explanation from my son's doctor. She wanted medical records proving that my son was sick. I drew the line, and I almost went back with my ex. I was this close [holding her thumb and index finger close together] because I thought, with his income and me working part-time, I could tell [my worker] to go to hell. But I'm trapped. That's not an option either. It's either deal with this abusive woman or deal with a previous partner and I'm stuck in the middle. And I just find she's been very militant since this whole concept of Ontario Works came in play—very, very militant.

The final straw came during the fall of 1999 when Veronica was served with an eviction notice. (Although a new tenant had moved into the house who did not pay a share of the monthly rent, Veronica's signature was still on the lease.) Tired from fighting for care for her son and from responding to the demands and accusations of social assistance, she now had to face her landlord. Veronica had intended to appeal the decision, but ultimately decided she would move to Northern Ontario, where she hoped that a slower pace of life and a cheaper standard of living would alleviate some of the stress she and her family felt. However, after further thought, Veronica realized the move would only separate her from the support network she relied on.

Throughout the three years of the study, Veronica maintained a brave face, always consoling herself with the fact that things could be worse; she reminded herself that she was surrounded by people who loved her and that she had a job she enjoyed. In our final interview, Veronica reflected that her hopes and dreams of a university education were on hold.

Angie

Angie was a thirty-six-year-old white sole-support mother of two teenaged boys—Steve (sixteen years old) and John (fourteen years old). All were born in Canada, of German ancestry. When we met Angie in June 1997, she had a permanent full-time job, with extended medical and dental benefits, as a property/building manager of a social housing cooperative in a medium-sized city. In addition to working in the social housing sector, Angie lived in a housing cooperative in a suburb. Her youngest son had a series of ongoing medical problems that affected his ability to succeed at school, and caused Angie a great deal of anxiety. Compounding these pressures, Angie felt that her income and housing situation were insecure:

> I'm a single mother of two boys. I worry all the time. It's difficult because both

of [my sons] are going into puberty, and I worry about them. I worry about whether or not I will be able to make my payments—but I worry about my boys more. Sometimes I just close the door, sit on the floor and have a big cry for about an hour. And then I pick myself up and start all over again. What keeps me going basically is the fact that I have two children that need someone to look after them.

When Angie asked her ex-husband to leave the home, she was left with the sole responsibility for repaying a large personal debt. She paid $1000 a month towards servicing the debt, $800 a month for her housing, $269 a month for her car and put some money into an RRSP; at the end of the month Angie used her credit cards for other expenses. These financial pressures were exacerbated by new policies that threatened her home and job. In June 1995, the newly elected Ontario Conservative government terminated some 300 developing social housing projects. At the same time, the government made it clear that provincial social housing policy would be changed:

I'm really worried because if I stay here, living in this cooperative, then it's possible that I could lose my job and my housing at the same time. That's very, very scary. I mean I am taking precautions to ensure that I have other skills, and I'm beginning to look for other work, but the uncertainty around all of this stuff is really scary. I don't like to think about it too much because it's just too much. I don't know where I would go. I have to plan it day by day.

Angie's tenuous employment and housing situation were compounded by her fragile relationship with her ex-husband. Glenn was unemployed and therefore unable to provide any child support. Since leaving her ex-husband in 1994, she had received no form of financial support.

Angie's youngest son suffered from Attention Deficit Disorder (ADD), among other medical conditions such as asthma and migraines. Correctly diagnosing and subsequently managing John's ADD was a constant struggle for Angie. In early 1997, she had to petition education officials, as well as doctors, in order to secure the resources her son needed at school. In December of 1998, she said, "The support at the school is next to non-existent. They keep making all these promises about what they will be able to do for John, but they keep reneging on them." Her son's condition consumed a lot of Angie's energy, she said, "I have had to give up my social life. I don't have a social life. And, even if I did have the time, I don't really have any extra money to go out and do things—like movies and stuff."

In September 1997, however, Angie met Travis and began to date him informally. By December 1998, their relationship had become serious: they were considering a long-term commitment. Feeling confident about the relationship, Angie decided to share a home with Travis. He owned a house in a community about thirty minutes outside of the city: they decided to live there. They made plans to build an addition to the existing structure and live together by August 1999. Having given her notice at the housing cooperative, Angie looked forward to her new life with Travis. She felt that the time had come to leave the supports she had found in cooperative housing:

> When I initially moved into the co-op, I was still with my ex-husband. I was going back to school to upgrade my skills after I had been home with the kids for an extended period of time, and my ex-husband wasn't working. The co-op provided us with subsidized housing. It also gave us a sense of community and we had a sense of giving back to the community because we were involved in the life of the co-op, on committees and stuff like that. Then, after I asked Glenn to leave, the co-op gave me an opportunity to get back on my feet. I was able to be independent but live in an environment where I was safe, and I knew the rent wouldn't be beyond my reach. I knew that I wasn't going to get tossed on the street. But, as I continued to grow, the co-op was definitely not the way I wanted to live. I had just grown beyond it, and it was time to move on and try new and exciting things.

In March 1999, however, everything came to a sudden halt. A massive fire caused their house to burn to the ground; dreams of an addition had to be abandoned. After a spring and summer of rebuilding, the family did move into their newly constructed home. Angie and the boys flourished in their new surroundings. Angie felt that John's ADD was receiving much more attention, compared to his previous experience at the other school. Living with Travis meant that Angie's tenuous financial situation seemed to be behind her. Their combined household income was much higher than anything Angie had experienced; their mortgage payment was lower than Angie's housing charge at the cooperative. With more disposable income, Angie bought a new car and hoped they would be able to have a vacation in the near future. Despite her financial security, significant challenges remained:

> It's wonderful living here with Travis—but it's also not wonderful at the same time. We are still two separate families and we are trying to become one. You know, if we had been married and had kids together, then the kids would be a common expense. But the boys are my kids, and they will be living here for a while longer yet. So, I'm really conscious that I make sure I am paying for my share of the kids expenses. Travis doesn't seem to think it's a big deal. Like he doesn't care if he pays the mortgage and the hydro and stuff, because he'd be paying those expenses anyway. But, still, it makes me feel a bit odd. This is still his house. It's a bit uncomfortable, but it's wonderful at the same time.

During our last interview, Angie reflected on how her life had changed. Although she continued to work in the social housing sector—but felt that her job was insecure—she was no longer living in social housing. Moving in with Travis meant that she was finally getting close to having a "normal" family.

I just want that stereotypical TV family. You have a nine-to-five job, a nice husband, and you come home from work and just spend time with your family. I feel so much better than I did about five years ago. The whole financial thing has made a big difference, but also the whole sense of security and family and community that has been added to my life. My relationship with Travis makes my life so much easier.

Jenny

Jenny was a twenty-seven-year-old white woman who grew up in a medium-sized community in Ontario, where she now lives with her three young children. Her ancestors had immigrated to Canada in the early 1800s, part of an early wave of Irish immigrants. Jenny did not complete high school, and married quite young; her relationship with her spouse dissolved in the early 1990s. On her own with little financial support and limited work experience in a recession economy, she managed to move into subsidized housing and began receiving Family Benefits Allowance.

Despite the disruptions in their lives, Jenny had kept her household stable and described her children as well-adjusted and contented. However, new provincial policies and regulations were making it harder for this household to manage. When we first met Jenny in 1997, she was struggling with a reduction of social assistance, along with the unpredictable amount of her cheque, month-by-month:

When I was on my own with just Tamura and Nicholas, I would get $951 a month, that was for me and two kids. Now, with three kids, sometimes I get $950, sometimes it's $970. All the time I get these deductions and overpayments. I don't know why.

The administrative requirements of social assistance were complex and challenging to navigate or predict. Jenny's ex-husband paid her $100 a month in child support, which was deducted from her monthly social assistance payment. The irregular payments from her ex-husband were not taken into consideration by social assistance:

I was mailed a support payment from my ex who was owing for child support. It was $600. My cupboards were empty and I'm thinking, "Great, my name's on this cheque, right on." About a week later, Welfare says, "Oh, you shouldn't have cashed that and we're going to have to deduct that from your cheque." That's ridiculous. $600 is a lot. That really screwed me up there.

For Jenny, access to affordable child care was a significant barrier to her finding and keeping paid work. She had worked at a number of part-time jobs over the three years before the study started, but all had been short-term or inflexible to the demands of her family life. At times Jenny had trouble envisioning ever moving her family out of poverty:

> I heard of a job not too long ago and I thought, "I could do this, make some money." Say I make $40, at $7 an hour part-time. In that amount of time, I would have to pay for child-care costs that would be more than $40. So it didn't make sense. I can't just go out and find the first job that's out there! It's not that I'm being picky because I'll do any kind of job. I've done really crappy jobs too. It has to be enough to pay for child-care costs. That is what's stopping the majority of single parent families from going to work. If child care was available you would have so many more people out in the work force, in school.

Jenny had had to give up a lot; her own health has suffered, resulting in significant weight loss:

> If I eat a regular amount of food a day, my kids wouldn't have any food. And I can't send them to school without lunch. I'm lucky if I have a glass of milk in a day. Like, those are things that you have to give up, too, just so that there's going to be enough. I did need to lose weight, but I'm not trying to diet. It's a drain on my energy, that's reduced.

Jenny and her family used food banks on a regular basis and had been turned away on a number of occasions because the food bank did not have food.

Being involved in community life was challenging for Jenny. Because she felt lonely, she wanted to attend her church, but she felt embarrassed by the family's obvious poverty:

> I feel isolated. I have the sense that there's a lot of things that I cannot do because of my financial situation. Like we can't go to church every Sunday. I would like to but I'm thinking I don't have any clothes to wear there. My kids don't have any clothes. Are we going to show up in our grungy clothes to church?

A relationship with her closest friend fell apart in 1998, severing an important emotional connection as well as her main access to transportation. Activities, such as getting groceries, filling a prescription at a pharmacy which waived the co-payment fee, getting her family to appointments and getting her kids to and from after-school activities became very difficult because of the lack of transportation.

In 1998, Jenny went back to school for adult upgrading. Coordinating day care, transportation, new fees and school schedules proved difficult. The province-wide teachers' work stoppage caused Jenny to decide to withdraw from school.

School and quality of education were important to Jenny. She wanted her children to have the best life chances she could provide amd saw school as one avenue forward for them. Jenny was concerned about the effects of cuts in education spending. Her eldest daughter, Tamura, had been diagnosed with Attention Deficit Disorder (ADD), and the medication she took decreased the child's appetite. Tamura's barriers in the education system were compounded by health barriers:

> A lot of parents probably notice the cutbacks, how it's affected the schooling. I'm having problems with Tamura eating her lunch. Because of her Attention Deficit Disorder, it's very difficult for her to sit still. Lunchtime is difficult for her. I've spoken to the school and asked if someone could please sit with her just to make sure she's going to eat her lunch. She's coming home still with nothing touched in her lunch all day. You can see how thin she is. I'm always on her about her eating. I guess the teachers just cannot spare that extra time. If you have to get hold of the teachers, it's during the school hours. They're not there after 4:00 p.m. They're not there for very long. And that has to do with the cutbacks too.

The effects of little income on her children's involvement in school activities were significant. In late 1998, Jenny explained that she had to tell her kids that they could not participate in hot dog days or popcorn days at school:

> They have popcorn orders for 25 cents a day and they have to bring it the week before. 25 cents isn't a whole lot of money, but when you have zero, zero, zero, that's money one day a month and it's just another thing. There's pizza day, hot dog day, popcorn day, book day and they miss out on all of them because I don't have the money. They say, "You're mean," and I say, "Hon, that's not the way it is. If I had the money I'd buy you a big movie popcorn vending machine to have in the house all the time."

Jenny lamented that her daughter had too little of a childhood. "My daughter knows more than I wish she did," she says. "She comes home saying, 'Mom, I just wish we weren't so poor. I wish we had some money.'" Jenny recalled that she was mocked as a child for her family's poverty and hated that her children were as well:

My children want things that I can't provide for and, not only does that affect me, it affects them. When they're at school and they don't have the things that all the other kids have, it's the self-esteem thing. They're put down, they're made fun of and sure you can say, "well, honey, we can't afford it, maybe some day," but you know that only goes so far. I remember what it was like going to school too and kids are cruel. I'm worried about how it's going to affect my children.

In late 1998, Jenny got engaged; in early 1999, she had her fourth child, a girl. She hoped to enrol in a college nursing assistant program once her daughter was a little older: she wanted to become a midwife. At the end of our study, she was managing day-to-day and planning what she hoped would be a brighter future:

I don't really have a choice, I just have to cope. Some days I have great days where I can accomplish a lot and then other days I just, I can't get it done. I just don't worry because, with the mountains of laundry for four children and dirt on the floors and spilt juice and dirty dishes, I can never keep up with it. I can't, it's not possible, it's not possible. I don't have the most spotless house on the block, but I don't care. The way I see it you know when I'm sixty they'll be out of the house and I'll have all the time in the world to have a clean house!

Sadan

When we first met Sadan, she had recently separated from her husband of over twenty-four years. She and four of her six children, whose ages ranged from two to twenty-two, resided in subsidized housing. After becoming a Canadian citizen, she sponsored her husband's immigration from Eastern Africa. Not long after their reunification, however, they began experiencing marital problems. Finances were tight; he often mismanaged what little money they received from social assistance. Despite the addition of another household member, the family experienced a decline in their benefit level. Prior to Ontario Works, social assistance recipients were either in receipt of General Welfare or Family Benefits. When Sadan's husband moved in with her, welfare transferred their case file from Family Benefits, which paid a more generous benefit level, to General Welfare. It wasn't long before the rent was in arrears. The pressure on the family intensified when Sadan found out she was pregnant with their sixth child. Sadan described the run-down conditions in her building and how their crowded living quarters were about to become more cramped.

Because she had good language skills, Sadan worked occasionally as a cultural interpreter for a local community agency; she also worked in a community kitchen assisting with catering orders. She took pride in this work and relished the opportunity to work when it was presented. While the local community provided employment opportunities, it also brought its share of problems. Community members and local agencies had long complained about problems in relation to police violence and racial profiling in this area. Not only did Sadan have to deal with the challenges of coming to Canada as a refugee, her family now became subject to a close police presence. As her own son began to experience "run-ins" with the law, Sadan began to seek out alternative housing. She feared the other children would follow their brother's example. In response to an incident at school, the Children's Aid Society was called in to monitor the family. Sadan continued to concentrate on moving out of the area, in the hope that it would give her and the children a fresh start. In addition to these difficulties, Sadan's youngest daughter, Minera, was having difficulty at school. Minera's teachers felt she had a learning disability and required additional tutoring; Sadan was unable to afford this added expense.

Shortly after the birth of her sixth child, Sadan's husband moved out, and she and four of the children moved to subsidized housing in another community. Her eldest son and daughter did not move with the family but set up separate residences. Sadan was relieved to be out of the old neighbourhood. However she also felt separated from her supports, including those from her own ethnic community. While experiences of racism in relation to housing availability are well-documented, her racial difference in the new community caused her to feel very isolated:

> In [the old neighbourhood] if I don't have food [I] go to a parents' drop-in and they give you a voucher. It helps you out. Here [there is] nobody. I [used to] go to a friend, please [lend] me $20 this month. This area I don't know anybody. In the fridge is nothing. Nobody helps you. That's very strange. And [in old neighbourhood] you go across the way to get a little food for your kids. At the food bank here, nothing; and everything is far away. This is a nice place. I like the place. It's quiet, no violence.

Nevertheless, Sadan continued to struggle with the daily grind of poverty. Her rent was in arrears, collection agencies were hounding her, utilities were cut off and there were frequent visits to the food bank. Money, or rather the lack of it, remained the constant preoccupation of her household. Sadan talked of her children going to school hungry and said that she did not have enough money to buy them warm clothing for the winter. Unlike the public school in their old neighbourhood, the children's new school did not offer a breakfast program. Sadan also lamented the loss of dental coverage under Ontario Works:

> Nobody goes to the dentist because we can't afford it. Social assistance doesn't cover it. I [would] have to pay, but I don't have money—so I don't take them [to the dentist]. It's been a long time since my kid's teeth were checked.

Sadan's money problems were compounded by intra-familial conflicts. Her eldest son returned to the household several months after he had moved out. Clashes and violent episodes between two of the children meant that the Children's Aid Society (CAS) continued to be a presence in the household. Sadan feared that the CAS would find her an unfit mother and place the rest of the children in foster care. She felt powerless to change the destructive course on which the family found itself and spoke of having little control over what was happening to her and her family.

On numerous occasions Sadan attempted to get back into the labour force, using temporary agencies to find work in factories. As she explained, these positions were poorly paid and the work was physically demanding:

Because there's no jobs. The jobs are factory jobs, and the agency takes out like a lot of the money from the company, and give you little. You have to work hard—like three days of work in one day.

After a number of failed attempts at securing employment through temporary agencies, Sadan requested that social assistance place her in a job under the much-advertised Ontario Works Program. She was disappointed when they recommended that she do more volunteer work to improve her English. Sadan had already spent years doing volunteer work, accepting a plaque the previous year from a local councillor in recognition of her contributions to the community. Her language skills were sufficient enough for translation, volunteer and factory work, yet Ontario Works refused to support her need to work. Sadan was angry that she was, on the one hand, not considered "job-ready," while, on the other hand, the welfare system continued to apply pressure on her to work. She wanted to be gainfully employed. She also attempted to enrol in upgrading for adult learners; however, her health prevented her from completing her program and she lost her subsidized day-care space. Sadan grew increasingly frustrated with the welfare system:

I had a nice relationship with my worker where I lived before. I moved here and I don't know what happened. They want a doctor's letter; I take the doctor's letter to show them I need treatment. I need to see the doctor often. Welfare said they want another letter, my doctor sent them [another one]. Now my doctor is tired of them and doesn't send nothing. [Welfare also] wanted a school letter, every day I have to go to school. They wanted an income tax return letter or they would kick my baby out of day care. I went to school to register, they said they need last year's attendance. Where am I going to get last year's attendance? They ask for so much. They need an excuse to kick you off. No, they're not supporting me. They do not listen to me.

Sadan found that it was becoming more difficult to maintain her benefits. Relations with her welfare worker were poor. Sadan did not know her worker's name; she only referred to her by her worker number. The escalation of information requirements by Social Assistance, also known as the Consolidated Verification Process, has resulted in welfare recipients being asked repeatedly to submit collaborating documentation to ensure their eligibility. As Sadan explained, this bureaucratic assault increased her stress and frustration level. She interpreted it as yet another way to cut people off of social assistance.

Anne

In early 1997, Anne was living in a three-bedroom rent-geared-to-income townhouse on a busy street. She was a white women who had immigrated from England at the age of eight; she now had four boys ranging in ages from infancy to seven years old. Anne talked with intensity and energy about her devotion to her high-needs children, her struggle to leave a damaging relationship, her efforts to make ends meet and her dreams of owning a home and returning to school. Accessing enough resources was Anne's biggest concern when we first met. In late 1995, when the Progressive Conservative provincial government cut social assistance payments, they also added a co-payment fee for prescription drugs for social assistance recipients, de-listed some drugs from among those covered and changed regulations governing access to dental care coverage. Anne talked about the difficulties these changes caused:

> I live literally cheque to cheque and once the money is gone, there's no more money. If they hadn't cut back our cheques, [we'd be in better shape]. I don't want handouts. If they allowed you to have maybe $150 more a month, [we could get by].

Throughout the study, Anne and her family were trying to patch together enough money to meet household costs, including high health care expenses and food for growing children. She explained that she thought she could manage without social assistance if her husband paid support:

> I wish he would pay support. He should be paying $800 support right now. If he was paying me support I'd have my baby bonus and I wouldn't need assistance. I'm doing it right now on $1100—barely—but I am doing it. At least I'd feel good about myself.

Anne employed a variety of strategies to stretch household income. She went to food banks and to a non-profit organization which provided diapers and formula. Anne and her best friend pooled resources and sometimes sold household goods. "We have to do things like take our kids' toys to the pawn shop to get $5 for a bag of milk," Anne explained. "A friend of mine sold her swing set last week because she had no money." Anne and her friend share child care and children's clothes, buy in bulk together and bake their own bread: "A lot of times we'll shop at each other's cupboards at the end of the month—a can of juice, diapers, formula. I'm trying to put a little bit of money up each month starting in July for Christmas." Anne's concerns with making ends meet were compounded by her worries about how she was faring as a parent. Suddenly finding herself a single parent with four young boys who had serious health problems was overwhelming. In addition, she had been in a car accident several months before our first meeting, which caused anxiety attacks. "I was doing more yelling than talking with the kids," she said. "This medication for stress has helped: if the kids do something, I'm now going from zero to ten, not zero to one hundred." She still questioned her judgement and decisions.

Anne's children suffered from chronic asthma, a condition their father also had. Two of her boys had been diagnosed with Attention Deficit Hyperactivity Disorder (ADHD), affecting their behaviour and learning possibilities. Her second youngest son had a bowel condition, and her infant required eye surgery in 1998. It was no exaggeration to say that her children were in and out of the hospital on a weekly basis. Anne managed multiple medical needs and had to dispense large amounts of medication on a daily basis: "I got seven prescriptions from the doctor yesterday." She added, "I've got like thirteen different medications for four kids, three or four times a day." In early 1997, Anne had pulled together a good team of professional supports around her; in addition, she was able to rely on friends. Anne had to be very resourceful and persistent to get these services:

When I needed help with the kids after the car accident, I begged the social service agency, "Please just don't put me on a waiting list." I said, "Please help me, I need your help. My family is in a crisis. I'm losing my marbles. My patience with my kids is going. I need your help." It was very important that they didn't just shove me on a waiting list. And they didn't, thank god! I was accepted within two weeks and they were coming to the house. So that's been a massive, massive relief just to know that there is professional support—not just your personal support.

Major changes in provincial policies, spending initiatives and regulation changes affected Anne's family dramatically over the last three years of the study. She described what happens when regulations change and service agencies are understaffed and workers are overburdened:

I used to be able to get certain medications covered on my drug card and now

I can't. I have to pay for those medications. And my kids have chronic asthma so that's a constant expense for me. The waiting lists are phenomenal for appointments [with medical specialists and social workers] because of the cutbacks. There used to be five intake workers. Now there's only one, so if your crisis isn't as bad as the next person's crisis, you're on a waiting list. They say, "I'm sorry, there's a waiting list due to social cutbacks." Everybody says it.

In 2000, the provincial government announced that it was considering barring social assistance recipients from receiving housing subsidies—a situation which it called "double dipping." Anne noted in 1997 that she would not be able to survive without a housing subsidy, "If I were living in a place paying $700 a month I wouldn't even have food money," she said.

Ontario established a welfare fraud hotline in 1995. While social assistance programs like Family Benefits have always been intrusive, the suspicion of poor families intensified. Anne explained that, when she was in the hospital in 1997, her ex-husband stayed in her home to care for their children:

Somebody reported to the Mother's Allowance hotline that my husband was living here. I flipped. I was in the hospital! I have four children that I could not take care of! Yes, he was here, but normally he isn't here at all. He was staying here to care for his children for the three days that I was sick in the hospital! He doesn't even pay support. It took me two years to get away from him. Did they think I'm just going to let him move back in here?

In late 1997, the children's medical needs intensified. As a result of the efforts of her children's pediatrician, Anne began receiving Handicap Benefits for two of her children's medical conditions and applied for benefits for her youngest son. The provision of respite money and ex-tended drug coverage made a significant difference to her finances.

Two other major events were occurring in Anne's life at the time of the study. Anne had to take her ex-husband to court to try to get his wages garnisheed for child support. His boss hid his earnings and lied for him, so Anne had no access to his wages. In addition, Anne's doctor, her child psychologist and the family service agency all recommended that William, her then four-year-old son, be put in a foster home. Anne wanted the best for her son but lacked the resources to care for him when she was always "putting out fires." Since she wasn't sure foster care was the answer to her problem, she consulted with the boy's father, with little success:

They want to place him in a foster home because of his severe ADHD.... They think that he needs to be in a two-parent, one-child environment. They say that the energy level in this house is too fast paced. They're saying, "It's what you can cope with, Anne." They have major high needs, mentally, physically, healthwise. They're saying, "What's William's best interest? Put your feelings aside." But what do I say? "Do you want to go live somewhere else William?" They ask, "What are you doing for your kids? Is it best for your kids to be in this environment where you're just putting out fires all the time?" That's basically what I'm doing; I'm just around to take Joseph off the covers, William out of the fridge, turn off the burners, shut my car doors. I don't know what to do. I have been telling their father that they want William to go into a home. He says, "Oh, he's going to hate you, and you'll be some worthless mother if you do that."

Anne's sources of support as well as her personal sense of confidence became seriously frayed during this period. Many of those who were involved in her case had changed jobs, and there was little continuity in the programs and supports that she had managed to pull together for her family. Her handicap benefits were decreased by $300. Anne dreaded having to go through the paperwork and hassle of figuring out why it had been cut and if it could be readjusted. Anne explained that the benefit for Joseph made a big difference; the letter about the cut came just as Joseph's behavioural, health and educational problems intensified:

Joseph was ripping his books up, throwing chairs at the teachers, leaving the school grounds. The principal was driving around looking for him. He's really bad. They can't get, you know, an assistant teacher to spend more one-on-one time with Joseph for him to feel more comfortable in there. So that's the major problem. If they would provide that, he would be fine. That's all the doctors recommended, an extra special pair of hands for Joseph, but with the cut-backs....

When we met for the last time Anne told us that her son had been placed in a treatment home. She was much calmer and had begun working part-time at a retail store. For the first time in three years, Anne felt okay, although not stable, financially. She remained very concerned about her own and her children's futures. She had coped against striking odds to hold this fragile unit together. She said she holds her breath every time the phone rings at work, for fear that she will be called to get a child who is ill and it will cost her her job.

Discussion

- When households such as these are routinely viewed as "social prob-lems," what does this help us see? What does this obscure from view?
- Women, such as those described in this chapter, are frequently por-trayed by the media and elected officials as being unable to respond to

the "ordinary" demands of raising children because of making poor choices. What are the ways in which "choice" is constructed and limited by race, gender, sexual and class oppression?

• What kind of value do we place on the work these women do: running households and informal economies, navigating health care and education systems and participating in the labour market and the volunteer sector, while caring for children?

• How does social assistance policy shape the options and level of security and personal safety available to sole-support mothers?

A central task of policy development and analysis is determining which differences among people and which conditions of their lives are important to recognize and address. By definition, policies ignore certain aspects of social life and focus on others. Since the female-headed households in this chapter encountered myriad policy regulations, their experiences are particularly rich analytical sites for understanding policy effects on women. In just these five households at least three elements can be seen: (1) Welfare changes and regulations have thrown sole-support mothers into the worst jobs available and into a state of constant crisis management; (2) Child care and child support programs continue to fail these families, leaving women without flexible and appropriate child-care arrangements while having to extract support payments from former partners. A gender-specific policy to "crack down" on "deadbeat dads" acts to increase rather than decrease the dangers and costs to women, with minimal financial gain; (3) Policing motherhood continues to utilize gender, race and class hierarchies to punish sole-support mothers while continuing to demand that they bear all responsibility for raising children, running households and participating in the labour market.

Unlike some of the households selected for other chapters, all these households were pushed to the margins of Canadian society—no matter what the indicator used, this was true. The lives of mothers raising children under conditions of poverty and systemic violence have been exacerbated by the harshness of recent policies: the precariousness of getting through the day, week, let alone month for the mothers in this chapter demonstrates this very clearly. Indeed, the demonization of these citizens over the past few years helped facilitate the public appetite for "cracking down" on the poor. Sadan's story shows how

> the odor of dishonesty that haunts the world of "the poor" in general is most intense around those who are non-White. Whole communities live under suspicion and surveillance—Somalis, Tamils, Jamaicans, and so on. This raced poverty is both masculine and feminine, and even its feminine face does not fall within any code of chivalry or compassion and charity. (Bannerji 1997: 30)

Since the early nineties, the dominant discourse surrounding single mothers views them as problematic to their children and themselves and indeed as a threat to the social well-being of the larger community. This is not a new phenomenon, but it has intensified. Their poverty is no longer viewed as a result of inadequate social assistance and/or low wages; it is seen as more or less inevitable, to be expected as a consequence of the lifestyle the single mothers "choose." Single mothering continues to be constructed as a matter of individual choice, made by women who disregard the welfare of their children. In this stereotype, poverty is to be expected and thus is not an unacceptable outcome: this conceptualization results in the "reassertion of the legitimacy of inequality" (Luxton 1997: 21).

Government, as a player in the lives of single mothers, has become more intrusive, operating as a policing agent bent on the punishment of those who do not subscribe to a two-parent family. This punishment is inflicted only upon the women, however, even though male parents of the children in these households offered few supports toward the care of their children. Their literal absence is reinforced by how they disappear from public policy concerns, even when attempts are made to retrieve financial compensation. For example, in Veronica's situation, focusing on mechanisms to collect child support from "deadbeat dads" not only disregarded, but exacerbated, the violence in her life. Anne spent months in court trying to collect child support, while the inconsistency of Jenny's support payments only disrupted her welfare payments. The precarious situation of both Anne and Sadan meant that the Children's Aid Society became involved in their lives, which only compounded for Sadan the reality of police violence and racial profiling she was already experiencing in her neighbourhood. All of these women bore the daily and punishing effects, financially and otherwise, of broken relationships. For Angie, on the other hand, a new relationship resulted in a substantial increase in her finances and security. However, a shift in that relationship could quickly jettison Angie out of that security, in ways that her male partner would not experience. Interestingly, she continued to feel responsible for paying the full expense of her own children, in spite of the "partnership." A market economy and social assistance system that mutually reinforced gender inequities harmfully compounded the relationships these women had with the men in their lives.

The challenges these women face are most often articulated as the result of "personal problems" or failed "relationships." In this way, we do not see how labour policies or welfare policies shape the possibilities and kinds of choices available to these women in the first place. Although it is evident that women and children are being harmed by policy shifts, the women themselves describe feelings of inadequacy and self-doubt when it comes to caring for their children or running a household. For Sadan, the loss of control over her family was rooted in the everyday racism of living in a heavily policed neighbourhood and attempting to work in a labour market that excluded people through race and language. While her "language skills" were fully utilized in a volunteer capacity, these same skills were seen as a deficit by social assistance, who used this excuse to bar her from training and full-time stable employment. Her story of racial exclusion, intersected with poverty and gender issues, resulted in a move which brought increased safety yet enhanced her cultural isolation in a new and unfriendly community.

Clearly these women go to great lengths to survive. Veronica never stopped. In fact, her daily schedule had every minute accounted for! Anne worked constantly with the health care system to ensure that her children got treatment when needed, not weeks down the road. Jenny actively intervened to minimize the effects of poverty on her children's identity. As neoliberal restructuring took hold during the 1990s, single mothers were increasingly "conscripted" to play a role in proving the need for reduced social costs and for the recasting of citizens as "workers." Furthermore, a family life model that equates the problems of children with family structure, along with a rhetoric about the "rising tide" of single mothers, immigrants and refugees invites "moral panic." These portrayals strengthen the state's ability to control, reshape and reposition "problematic" groups in ways that justify a cost-cutting political agenda. Because of the alleged illegitimacy of their presence in Canada, immigrants and refugees are not candidates for social supports. This "segment of the 'Poor' is thus quickly covered in a mantle of crime" (Bannerji 1997: 30).

This chapter raises questions about what counts as work and productivity in Canadian society. In the 1990s, paid employment was reinforced, once again, through both employment and tax policies as the only legitimate form of valuable work. This narrow definition of productivity erases other ways of thinking about provisioning. The participants profiled in this chapter engaged in mental, emotional and physical labour, as they cared for children and negotiated repeatedly with health and educational systems in order to secure the type and amount of resources that their children needed. Although this contribution was recognized as work in the 1996 census for the first time, it continued to be denied in every social policy area.

Feminist policy analysts note the significant problems involved in addressing the economic needs of women, when viewing them as female equivalents of male breadwinners (Lewis 2001). Such a model fails to incorporate the unpaid work done by women and undervalues caring labour, whether paid or not. Further, it ignores the fact that poor women and women of colour have always worked and been essential to the waged labour market and the household economy. All of the women in this chapter held down multiple jobs in the labour market, even though it disqualified them from or interfered with their receiving benefits. The experiences profiled here are consistent with international findings that households use an informal economy as part of an overall strategy to make ends meet (Elson 1998). However, in both economies, the caring responsibilities women carry still affect their ability to acquire resources. Survival strategies used by women to meet daily needs all too often result in the loss of long-term goals, while gender, race, sexual and class patterns of inequities are reproduced and reinforced. Making ends meet today by taking a series of low-paying, contract jobs that interfer with child care and increased the chances of bureaucratic mistakes does not help build a secure tomorrow. Such policies negate the contributions of women's caring labour and deny such contributions as a basis for making citizenship claims that are as valid as those based on one's market activity.

Notes

1. The rampant prescribing of Ritalin by U.S. and Canadians doctors during the 1990s is well documented. Many have linked the psychiatric and pharmaceutical control, or policing (Armstrong 1993), of young children to the "tendency to increasingly pathologize annoying childhood behaviour" (Oliverio 1998). Rooted in discourses of maternal responsibility and risk, Malacrida argues that pharmaceutical and alternative therapies continue to portray mothers as inadequate and responsible for children increasingly viewed as a risk to society (2002). Others have found Ritalin has become the "sit down and shut up drug in classrooms" (Bongers and Palmer 1997).

2. In partnership with Anderson Consulting (now Accenture), the provincial government, in 1997, began to redesign the delivery system for social assistance, of which the CVP is one element. The CVP provides an ongoing review of every aspect of a recipient's case history, which for sole-support parents was undertaken before transferring them from Family Benefits to Ontario Works. Considerable evidence indicates that numerous cases are being closed improperly and unfairly. As of January 2002 CVP generated $345 million in direct program savings through caseload reduction (Herd and Mitchell 2002).

3. Case reviews, once performed based on need, are now prioritized by the risk of committing "fraud." Herd and Mitchell note how risk factors, such as high shelter costs in relation to benefits and being in receipt of assistance for over thirty-six months, automatically place one into this category (2002). Welfare fraud hotlines were also introduced throughout the province.

4. Regulations introduced by the province in 1995 (O. Reg. 409/95) reinstated a rule making a woman living with a man ineligible because she is assumed to be supported by him.

Chapter Five

The Barriers to Good Jobs
Dashed Hopes after Years on the Job

In Chapter Three we examined issues of income security facing participants. This chapter focuses on paid work and its centrality in people's lives. It puts forward the idea that the restructuring of the 1990s was in part driven by a desire to create a labour force available to work in precarious jobs; in short, "bad" jobs are central to the new economy. In Canadian society paid work is more than a source of income, it is also a source of identity and status. As illustrated dramatically in Chapter Four, social policies like social assistance and workfare are possible because they rest on the premise that paid work is the only legitimate source of income; others are suspect. The breadwinner model of employment, with its gendered image of a man with a steady job earning enough to support himself and his family, never did reflect the experience of many citizens; for example, poor women and women of colour have always worked outside the home. Indeed such a model was available to only a privileged few. Yet it remains ideologically powerful. An examination of paid work, then, must look at more than level of income. Employment is one of the major institutional mechanisms for regulating different sectors of society. As such, it is a site for documenting how the dynamics of gender, race and class get produced and reproduced. In this chapter, some of these processes are captured in household narratives.

This chapter is about the labour-market myth that a job is the way to security as this idea is applied to the select vulnerable populations of youth, older workers and immigrants. Thus, this chapter shows how social location works in practice. Documented are some of the struggles of young participants trying to establish themselves as members of the labour force, of middle-aged employees who faced plant closures due to companies moving elsewhere or of recently retired persons whose incomes proved less than adequate to meet rising costs. Over the three years of the project, participants encountered an array of barriers that they had to overcome as they tried to secure stable, well-paying jobs. The social policy climate with regard to the labour market changed substantially in the 1990s—particularly after 1995 at the provincial level. As Canada intensified its integration into the global marketplace, some segments of the population were forced to adapt to a rapidly changing labour market. For many of the participants in this chapter, this meant changes in the types and organization of their jobs. It also meant lowering their expectations of public services, benefits and employment.

National governments are increasingly powerless to influence decisions made at the supranational level. However, federal and provincial governments can make political choices that influence how these changes are dealt with in the local economy and that ensure that policies are in place that protect workers. Significant decreases in investment in education and training, as well as inappropriate training; a growth in nonstandard jobs, along with legislative initiatives that decrease wages, health and safety; and changed hiring and firing practices have all posed new barriers to workers and have made carefully planned income and work strategies untenable. Policy changes in areas like municipal taxation significantly affect those on fixed incomes.

The following household experiences document how individuals and their support networks coped with job barriers and restructured plans. We start with the story of *Frank* and *Michael*, a same-sex professional couple, who changed jobs with minimum turmoil a number of times before and during the study. By contrast, *Patrick* and *Denzel* were two young men with some post-secondary education who could not cope as successfully with a shifting labour market. A move to a new city proved disastrous to Patrick's career, while limited family support and heavy student debt resulted in major stressors that took a toll on Denzel's mental health. *Michelle* was in mid-career with school-aged children to support. Until the company she worked for downsized, she had enjoyed stable, full-time employment. She was then caught in a web of short-term contract work, social assistance and unemployment insurance. *Leo*, an older worker in the manufacturing sector, experienced a constant decline in his standard of living, while *Liz*, a long-time school-board worker, retired early from a chaotic educational system only to discover that her expenses outstripped her pension income.

Frank and Michael

Frank and Michael, two white men, lived and worked in Toronto. In a committed relationship of over seven years, they shared all aspects of their lives with each other. At the time of the study both men were in their late-thirties, held graduate degrees and worked in senior positions for agencies serving the gay/lesbian/bisexual population. Their annual gross household income was approximately $100,000. They were particularly concerned about how policy changes were affecting their clients.

[Frank:] I work with people who are pretty marginalized in the world—lesbians and gays living with HIV and AIDS, and often they are dying. My concern is that, for people that are in difficult life circumstances, things are not getting any easier.
[Michael:] I have come to realize that we are living in an historical context

where decision-makers are saying through their actions that we—as a society—are no longer responsible for vulnerable people. I find that very disturbing. There is something wrong with that kind of society.

On a personal level, however, Frank and Michael were not directly affected by funding cutbacks. Although a succession of cuts by federal, provincial and municipal governments resulted in many community-based agencies closing, Frank and Michael were never without employment and income. When we first met Michael he had been employed for more than five years at a community-based agency. He enjoyed his work and felt fortunate to have a stable, full-time job with medical and dental benefits. With his skills in demand, Michael was also employed as a part-time college instructor and undertook some private consulting work. In September 1997, with the financial support of a fellowship, Michael began part-time doctoral studies; a year later he switched to full-time studies. He was earning approximately $50,000 per year.

At the start of the study, Frank was working two separate permanent, stable, part-time jobs, as well as doing some teaching at a local college. While his goal was to secure a permanent full-time job, he enjoyed the flexibility associated with two part-time jobs. In April 1998, however, Frank decided to quit one of his part-time positions and take a second part-time job with the same agency as his first job. The agency was funded by the municipality and was undergoing many changes, primarily as a result of funding pressures. Because the provincial government had downloaded the responsibility and costs associated with many services, municipalities had to make decisions about the allocation of scarce funds. Frank became concerned that the future of the organization was in jeopardy. As a way to get involved in the decision-making process, Frank took over labour-union steward responsibilities. Later that same year, Frank changed jobs again. With his skills and education in demand, Frank secured a permanent, full-time job at another prominent community-based agency. His income increased 40 percent; he had the protections associated with union membership; and he received full medical and dental benefits. He was, however, no longer actively involved in union activities.

Throughout the time that Frank and Michael were experiencing career opportunity and growth, Michael's health status was unstable. He had an ongoing chronic condition that required constant attention and drug therapy. He took steroids which caused him to gain weight and changed his personality somewhat. Michael decided to undergo a delicate and risky surgical procedure requiring two separate operations. A minimum six-month recovery period was required. This meant a drop in income and increased demands on Frank to be flexible with his own work schedule.

Frank put in place their own in-hospital support system comprised of close friends and family. He said,

I've been involved with AIDS work since the late 1980s and I'd been on a number of care teams personally where I'd been a caregiver until somebody died. They chose to die at home, so it was palliative care. When Michael went in for his surgery, I knew that the health care system was under a lot of stress and there were lots of changes going on, so I suspected that there would be fewer supports available in the hospital. I think I knew what to expect. I also knew that I wouldn't be able to bear all of the responsibility for supporting Michael through his surgery and recovery period. I knew that I'd need some support and resources. So, we got a bunch of friends and family that were comfortable helping out. We rolled up our sleeves and dug right in there. We found out where all the supplies were and how to do things for Michael. We provided a lot of direct physical care—which wasn't a problem because we wanted to do it. But I remember thinking that if you were an elderly person, or a single person, or if your family wasn't around, it would have been a very different hospital experience. You just would not get the same kind of care.

Aside from having to provide his own in-hospital support system, the scheduling of Michael's surgery was also directly affected by hospital cutbacks. Two weeks before his first surgery was scheduled, Michael went on sick leave from his job, and his studies. Three days before the surgery, however, it was cancelled. As the new date approached, the hospital cancelled the procedure a second time:

I pushed hard with them the second time. They wanted to move the surgery date a month into the future. I just told them that it was unacceptable because I had made arrangements with my employer and with school. If it was delayed any longer, I would lose my academic term. And Frank had taken vacation time to be with me during the hospital stay. If it was delayed any longer, that would have been all screwed up. I just pushed and pushed and pushed and they found a way to do it.

During his recovery, Michael required the support of home care. Michael found that the quality of the home care he received was excellent, although he had to constantly advocate on his own behalf to retain the same level of service. Carrying large case loads with reduced staff, the agency wanted to terminate his care not long after he started receiving support. Michael's post-operative recovery was excellent, and Michael and Frank began to think about the future, including investing in their own home.

As our study concluded, Frank and Michael were enjoying their new home, their expanding careers and an active social life. They both felt, however, that they were living in a society full of more and more contradictions. It was these contradictions that they often found difficult to reconcile. Frank explained,

I know that we are now better off materially than compared to five years ago. There is no question about that. I know that over the course of the 1990s, I have developed more personal material wealth. I know that during some of the toughest social and economic circumstances for many people, I have prospered personally and benefited financially.... So I'm better off, but I don't think that we are better off as a society. I really don't. Some people have prospered a lot, while many, many others have just found it more and more difficult to get by.

Patrick

Patrick, a divorced white man in his early thirties, moved to Ontario from western Canada in 1995 to be closer to family members. Given his eclectic work history as a desktop publisher, community-worker and landscaper, he did not anticipate having problems finding employment. He was surprised when his savings ran out and he still had not found a job. Since his most recent position was business for himself, he was not eligible for employment insurance. After living with his brother and sister-in-law for a month, he turned to social assistance. He struggled to make ends meet on the $520 he received from Ontario Works. His rent, $458 a month for a bachelor apartment, only left him with $62 a month to pay for his groceries and utilities. He could not afford to keep his van on the road. Patrick managed by scrutinizing each and every expense. This frugality limited his options in pursuing job leads. Keeping transportation expenses to a minimum meant limiting job interviews, unless he could obtain help from social services for the fare for public transportation.

While receiving assistance Patrick picked up temporary odd jobs. While such work eased the financial pressure he felt, it failed to lead to more permanent employment. Throughout the study, Patrick talked about the difficulty of finding work. Having been in the work force for a number of years, he did not expect to have to re-enter the labour market in an entry-level position. He felt that his labour-market experience worked against him. He explained that employers were reluctant to hire those with years of experience for entry level positions because they feared they would not be able to retain them for long periods of time. Getting his foot in the door proved harder than he thought. He said,

People are not willing to pay. They want you to have two or three years experience, but still at $7 an hour. If you have four or five [years of experience] then they go, "Well, you're not going to take this job," even if you say you are going to take the job. You want the job, right? They're going to say, "No, I don't believe you."

While in receipt of social assistance, Patrick attempted to enrol himself in numerous training and upgrading courses. To his dismay, the courses that were offered were short on employment potential and long on disappointment:

> I went [to the training program] for the first two months and it was disastrous. There were so many things wrong with it. I ended up writing an eight page letter to Social Services, the Employment Office, basically saying what was wrong with it. They didn't have the co-ops. Basically what they did was lie about everything. The teachers did not know what they were teaching. If you had a question they'd go, "I don't know, look in the book," right. So what you ended up doing was self-study. There was no monitoring process for that.

Patrick, who had some post-secondary education, felt there was a lack of fit between the programs that were being offered and his skill set. Not only did his interests not mesh with available course offerings, but his experience underlines one of weaknesses in current employment policy, namely that people are directed toward meaningless training programs while little effort is made to leverage the considerable experience and skills that some like Patrick already possess. Furthermore, having access to training programs offered to those on Employment Insurance, he commented on the disparity in course offerings between EI and social assistance. Whether your income was from social assistance or employment insurance, Patrick reasoned, you are still unemployed; any program that may benefit you should be made available.

Frustrated with the lack of assistance he was receiving from social services and disillusioned with training programs that he felt were based on an outdated model of the labour market, he sought to teach himself computer animation. Patrick was disappointed to learn that welfare recipients could no longer be full-time students in post-secondary institutions. His only option was to forego social assistance and finance his education through OSAP, a proposal he was not about to consider since he had only recently paid off his earlier student loan. He asked his welfare worker about the possibility of participating in an Ontario Works jobs placement, thinking it would provide him with on-the-job training in a computer field. Once again he was disappointed:

> If you want work experience, guess where the work experience is, the non-profit sector. So you've got to go down to the Alzheimer Society and volunteer your time there. To do what? Computer animation? Are they going to have the equipment? No. Are they going to have the experience that I want? No. They are going to have the stuff that I already have.

Patrick feared that the intent of programs offered through Ontario Works was not to offer welfare recipients a hand up, placing people into sustainable jobs, but simply to move people off of assistance:

The government is interested in quantity not quality. They want to herd everybody out like cattle, get [social assistance recipients] to work. [That enables the government to say] "See how great we are" rather than [considering] a year later they are all going to be back on the system.

Despite taking issue with Ontario Work's hollow claim that people should work for welfare, Patrick was in favour of the reduction in benefit level. By reducing benefits, he believed the government was successful in dismantling the welfare wall, that is, removing the disincentive from working. He observed in one of the interviews:

I was thinking about this the other day. Welfare went from something like $640 down to $520 and I'm thinking, yes, there's cause. It was short-term stress. You're thinking, "Oh my god, how can I survive?" You've already allotted your budget. Your rent is taking up 80 percent, 90 percent of your budget. How can you survive on this? In retrospect, when looking back if it was still $640 and I'm making $800 and $900 [working] I would still be on the system. So, I mean, in some ways it's a good thing and in some ways it's a bad thing. I mean it helped me to get off [welfare]. I mean, it inspired me. I said to myself, "Well, wait a minute—$520. You can't survive on that, let's do something about it." You know, take responsibility and get off of it.

Although no longer in receipt of social assistance, Patrick continued to struggle financially. Barely earning above minimum wage, he found part-time employment in the service sector. The flexibility of the job allowed him to pick up extra hours when they were available and continue learning computer animation. But, as Patrick discovered, work in the service sector seldom comes with work-related benefits such as pensions, health benefits, such as a drug plan or dental care, or long-term disability protection. Even with picking up extra hours, Patrick found it difficult to manage without the assistance of social services:

You cannot work at $7.25 full-time and make a living in Toronto, it is absolutely impossible. Unless you don't take the taxes off, that's the only way, but then you're going to be penalized at the end because you're going to have to pay the taxes.

Despite working full-time hours, Patrick continued to be classified and paid as though he were part-time. He became disillusioned with the company's promises of advancement and soon started a bid to unionize his work place:

Well, my issue was part-time people getting paid less than full-time people. Bottom line is I was doing the same work as the full-time people except I was getting less pay for it. I didn't like that and I expressed my concern. The owner couldn't understand why. We put out this newsletter about all our concerns and some concerns were cleaning toilets and things like that. They [told us that we] have to clean toilets because they got rid of their porter. They wanted to save money on that end and give us more duties. So the owner came running in one night and said to me, "I can't believe you did this," right. Like, "I read what you said and I understand where you're coming from but I just don't believe it." I said, "Well, look at it from my point. I'm in a part-time position. This is the first job where I've ever came into, where I'm getting paid less than someone else and I'm doing the same damn job." I'm getting paid $7.50 and someone else is getting paid $8.25. I want that same amount of money, you know, and it's not about the money, it's about equal work for equal pay.

Patrick's conception of equity did not apply to all workers. He felt that he was singled out, mobilizing a discourse of merit to justify a position that normalized his identity and constructed others as "different." Thus, he believed that the *Employment Equity Act* fostered an environment in which the best candidate was overlooked in favour of less qualified candidates who were from the targeted groups. According to Patrick, a white male goes without a job, not because there are fewer opportunities, as employment creation figures seem to indicate, but because designated groups such as visible minorities and women are given preference.

While his bid to unionize was narrowly defeated, Patrick still remained in his position, scaling back his hours to devote more time to teaching himself computer programs. Conditions that management had promised to address were still unresolved by the final interview in 1999.

Denzel

Denzel was a twenty-eight-year-old single black man. In 1996, after completing two years of university, Denzel was expelled for poor academic performance. Since that time, he had received social assistance, lived in a variety of housing situations and worked a variety of temporary jobs—all of which paid close to the minimum wage. Denzel constantly struggled to find stable, full-time, permanent employment. In May 1999, he secured a full-time job in the telemarketing industry, which paid barely above minimum wage; he was living on his own. Despite finding a relatively stable job, Denzel knew it was not a career. The last time we spoke with Denzel, he was worried about his future—in particular, the possibility of finishing his university studies, and his ability to secure meaningful, long-term employment. He said,

I know that down the line I want to have a family, but I'm not sure how I will support them. I don't have a trade or anything like that, which you need to find a secure job. I have some job experience, but it's all from small jobs. I don't have good experience for permanent, long-term jobs. I think about that a lot.

Denzel grew up in the greater Toronto area and lived with his father, who had divorced from Denzel's biological mother when he was young. Denzel's younger brother and sister lived with their mother, so Denzel had very little contact with them. Denzel was an average student, and after completing high school, he decided to pursue a post-secondary education at a university in another city. Denzel's relationship with his father was strained, and he was looking forward to beginning a life independent of his family. With a student loan from the Ontario Student Assistance Program (OSAP) and some financial support from his father, Denzel lived off-campus for two years. Since he found living on his own difficult, his university studies suffered. In 1995, the university notified Denzel that if his academic performance did not improve, he would be expelled. As his academic performance did not improve, the next year he was asked to leave the university. Denzel found himself alone with no source of income, no place to live; meanwhile, he had incurred almost $20,000 in student loans and credit card debt. His relationship with his father had deteriorated, and he was no longer willing to provide Denzel with any financial support.

When we met Denzel in 1997, he was in receipt of social assistance benefits and was living in a rooming house. In 1995, the Ontario government cut social assistance benefits by 21.5 percent, so Denzel was receiving the minimum payment of $520 per month for a single able-bodied person. His rent was $325 a month, which left him $190 a month for groceries, transportation and so on. He found it very difficult to make ends meet, and was not happy with his living situation. In particular, he found the neighbourhood in which he was living unsafe and often witnessed violence, drugs and prostitution.

Throughout the time that we spoke with Denzel, he faced many barriers, especially to employment. He was very aware of the racism around him and wondered how this affected his ability to get meaningful work. He had a pragmatic view of the situation, but said that it was something he faced every day:

I don't think that because I have a different skin colour, I should be treated any differently. It's not a big deal to me. I don't want it to be a big deal. But I know that I have been the victim of racism. Every day I'm the victim of racism. A few days ago, I was walking down the street and two guys in a car passed me and starting yelling "nigger" to me. I don't get it, I was just walking down the street. But, it's a lot better than it was ten years ago. I just try not to think about it, but it does hurt. I'm not going to kill myself over it though.

During this period, Denzel used community-based services to help him find a job. In June 1997, while receiving social assistance benefits, Denzel enrolled in a job-readiness training program offered by a community-based employment agency. He had an employment counsellor who was helping him prepare a résumé. In addition, Denzel was participating in a one-month job placement with the federal government. He was sorting mail in a large departmental mail room. While he did not like the work very much, he enjoyed getting out of his room and meeting new people. At the time, he hoped the job would eventually lead to a more permanent position.

Denzel's job placement ended without his securing a permanent job. He spent the summer working a variety of under-the-table odd jobs as a way to save some money. His housing situation at the rooming house deteriorated. In September 1997, he used the money he had saved to move to Toronto. Denzel felt that the Toronto labour market was better suited to his skills and he would, therefore, secure a stable, full-time job. In addition, his mother agreed to provide Denzel with rent-free housing for an indeterminate period of time. Denzel had a distant relationship with his family and he wanted to live on his own, but he could not afford to pay rent. Thus, he decided that this was an opportunity to both rebuild his relationship with his mother and save some money.

Within a month of moving to Toronto, Denzel had found a job. In October 1997, he secured a full-time, temporary clerical position through an employment agency. He was no longer in receipt of social assistance benefits and was relatively happy with his situation. He said, "It's not the greatest work, and it's not that secure, but at least I'm working, and there is money coming in. It makes me feel good." Denzel was making $9.50 per hour; he began to feel more confident about making plans for the future. He decided that he wanted to return to university in September 1998 to finish his degree. In March 1998, with two years of university education completed, and a $20,000 debt, he expressed concerns about the size of his personal debt load and his ability to repay it. These concerns, however, were counterbalanced by his belief that an education was worthwhile and necessary to secure stable employment:

An education should make you feel confident that you can conquer the world. When I went to university I was so happy because I figured it was my ticket. Even all my family told me it was my ticket. My father told me to go to university and work really hard. Well, I did that and now I owe about $20,000. I just hope that it will be worth it in getting a good job. I think it is still worth it.

As our study proceeded, Denzel's commitment to a post-secondary education began to fade. In 1998, he placed a ceiling on the size of the personal debt he was willing to incur:

I have made up my mind that I will only go $50,000 in debt because I think I can handle that. I'm not saying that an education should be free. I'm not even saying that it should be handed to you on a silver platter. I agree that you should have to work for your education. But, if the first obstacle you face is $20,000 in debt, and you have no choice in the matter, then that's a problem. It's not whether or not I can get into the school, whether or not I can handle the work load, or whether or not I am willing to do the work—the key issue is if I can handle the debt. I have to worry about that. I have no money. It just raises the bar, and that bar is too high for lots of people. No one should have to worry about their next meal while they are in school. It's just not right.

Denzel continued to work in contract and temporary positions that he secured through temporary agencies throughout this period. The nature of the industry, however, meant that he had no job security. In May 1998, for instance, Denzel lost his contract position after seven months of work. He was surprised that his contract ended. He said:

They hired two other people through the temporary agency and they let me go. That's the way that business works. If they like you, then you keep working, but the moment they don't, they can just make a phone call and you're finished. You have no security. I thought I was better than the people that they hired, so you just sort of ask yourself what you were doing wrong. I thought I was being successful. I just feel like no one respects me.

While the jobs Denzel secured through the temporary agency offered no security and no extended medical or dental benefits, they did offer him some labour-market flexibility. He was able to pick the jobs he wanted to work and choose the sort of schedule he was willing to work. He also found that there were a lot of these type of jobs in the labour market. He felt that, unlike the type of work he was getting through social assistance, finding work through a temporary agency was an efficient way to make contacts and get job training that could lead to a full-time, stable job. The quality and rate of pay for these jobs, however, was poor. In May 1999, after working a variety of temporary contact positions, Denzel secured a full-time sales position with a telemarketing firm. Like all his previous jobs, this position offered no security and no benefits, but the $11.00 per hour rate of pay was more money than Denzel had made up to that point:

I decided that I needed to find a real job to pay rent and live on my own. So I did some temporary work for a few months, and then I found my current job. There is no security in this job. Like there is only security as long as I'm making sales, but the money is good. I hate the work and there are no benefits, but I like the money.

The same month he secured his new job, Denzel moved out of his mother's apartment and into his own room in a large college dormitory. While Denzel was not a student, the college rented out rooms to non-students on a monthly basis. He had a private room with a shared kitchen, bathroom and television. Unlike his former rooming house arrangement, this housing situation was safe and clean. Denzel said, "I really like it here and want to stay here as long as I can. I can't afford a big apartment, but I don't need it because this place meets all my needs."

With a new job and a new place of his own in which to live, Denzel was feeling very confident about his future:

> I feel a lot better about myself. I moved out of my mom's place, I have a job that pays $11 an hour. I can afford to pay rent, I have some spending money and I have savings for the first time in my life.

His student loan and credit card debt, however, continued to haunt him. He decided the only way to succeed was to ignore his personal debts:

> I'm just hiding from that. I have about $900 in the bank, and it's just there and I don't want to touch it. I have to find a bank trustee so that I can declare bankruptcy. I could pay back my loan but then I would have no money left over and nothing to show for all my work. I would just be paying off my debts and that's it. I don't even have the degree. It would put a big crimp in my life, and I'm getting older so I don't like the thought of that.

Denzel mused that he was not sure if he was better off now than he was five years ago:

> Five years ago I was in university with big, grandiose dreams, so it's hard to say if I'm better off now. I have my own place now, I have money and I can do stuff. That is all good. But, it's not exactly as I had envisioned my life. I thought I'd be corporate. I thought I'd have a shirt and tie on, and I'd be playing golf. But none of that worked out.

Michelle

Michelle was a forty-one-year-old black woman who lived in Toronto with her two children, a boy and girl aged seven and five. Michelle's aunt and her grandmother lived downstairs in the same apartment building. They had come to Canada years ago, sponsored by Michelle. Michelle herself was born in Jamaica, lived in England for awhile and immigrated to Canada twenty years ago. The two-bedroom apartment in which she was living at the time of the interviews was the only home she and her family had ever known since coming to this country. As the children grew, however, the apartment seemed to get smaller. Michelle had a high school education and had taken a few training courses. She was keen to sign up for any training or educational program that would improve her chances at getting a "better job" in a labour market where she had experienced both ageism and racism. Nevertheless, she was determined and positive about "making it," in spite of a government that, she said, was actively barring her and other single mothers from making a decent living. Her income fluctuated over the course of the interviews, yet remained well below the poverty line, reaching $18, 000 annually by the last interview. Her rent alone demanded 48 percent of that total. Michelle's children were the main focus in her life: she did everything she could to make sure they had every opportunity to be happy and successful. Michelle had them enrolled in French immersion and a heady number of activities, such as ballet, jazz, swimming, cubs, Sunday school, basketball, soccer and music lessons.

Throughout the nineties, Michelle's financial situation went from bad to worse. She described how she was caught in a round of layoffs by her employer, a telecommunications company that was hoping to maintain its competitive edge. "I really enjoyed it, you know, but unfortunately it was a time when other companies came into the market, so quite a few of us were let go," she said. Since then, she had found herself in the chaotic and insecure world of multiple contract jobs that often offered no benefits and hampered her ability to plan for her family's future.

Because of the unstable job market, Michelle was launched into the equally chaotic and changing world of social programs. The nexus of temporary jobs, EI and social assistance required an endless paper trail to satisfy workers and to hold onto a day-care subsidy. On top of this, each new job with its different hours, locations and demands meant that her schedule and her children's were turned upside down—transportation issues, babysitting, meals, shopping, doctors' appointments and all of her children's activities had to be re-organized. Michelle explained,

> On the government data base it says I'm working, but I'm working part-time or on a contract basis. Mentally, I'm concerned with what's going to happen in the next six months. I have to think about my rent. I'm still having the struggle over whether I am saving enough if this contract should be up before the six months (May God forbid!).... You're seeing on the news how many people are back to work, but really they aren't. One of the counsellors said to me, "You have to keep changing your résumé and you have to be prepared because there are no long-term jobs any more. We are all on contracts.

Michelle had some clerical and computer skills but felt she was easily replaced by younger workers who were more adept in this area. Few training programs were available to her and she could not afford private training. At each interview, it seemed she had to clear some new hurdle if she were to secure any kind of an income for this household. Since the loss of her full-time telecommunications job, most of Michelle's savings had disappeared. Although she remained optimistic, in every interview she talked about how her dreams of having a house were fading: "My biggest dream is to see my children grow up in a home," she said. "I wanted to get them out of this apartment." For Michelle a job was synonymous with having a house: "I want to get a better-paying job. It's really starting to bother me now because once the children get in from day care they are locked in. So this is why I tend to take them to the park as much as possible."

At the time of the first interview, Michelle was receiving Employment Insurance and had one week to go until she would lose her day-care subsidy. She had relied on a drug plan from Family Benefits (a program replaced by Ontario Works and the Ontario Disability Support Plan in 1997) while she was working to help out with things like her daughter's asthma medication, but the plan was suspended while she was collecting EI. The drug costs would only be covered if she went back on social assistance or held another low-paying job. Her main concern was that

> I'm not working right now and I'm only limited to six months to find a job or to be in school and, if not, they would just withdraw my children from the day care. My expiry date is in one week. Right now I have signed up for a few schools and I'm also looking for jobs. So whichever one comes up first, I have to grab it.

Michelle landed another job before her day-care subsidy ran out, but it was another six-month contract. She got this job through a government agency that placed temporary workers in various ministries. The government had recently privatized this job-placement service, which meant that hourly wages for these jobs had dropped significantly. Her new job, a full-time clerical position, brought in $10 per hour. As a result of this rate of payment, her day-care expenses had increased; Michelle was attempting to appeal this increase. She described how even making an appointment was difficult:

> I made this appointment to see them but they said it wasn't that day. So I said I had just started this job and I can't keep going back and forth to my employer and telling them that I need time off. I need my job and I need this space too, so can you meet me halfway. They were really pushing me around and said, "You know, we can't see you today, you'll have to come back next Monday." So now I have to go back and they want everything—my bank book, rent receipts, financial statements, "Do I have access to my kid's scholarship fund," etc. Last week they assessed me, it was $80 a day for the two kids. So what is that telling me, I should stay home with my children. So this is why I have to go

back to appeal it because I don't have that much. And I want to work. I am a single mother. I don't want to stay at home. I want to give my kids something for the future but it's like every door is closing on me.

Despite these problems, Michelle was thrilled to be working again:

It's fantastic. It was busy at first but I just love it. I love to get up in the morning, get my kids ready, drop them off and just rush in the subway. It's great because I get to read stuff, I get to read my manual on the subway, so I'm a working woman and using my brain, using it to think of what I've learned.

She was happy that, since more money was coming in, she could afford a few treats for her children. Michelle was much happier when she had a structured schedule to follow and felt a great sense of accomplishment from managing the fast-paced schedule she had laid out for her family. With her new job she qualified for the drug plan through Ontario Works:

They combine my salary and what they are giving me: I don't know how they make their calculation, but I'm sending in my statement. Apparently they calculated that I'm a thousand dollars overpaid. But they are not rushing in to take it, they take whatever at a time.

By the third interview, Michelle had finished her six-month contract, and, within a few months, had found another full-time job on her own. The new job was in a U.S. telemarketing company. The rate of pay was $10 an hour. With this job, Michelle received some extended hospital coverage, but no drug plan. The company had been in Canada for four years and had not laid off anyone to date. Earlier, when she had been laid off for two months, however, she started feeling quite angry about the Employment Insurance program into which she had been paying. Because Michelle was lacking the equivalent of three employment weeks needed to qualify, she was not eligible for Employment Insurance and was forced to rely on personal networks:

Well, their father did help me out, and I borrowed some money from my aunt and I used my savings. But it was really financially tough. You see other people move on, and you set your goals to accomplish, like, to get a home for my kids. And it's always a setback due to the fact that I'm not working for a couple of months and all my savings are gone.

To make it during these two months Michelle said they had to cut back: "My son wanted to go into ice hockey this year and I couldn't afford that and their other winter activities."

In the last interview, Michelle was once again looking for work. She was concerned about those who had to use food banks and prayed she would not have to resort to that. Although she thought of herself as poor, in the sense of not having adequate housing, she viewed others as being in more difficult circumstances. Michelle's comment on the re-election of the Progressive Conservatives in 1999 was, "It looks like it will be a nightmare all over again." Yet she believed in fighting back and

> getting our words across and banging on politician's doors and letting them know we are not going to sit quietly. We want our children to get a good education, we want our nurses back, we want to get jobs for ourselves. We want to know what they are doing to the welfare system. We have a right to, we are not criminals. I want to see the government put in non-profit housing where low-income families can buy their own house.

Leo

Originally from North Africa, Leo was a fifty-three-year-old father of two sons in their early twenties. He and his wife, Maria, had been married for twenty-seven years. Until the time of the study, they had owned and lived in the same semi-detached home for eighteen years. Leo had been employed in the manufacturing sector for twenty-five years, and his wife had been an elementary teacher for thirty-three years. Both their sons were pursuing post-secondary education. For most of their married life, Leo and Maria had a relatively stable middle-class lifestyle. Beginning in the 1990s, however, they faced labour-market challenges beyond their control. Leo's previously stable, full-time job in the manufacturing sector slowly shifted into a seasonal position in which he was laid off for four months of the year. In 1999 Maria accepted an early retirement package designed to encourage older teachers to leave the public school system. Their household income dropped from $78,000 per year in 1990 to approximately $38,000 per year in 1999. Shortly before the study began, Leo, Maria and one son had moved into a new sub-division north of Toronto; however, they were finding it increasingly difficult to make ends meet. In fact, Leo was borrowing money from the bank and/or extending his personal line of credit as a way to pay his monthly bills and help his sons with some of their schooling expenses.

Like many others in the manufacturing sector, Leo found that his job security had come to an abrupt end in 1990. The Canadian economy was in recession, and, in an attempt to cut labour costs, Leo's company began to contract out work, which had previously been done by unionized labour. Some months later, the company announced it was closing the Canadian plant to take advantage of cheaper operating costs in the United States. Leo was given eight weeks' notice and no severance package. He described his union as weak and unable to negotiate a settlement for its members.

After twenty-five years in Ontario's manufacturing sector, Leo found himself unemployed, in a shrinking economy. He was unemployed for two years.

During this period, Leo applied for and collected unemployment insurance benefits and enrolled in government-funded English-language training courses. He used employment services offered at community drop-in centres to help him in his job search; he tried to keep a positive outlook on his situation. Maria provided important financial and emotional support for the household, while Leo continued to look for a job. His union could not help him find a new job. Leo found himself looking for work in a labour market that no longer seemed to have a place for his skills. Recognizing that he needed to learn new skills, Leo took positive action. In 1992, he enrolled in a government-sponsored computer maintenance retraining program offered at a local college. When the year-long program was completed, Leo found a contract position installing computers in retail outlets across Ontario and Alberta. After a year, however, the contract ended, and Leo was once again out of work.

While looking for new work, Leo discovered that his newly acquired skills in the computer maintenance field were already out of date; he could not afford the time or money associated with more retraining. In 1994, Leo returned to the textile industry, a move he described as "winning the lottery." He was offered a full-time position at a Toronto-area textile plant. He quickly discovered, however, that the industry had changed considerably since his earlier experience working in it. His new position paid less money and came with no guarantee of full-time, full-year work. In fact, Leo was laid off for four months every year, and, in 1998, his hours were reduced to a four-day work week. He said, "My job has no security now, but it's what I know how to do, so I have to stay and keep working."

Leo told us that, when he is laid off, he never knows if he will be rehired the following year. In 1998, while unemployed and hoping to go back to the textile plant, Leo told us,

I haven't heard if I will be rehired yet. I never really know. I have a union, and I go by the union office once a week to see if there is any news about jobs. Every week the union has no news. I'm not the only one in this situation. There are about twenty or thirty workers and we are all waiting to hear when we can start working again. It's very hard.

Leo blamed the lack of work on free trade agreements, which make it more profitable for businesses to relocate their plants in countries where labour costs are lower.

Leo also expressed frustration about the so-called "active labour-market" measures in the new Employment Insurance program. As noted by other participants, these elements of the program required recipients to enrol in job-training and job-readiness workshops. While Leo understood the potential benefits of these workshops, he felt that they had not kept pace with the changing labour-market. His manufacturing job was now a seasonal position, so his needs were different from many others receiving benefits:

> Getting laid off every year is standard for me now. I never know if I will get called back, but I hope I will be. I know I won't find another job because there are no jobs for me out there. I don't understand why I have to go to these workshops. I just want to go back to the textile business, that's what I'm good at.

Although his wife's income remained secure throughout most of this unstable period, during the three-year period of the study Leo's family had to adapt to less money:

> We have to watch our spending. You know, when you own a house, you have so many expenses, so we have to watch our expenses very carefully. We don't go to the movies anymore. We don't buy new clothes. All we do is pay our bills—the hydro, mortgage, cable. That's it.... Even the small things, I sometimes have to use credit to afford them. We have big, big credit.

Over the course of our research, Leo's family would often use credit cards and his personal line of credit to pay for the necessities of life. He refused to borrow money from family or friends, saying that "it changes your relationship with people when you start asking them for money. I prefer to go to the bank and get a line of credit."

In 1999, Leo's household had to adapt to a new set of changes, when Maria took early retirement. Her decision was reinforced by several years of upheaval, strikes and low morale amongst teachers, as massive cutbacks were implemented to the education system from 1995 to 1999. As a result of the cutbacks, Maria's job changed three times in two years. Leo told us that Maria was not happy about leaving the profession she loved and which she had practised for more than thirty years:

> She can't take it anymore as a teacher. The pressure the government put on teachers is too much. She was a full-time music teacher, and then they cut that job and gave her ESL [English as a Second Language] programs, and then they cut that too. She has had enough, so she has to leave. She doesn't want to retire and is not happy about leaving. But, if she doesn't leave she will get sick.

Maria's retirement meant that her take-home pay dropped from $48,000 a year to her pension income of $25,000 a year.

In 1997, when we asked Leo where he saw himself and his family in the year 2000, he told us that he wanted to move from a semi-detached to a detached house in a new Toronto-area neighbourhood. At the same time, however, he said, "I'm not sure I will be able to move because my job is not stable anymore, and it's hard to find other work. I'm just not sure if we can afford to move." In 1998, Leo told us that his wife wanted to move into a new house in the coming year; he said, "A new house, that's her goal. My wife wants a new house, so we will get a new house." Leo expressed a lot of hesitation about this plan: he was uneasy about his job security, and his wife's upcoming retirement would mean less take-home pay for the family. Nevertheless, in July 1999, Leo, his wife and his son moved into their new house in a suburban development north of Toronto. At the end of the study Leo and Maria were much further in debt and had a considerably lower household income. Leo felt that his family had relative stability; however, with few retirement savings, he told us that he expected he would have to continue working well into his old age. He hoped there would always be a job for him in the textile manufacturing sector.

Liz

Liz was a fifty-seven-year-old single white woman who was born, raised and spent most of her life in the same large city. She lived, with her two cats, in a very small row house, which was over a hundred years old. In 1994, after a career as a full-time clerical worker, Liz accepted an early retirement package offered by her employer. She looked forward to slowing down the pace of her life and pursuing her first love—painting. Prior to retiring, Liz had arranged to work part-time as a means to supplement her pension income. However, this job disappeared a year later. Liz began to worry because her monthly expenses were increasing; for example, her property taxes had recently gone up, after changes in a provincial funding formulae left local governments with fewer tax dollars. Liz was frustrated because her early retirement now caused her unanticipated financial stress. On a fixed income, with rising expenses, Liz found it difficult to make ends meet and worried about the future. She said, "I'm really frightened about what's going to happen to me. Right now I'm at an age where I can cope, but what will happen to me when I'm sixty-four or seventy-four?" Compounding Liz's financial concerns was her deteriorating health.

Liz graduated from high school at age eighteen; she immediately started working for a public school board. In the mid 1990s, as a part of a plan to reduce the provincial education budget, the government offered workers with seniority (Liz had thirty-one years of service) a series of early-retirement schemes, which accompanied the resulting downsizing of staff across the entire public education system. Liz had been increasingly frustrated with work; this frustration, along with her deteriorating health condition, made the opportunity to retire a few years earlier than she had originally planned very compelling. Although Liz had concerns about living on a fixed pension (she especially questioned her ability to pay off her mortgage), she felt that a part-time job could help her to make ends meet. She said,

> I wanted to retire at fifty-five, that had always been my goal. But there came a time when the government wanted to get rid of the older people that had years of service and age. I was one of those people, and they made me an offer. I thought back and forth whether I'd go or not. I was also in quite a bit of discomfort because I'd been in a car accident and it seemed like every morning it was taking me longer to get up and get to work. I discussed the situation with my doctor and she thought that retiring early would be a good idea. As it happened, my doctor also had a secretarial position available in her office. She suggested that I take the early-retirement package and work for her on a part-time basis. It would give me stability, and I'd be able to pay off my house. So, that's exactly what I did.

Her part-time job provided her with some extra income and allowed her to keep control of her debts. In 1996, however, Liz lost her job at the doctor's office:

> About a year after I started the job, my doctor became ill and was forced to give up her practice. I lost my job. Since that time, I have been very concerned about my finances. I figure I can last the twenty-two months, which is the remaining time on my mortgage payments, but I'm worried. The municipality is talking about raising property taxes, and if they do that while I'm still paying my house off, then I'm going to be in trouble.

Liz's lost income from the part-time job meant that it was very difficult for her to stay on top of her monthly bills. To make ends meet, she began to use her credit cards and arranged with the bank to go into overdraft. By 1999, Liz was $10,000 in debt. To cope with her deteriorating financial situation and her rising personal debt, Liz tried to cut her expenses. Each time we spoke with Liz, she expressed concern about her ability to make ends meet on a fixed income, and, in particular, her fear about possible increases to municipal property taxes.[1]

Throughout most of Liz's working life, she lived in rental accommodation. While she wanted to own a house, her modest income made it difficult for Liz to save enough money for a down payment. Nevertheless, after years of saving, Liz was able to afford a very small two-bedroom row house. Liz's long-term goal was to own a house so she could retire and "grow old" with a sense of security—knowing that she would always have a roof over her head. She also knew, however, that all her disposable income would be spent on the house. Liz could no longer afford holidays, new clothes or a new car. She said, "I always figured that I should buy a house by the time I was forty years old. And I think I was thirty-nine when I bought this house. I knew that it would have to be paid for by the time I retired."

Liz's financial situation continued to decline. She started to look for another part-time job. She had concerns, however, that employers would not want to hire an older worker, favouring younger, high-school students. After five months of looking, in November 1997, she found another part-time job, working at a neighbourhood retail store:

I couldn't live on my retirement. I filled out a bunch of applications and one store told me that they would keep it on file for six months. I didn't hear anything for three months, so I went back and re-introduced myself. They told me that they had just hired a high-school student. I thought, well, that sort of leaves me out—I'm at the other end of the spectrum. But then they phoned me about a week later. They were interviewing to hire temporary workers for the upcoming Christmas season. I guess I impressed them, and they hired me. At the end of the Christmas season, I was told that they no longer had any more hours for me, and I was going to lose the job. That meant I'd have to start looking all over again and worry about my expenses. But, about the same time, a few people left the store, and they hired me on a part-time basis. I was very lucky, especially when you hear about how hard it is for other older people to find a job. It's worked out quite well. I just hope it keeps up until I get my debts paid off and then I can officially retire.

In 1999, Liz told us that if she had not found a part-time job she would have lost her house. Her part-time retail job brought in approximately $500 a month, which was enough to keep her financially solvent. She said, "I'm feeling a bit more secure now about paying off my house and paying my property tax bill. This part-time job has made me feel better about things."

When we last spoke with Liz in February 2000, she was mortgage-free, and her part-time job meant that she could begin to pay off her personal debt and that she could afford better-quality food. However, her fears about rising municipal property taxes came true: Liz faced a 180 percent increase in taxes, from $400 a year to $1600 a year. Luckily, she was able to manage this expense because she had paid off her mortgage before the tax bill arrived. Nevertheless, it was an expense that she had not originally considered when she decided to accept her employer's early-retirement package.

At that point, Liz was feeling more optimistic about the future, but resigned to the fact that she would have to continue to work for at least another five years:

I certainly didn't picture my retirement like it is right now. I thought I'd be able to stay at home and start to relax. I wanted to learn how to do things I'd never had the time to pursue. But my financial situation hasn't allowed me to do that, so I've had to work. I've got my house paid for, so now I just have to keep paying my taxes and get rid of my credit cards and overdraft. I think I'll be able to quit my part-time job in five years and officially retire. Not that I don't like my job. I do like it, but you get to a point in your life when you'd like to slow down. I'm at that point now.

Discussion

- How does social location affect the experiences of these participants in a shifting labour market? In particular, how do racist practices exclude some workers? How is racism used as a means to explain labour-market failures? What kind of labour-market policies would assist young adults like Patrick and Denzel?
- How do social assistance regulations impede the job-search efforts of individuals like Michelle?
- What kinds of policies would cushion older workers like Leo when the demands for a skilled trade disappear because an industry moves offshore?

The experiences of these participants raise questions about the focus on job-search skills in most training programs. Programs that emphasize job readiness, search skills and even specific skill training presuppose a post-World War Two standard-employment situation yet, at the same time, support an insecure contract-based job market. Such programs both reflect the realities of today's labour market and reproduce it by directing people into short-term contract jobs, which, as argued in Chapter One, characterize the economy in a period of intensified international trade and capital mobility. These jobs, however, did not provide the income needed by households to meet their monthly expenses. Many participants had taken very seriously messages about the need to retrain if they wished to find jobs in the new economy. Aside from specific training, they pursued opportunities for higher education, hoping that this would help them to find a "good job." However, the expense of college and university education is making such a plan permanently inaccessible to those who lack private means of support. Participants were carrying growing student loans; other household members, like Leo, were taking on a personal debt load to help their children with some of the costs.

The stories in this chapter highlight the importance that having paid work meant to the quality of life of participants. While, as shown in Chapter Three, insecurity of income pervaded the lives of many participants, these narratives document how the presence or absence of paid work affected all aspects of life. To speak of what was happening within the limited discourse of "employment policy" would capture a fraction of the issues faced by participants: their daily lives were ruled by efforts to secure and maintain income from some form of paid employment. Plans were completely reconfigured when paid work was interrupted; long-term goals were put aside when employment efforts failed.

Current social policies are foiling attempts by young people to carve out options for their futures in many ways. Patrick had the profile of the new ideal worker: he was a young white male, reasonably well-educated, had no dependants and could, if needed, follow jobs across the country. This image, however, assumes that the other side of the labour-market equation is in place, namely, that work is available and that it pays a living wage. In Patrick's case, this assumption proved to be false; the training to which Patrick was referred failed him, not because of specific program-matic weaknesses or a lack of skills, but because of a lack of employment opportunities.

Educational policies are also exacerbating existent stressors associated with pursuing higher education. Denzel, like many young people who grapple with the demands and expectations of adulthood, experienced academic difficulties. Unfortunately, Denzel was dealing with these issues at a moment in history when tuition was climbing and when there was little paid work to give him income; his opportunities to reconfigure his options were, therefore, very limited.

For Patrick, racist stereotypes were easy to employ, as he tried to explain the impediments suddenly facing him in the labour market. Patrick was drawing on a well-established history of racial exclusion by focusing on a single policy—employment equity—that attempted to redress this exclu-sion. Other public policies, such as tax cuts and changes to labour legisla-tion, which contributed to workers' vulnerability, faded into the back-ground and thus escaped his interrogation. Such conditions are fertile soil for aggravating divisions and entrenching hierarchies among people. By constructing the problem of the white male as an "us and them" phenom-enon, the realities of exploitation in the labour market are obscured and workers are pitted against each other. In the process, institutional racism is reinforced through the everyday practices of individuals.

Unlike Patrick and Denzel, Michelle's life seemed at first glance to be the picture of stability. Her job was steady, although the pay was hardly above the poverty line. The picture changed overnight when restructuring resulted in a major downsizing by her employer. Like Patrick and Denzel, the programs available to Michelle were premised on a labour-force model that assumed work stoppages were temporary and new work could be found with some updating of skills and job-search techniques. Training available under Employment Insurance (EI) is designed to address the needs of workers who are undergoing a temporary interruption in an otherwise steady work career. This image of a regular member of the labour force who is temporarily unemployed explains in part the superior training opportunities available through EI. Programs associated with social assistance are more coercive: they assume that the individuals are not regular members of the labour force. This distinction has always been dubious. Interruption is rapidly becoming a permanent feature of labour-market participation; many of those on social assistance already have plenty of labour-market experience. Most people receiving social assistance, unless they are raising small children, move between it and a stream of minimum-wage jobs (Ornstein 1995). Nevertheless, the distinction is maintained; thus the favoured policy mechanism has been to make access to EI more restrictive. By this mechanism, fewer people are defined as regular members of the labour force. The irony is that this conceptualization does capture the dynamics of a restructured economy, where full-year, full-time employment, with benefits, is no longer the norm. Increasingly, more and more citizens are excluded from such a labour situation: the injustice lies in the fact that policies designed to help workers in a changing labour market actually exacerbate their insecure employment opportunities. Participants' experiences tell a labour-market story wherein temp agencies are the new employment centres, call-centre jobs are considered steady ones and credit cards are sources of supplementary income.

Liz and Leo and Maria are older workers. Their experiences resonate with those of many others with similar age and work history profiles. Their steady employment patterns should have guaranteed them the "dreams" they shared with us. As steady, reliable workers, they had, so to speak, kept their side of the bargain, but the social and labour-market climate had changed. Amongst the households profiled in this chapter, only Frank and Michael were in a position to exert some control over the effects that job changes had on the quality of their lives. Although Michael changed jobs several times during this study, he was never worried about being able to make ends meet. His relative security allowed him to see these changes as providing new opportunities for jobs that he could choose either to leave or take. This ability to exert some control over one's life was not available to other study participants.

For those participants without resources upon which they could draw when they were unemployed, the future looked bleak. The unrealized dreams of participants were varied but modest: moving to a new home without a heavy debt load was a long-time dream for Leo and Maria; Michelle's desire was to own a home with a back yard so her children could play safely; Liz dreamed of retiring after thirty years or more to pursue a loved hobby. These aspirations were realistic in the post-World-War-Two period, when labour and social policies were designed to create social conditions that included predictable life-time earnings and a strong welfare state. For the most part, participants introduced in this chapter abided by the traditional rules of how to "make it" in such a market economy. Now their futures were uncertain as the "new" labour market and associated neoliberal policies, demanding flexibility and decreased expectations, took hold.

The relationship between paid work and quality of life requires rethinking. As suggested by the experiences of households profiled in this chapter, some of that rethinking will consider child care, types of training, levels of support provided to people changing jobs, the development of insurance and benefits schemes that are not tied to the work place and pensions that are not dependent on one's track record in the labour force. These social policies will need to be the focus of future "restructuring" if the next generation is to escape the destruction of hopes and dreams that marked the lives of so many participants in our study.

Notes

1. Throughout the late-1990s, many Ontario municipalities reviewed and adjusted their local property tax structures to equalize payment structures across their jurisdictions. For some homeowners, this process had the potential to increase their taxes by more than 100 percent. In 1997, as the municipality in which Liz lived began to assess property taxes, she was very concerned that a higher tax bill would force her to lose her home.

Chapter Six

Shut Out
Uncovering the Dynamics of Social Exclusion

This chapter is about people who are marginalized by the society within which they live. In recent years, this phenomenon has come to be called "social exclusion." The term is intended to capture the processes through which individuals are detached from the organizations and communities that make up society and from the rights and obligations that embody citizenship (Room 1995: 243).[1] The term is sometimes equated with poverty. For instance, it might be used to portray how youth and immigrant populations are pushed to the economic margins by their labour-market experiences (Bryne 1999; Mandanipour et al. 1998). However, lack of resources does not capture the dynamics of what is happening to the participants profiled in this chapter. Poverty is part of the picture but it may only be one of the more visible manifestations of processes that bar individuals from those systems that serve to integrate people into society, enabling them to exercise the rights of citizenship. A focus on exclusionary processes has enabled researchers to document how these processes work in differing ways in different populations, such as people with disabilities and aging women (Aronson and Neysmith 2001).

Social exclusion reflects the often precarious relationships people have to the labour market, to civic participation and to social networks. It describes a multi-dimensional and cumulative process with economic, cultural, spatial and political dimensions (Littlewood and Herkommer 1999). Although the forms these processes take vary, the result is predictable—disenfranchisement. A legacy of colonialism, racist immigration policies and discriminatory employment practices framed the experiences of participants in this chapter. In addition, inequalities and marginalization based on age, race and ethnicity, gender and sexuality were operating. Some of these dynamics emerged in the narratives that informed Chapters Four and Five. In this chapter, however, the effects are stark: participants' stories portray how political, institutional, community and family processes weave together in ways that reinforce social exclusion.

This chapter concentrates on household stories which reveal the structural processes that locate and push people to the margins of society. Revealed in the narratives are the dynamics of how changes in social spending and policies in the late 1990s built upon and intensified historical processes of marginalization and exclusion. *James*'s story shows how the historical dislocations of First Nations peoples become exacerbated in a climate of fiscal and social conservatism. *Richard*'s story documents the intense moral regulation of those receiving public benefits. The resultant feeling that one is undeserving eats at the very core of self-respect and erodes expectations of basic citizenship rights. These assaults were compounded by feelings of being burden to family. As a sole-support mother receiving social assistance, *Amy* lived in a society that denigrates women, and black women in particular. Although *Brad, Samantha* and *Nathan* were still in their teens, many options were already closed to them. As they struggled to complete high school, they became categorized as "at-risk" youth. *Antonio* and *Natalia* fled to Canada from Latin America because of political violence and persecution. However, they continued to confront the racial discrimination that operates in most Canadian social institutions, limiting their employment, housing and life chances.

James

James, an Inuit man in his mid-twenties, from the east coast, had been living in Toronto for two years when we first met. He did not have a phone or address. Contact was maintained via messages left at a social service agency. James's annual income was well below the poverty line; he collected social assistance on a sporadic basis over the three years. He had worked at repairing furniture, at unloading transport trucks, as a painter and in a warehouse in shipping and receiving. The latter job was the most stable, but he was laid off after a year. Other income sources included squeegeeing, selling a local paper for homeless people and selling crafts on the streets. Because he was precariously housed, James rarely qualified for the social assistance housing allowance of $325 per month. On occasion, he collected the non-housing portion of $195 per month.

Over the years, James had "crashed" at friends' places, stayed at a variety of shelters and rented rooms in rooming houses that did not come close to meeting any basic housing standards. Since, at the time of the study, social assistance no longer covered first and last months' rent, rent controls had been removed and non-profit housing was frozen, maintaining housing became almost impossible.[2] James explained his housing dilemma:

> If you're looking for a place to stay, you call up and say, "Hi, I'm looking for a place to stay. Do you guys take welfare recipients?" They'd ask for a deposit or first and last months' rent and welfare won't provide it. So most of the time you have to take what you get. [Most places are] ... a hole in the wall.

In every interview, participants talked about their daily concerns. Replies varied from household to household. However, James's answers were more stark than others:

Trying to get enough sleep at night. When they had the Out of the Cold program [a municipal program that opened extra beds when the temperature dropped below a certain point] I got a fair amount of sleep, but then I moved in with a friend. A lot of people came over and usually they drank, sometimes to four o'clock in the morning. I had to get up at eight o'clock.

James's daily schedule was filled with constant movement, since rest, food, shelter, health care and clothing depended on the hours and conditions of the agencies he frequented. As far as hostels were concerned, he said, "It's a place, it's a roof, but I wouldn't call it home." Friends and acquaintances who had tried to find housing had just given up. James busied himself by visiting a variety of city agencies, where he used the services and helped out staff with chores when necessary.

James remarked on the changes he had seen over the last few years,

Well, just people in general. They're a bit nastier, every now and again you'll see a few fights. Well, there's not a lot more but there is more violence than there was, say, a year ago. A lot more panhandlers than there was a year ago. I've noticed a whole lot more squeegee-ers, I tried that a couple of times but that's not my type of thing, and sometimes the police come by and they give out a $65 ticket. I was lucky, I didn't get any of those.

The most James ever made squeegeeing was $30 a day.[3]

Throughout the time of the study, James did not look to the future. "I haven't got anything planned at the moment. Maybe later on I'll do some planning." He had a couple of good friends on whom he felt he could rely. Describing his heritage, James said, "[I was] born over in Labrador, but I grew up in Newfoundland. I was born under the Inuit culture, but it doesn't really matter what culture I'm from. I'm still a Canadian." He explained his dislocation from the community of his birth:

The Newfoundland government had a policy back in the sixties and seventies. I guess they wanted Native children to adapt to different societies, and I was one of them. I grew up in a foster home. It wasn't too bad a foster home.

Racism continued to frame his life: James spoke at length about his sister's situation of having her children taken from her:

Well, last year she got her children back. There's a Native band group out there and they've been extremely helpful. The family and children services used this one psychologist and, in her report, there were a lot of lies. There was one part where it said that since she's Native, the children would not receive a proper upbringing. So we went to see if we could get a second opinion. Her lawyer dodged the subject for about a week and then we phoned the Human

Rights Commission, and then we phoned a Native band out there, and in the end she got her children back.

By the second interview, James had been incarcerated. A drinking episode ended with him being in the wrong apartment. When the police were called a fight ensued, which resulted in an assault charge being laid against him. James had been staying at his girlfriend's place after our first interview. He explained the circumstances:

> We had been drinking and I went back to where we lived. I didn't have my keys on me so I broke into the apartment but it was the wrong apartment. I got charged with break and enter. I'm lucky that nobody was home. They might've then charged me with one of those home invasion things. The police showed up a half an hour later. In the meantime my girlfriend had come home. She freaked out. I also got charged with assaulting the police.

Unable to hire his own lawyer, James was appointed a lawyer who was referred to as the "dump truck"—a person to whom cases like his are delegated. James pleaded guilty and assumed that his lawyer would ask for six months. On the day in court he asked for seven to ten months without telling James. In the end, James was incarcerated for five and a half months:

> Those months were long and I hope I never go through those months again, tap on wood. If you're not warped, well, if your mind isn't warped and you go inside there, when you get out you may have a different way of thinking. They're there twenty-four hours a day and they tell you what to do and it's not a good place to be. Day in and day out the same thing.

Once out of jail, James had to survive the same cycle of struggling for work, food and shelter. Unfortunately, he lost all of his identification; as a result, he was barred from collecting $195 of welfare for the next month. James had to send money to another province for a birth certificate and get a new health card.

By the third interview, James had missed reporting for parole and a warrant was out for his arrest. He was sharing a one-bedroom apartment with another man for $330 in a different area of town. James was busy making dream catchers and talked about finding a full-time job. He had a couple of friends on whom he could rely for support; he was trying to stay away from "bad influences." At this point, he said he had few concerns: "I know I am on borrowed time, so I have no real concerns." At the time of the final interview, James had just completed a three-month Native rehabilitation program. He had been picked up on the street a couple of days after our third interview. He described how an Aboriginal treatment program really helped him:

I probably spent about thirty days in jail, and a Native youth worker came down to court, and he went to bat for me, and I went through a court-ordered treatment. I'm quite thankful that he got me into it. It is a pretty good program and I would recommend it to other people. They have Native traditional teaching throughout the week. My probation officer gave me a choice between a twenty-eight-day program and the Native program for four months. It's a pretty good program.

After the treatment program, James shared an apartment with a woman. Together they worked on painting and decorating their home. James's schedule remained busy, and with a little more combined income they managed to rent a movie once or twice a week. Since he did not have a permanent address, James received the basic social assistance allowance ($195); he wondered if living in this new place would qualify him for the housing allowance. "I've just started a relationship with my caseworker so I'm not sure how it's going to go," he said. "In their records for the past couple of years I'm down as homeless." James did not know whether or not his proposed housing arrangement would be approved by social assistance. He said, "I think I'll try and say I'm just renting from this person." He talked about how cuts to programs and tax cuts were borne on the backs of poor people: "Some people think we shouldn't have a safety net, and I think some people think it's great that there is a safety net there. I have no expectations of government."

Samantha and Nathan

Samantha, her two-year-old son and three-month-old daughter, resided in subsidized housing in an area of a city that she felt was unsafe. Samantha's maturity far surpassed her sixteen years. She was a sole-support mother, receiving social assistance, who described herself as Latin American in heritage. Her daily life was very different from that of her friends. While she continued to maintain contact with her high-school peer group, many of her friends just did not understand what it was like to juggle Grade Ten course work and a family. Although Samantha did not feel that she was missing out on anything, it was clear that her concerns were not typical of most sixteen-year olds. She felt an incredible amount of pressure to provide for her children. While most teenagers her age were managing allowances, she managed a household. She resisted spending money on clothes and shoes and, instead, made sure she had enough for diapers and formula. She talked of social assistance being a temporary measure: she planned to go to university or college to study nursing after high school.

Samantha's family helped her negotiate the student-parent transitions that were part of her young life. Her mother and grandmother provided child care when she was at school, and they assisted her financially with diapers and groceries. Even with this support, Samantha found she could not always rely on family members:

> I tried to rely on my mom for baby-sitting when I started school in September last year, but she had doctors' appointments and stuff, so then I couldn't go to school that day. It's hard to rely on [family]. I like day care better.

Samantha made regular use of formal support services, particularly those geared towards young mothers. At one centre, she learned about infant care, socialized with other mothers and received support regarding practical issues such as housing, education and social assistance. These young mothers also became indispensable sources of advice, providing each other with information on a range of issues from how to negotiate with social assistance workers to where to go for cheap dental care. Despite the services available and the support she received from family, which Samantha characterized as adequate, she still needed to use the food bank once a month. The material needs of her family often went unmet. While she was not in receipt of child support, the children's father was emotionally supportive and provided some financial assistance when he could. However, the young father continued to live at his own parents' home while finishing his high-school diploma.

By our second interview, Samantha and her partner had decided to move in together. The young couple applied for social assistance as a family. While Samantha looked forward to Nathan moving in and spending more time with the children, she was concerned about her loss of control over familial finances. Nathan was required under Ontario Works to participate in a work placement. The benefit would no longer be administered in Samantha's name but rather in Nathan's. She worried that this would change the household management and budgeting of money. She also worried that if the relationship were to break down, she and the children would probably have some interruption in assistance:

> I'm kind of worried about me and Nathan going on welfare together. Right now the cheque has to be under his name because he's the one who's going to be looking for work. [He] has to go in the Work Program.... I'm going to school. What if they deleted me from the files? Or if he ends up leaving? Then I'd be stuck trying to get back to where I started [from].

Nathan was enrolled in Ontario Works, working part-time at a community centre, while Samantha continued with her high-school studies. Upon returning to high school after the birth of her daughter in the fall of 1998, Samantha expressed concern about the changes she saw to the education system. She felt she was missing out on extracurricular activities because of the 1998 teachers' work stoppage and she worried about the fate of alternative high schools and programs that allowed students more learning flexibility. At the time of the last interview, Samantha continued to pursue full-time schooling despite the challenge of raising her young family. She also wanted to move into an area where she didn't have to fear for her or the children's safety. Nathan was no longer participating in Ontario Works but actively looking for a full-time job. Their main goal was to be independent and no longer in need of social assistance.

Brad

Brad was a nineteen-year-old white youth who was in school and trying to make money squeegeeing and panhandling. He was interviewed only once; further attempts to contact him at his school or on the streets failed. Brad had finished Grade Ten; he was taking some English courses and collecting social assistance. With stricter guidelines for youth to access social assistance, Brad had limited access to formal income supports. Under new social assistance regulations introduced at the time of the study, an adult had to be responsible for and verify a youth's situation. While this change was aimed at increasing accountability amongst system users, Brad explained that, before t he change,

As long as your parents didn't want you there, you could get it. Now if your parents want you, or even if they do not, you have to go through this huge process. You have to be with an adult who's over twenty-one, who's going to look out for you.

Brad had left his home town and had come to Toronto where he had lived on, and off, the street since his arrival. Many of his worries were the same as those of other youth: he fretted about a relationship that had just broken up and felt that he didn't know what to do with himself. Unlike many other nineteen-year-olds, however, finding enough money was a constant struggle. He said, "I never really have any money. Every day I wake up and I'm pretty hungry. I don't know how I'm going to get money." His social assistance was $470 per month. He paid $275 for rent plus hydro and shared the two-bedroom apartment with a few friends. The money he made on the street netted him $20 to $25 a day, when he worked. He had been an extra in movies, shovelled dirt (a fertilizer place regularly employed people on the street to shovel dirt into bags), emptied boxes from huge trucks and mopped floors:

If you hang out on the corner long enough you'll have people come up to you. Two days ago this guy was like all frantic: "Come and help me and I'll give you money," [he said]. And so me and this guy went up and we took his stove up the stairs and then we took this fridge down the stairs. And then we took another fridge up the stairs. It took us about 20 minutes and he gave us $25 dollars between us.

Nevertheless, the pressures of trying to get some high-school credits and make a living on the streets were getting to him.

Brad's application for transportation coverage so he could get to school finally came in. He said, "I'd been waiting all year. I used to have to make the money to get to school. A couple of times I walked; a couple of time I hopped on the subway behind the ticket guys." In terms of the future, Brad worried about how he could ever get the kind of education he wanted:

It's going to be difficult for poor people to do anything really. We're not going to be able to get welfare. There will be more people on the streets. Even if I do finish high school, if I choose to go to college, it's going to cost a fortune. I'm going to have to get a loan and owe them money for the rest of my life. I don't know. I can't see that far into the future any more.

Getting some high-school credits was important to Brad. He explained, "The only reason I really want to finish school is to impress my mother. And it's really pissing me off, because she's really helped me out a lot. And she's really happy I am in school." However, Brad had been living on the streets for a couple of years, had become involved with drugs and felt that he could not get off them. While he talked to other students, he did not socialize with them outside of school. They had a completely different reality:

School's hard when you have been living like this for a long time. You're just basically an addict. Everything just kind of builds up and you just want to party. Then I also want something to do but it's just too much.

Although he had difficulty getting to school and remaining motivated, there was no doubt that Brad really enjoyed the alternative school he attended. He was much more able to cope in an alternative setting where the teaching model was less authoritarian. His previous three high schools had not worked out. He said, "Schools are like jails basically. You are forced to go to school. It's the law. Your parents can be charged with truancy. What the hell is that?"

Brad commented on the language used in the restructuring of primary and secondary education in Ontario. He felt that the "taxpayer" and "cost savings" were more important than students:

Governments are ignoring the homeless while banks post billion-dollar profits and there's people sleeping in them, there's people sleeping in bank towers.

And they don't like it and they get kicked out, it's ridiculous. People think so backward, they just don't want to help people.

So, while the government will save money on social assistance, Brad asked,

Where do they think these people are going to go? There is still the problem of underemployment; educated people who do not have jobs. Like my perfect vision of the world is not one person working eight hours a day five days a week, but eight people working one hour a day. There would be no homeless, no unemployment and everyone could do what they are good at.

Brad had been to his share of rallies against the provincial government and went to Ottawa to protest homelessness. He noted that single mothers had it particularly bad since they did not have enough money to feed their children properly.

Richard

Richard was a fifty-four-year-old single man of northern European and Acadian heritage. In 1992, he tested positive for HIV, and, in 1995, he was diagnosed with AIDS. When Richard discovered he was HIV-positive, he went through a period of denial and seclusion. In 1993, he applied for and received federal Canada Pension Plan disability benefits, and a provincial social assistance supplement. From 1993 to 1996, Richard lived in Toronto and managed his HIV-positive status. Finding it difficult to make ends meet on a fixed income, Richard decided to relocate to a Toronto suburb where rental accommodation was more affordable. When we met Richard in 1997, he had been diagnosed with full-blown AIDS two years previously. He was living with his boyfriend, Robbie, in a rented one-bedroom apartment in a city just outside Toronto. Richard's health was fragile and deteriorating. He said, "I feel that, health-wise, things are going to get worse, and I'm really worried about my supports." Robbie was twenty-six years old, and his low literacy skills made it difficult for him to secure a job. He had been in receipt of social assistance benefits for a number of years. Richard said,

By the third week of each month we run out of money. We try to budget very carefully, but there just isn't enough money. After we pay the rent, and our bills, we have about $50 left. We can't go to a restaurant or spend $16 on a movie.

When Richard was first diagnosed with HIV, his family was not especially supportive. They found it difficult coping with the fact that Richard had a terminal illness, particularly one which had so many stigmas attached to it. As time went on, however, his father and sister became more comfortable with his condition. Richard's eighty-five-year-old father gave them some money for groceries but, by the end of the month, Richard and Robbie were usually forced to use the local food bank. Due to Richard's declining health status, he decided in October 1997 to move to the same town as his father and sister. Richard and Robbie's combined monthly household income was $1400, of which $790 went to pay for their one-bedroom apartment. Nevertheless, Richard was confident that being closer to his family would be beneficial.

Richard's family did provide support, but Richard was unhappy with the situation. He found that moving closer to family had cause intrusions into his private life, and it was putting a strain on his relationship with Robbie. He found the community homophobic, and he did not feel comfortable walking down the street. Neighbours gossiped about his AIDS status and his relationship with another man. Despite some job offers, Robbie was still in receipt of social assistance benefits largely because of lack of transportation. Costs for Richard's transportation also grew unexpectedly by $90 per month, since his declining health meant more visits to Toronto for medical appointments. Richard and Robbie continued to rely on food banks for their groceries. In this town, while the food was of better quality, only one visit per moth to the food bank was permitted. Richard felt the strain of the situation on his relationship:

> Robbie and I don't talk about AIDS very much anymore. He is really scared of it, and I'm finding that he's not as supportive as he used to be. He feels like he has no hope of learning anything because of his learning disability and the fact that he can't read. He's just twenty-eight years old, but he's in a rut and he doesn't think he'll be able to get out of it. He thinks that he will be living on welfare for the rest of his life. And, no matter how much I support him in all the ways that I can, he still feels that, because I'm going to die, that there is nothing much worth living for. But, he can't live on $520 a month for the rest of his life. You just can't do that. I'm trying to encourage him, but it's very hard. I worry about Robbie a lot. I don't know what is going to happen to him.

In April 1998, Richard and Robbie's relationship went into crisis. Unable to find work and frustrated with his living situation, Robbie went into a depression and began abusing drugs and alcohol. Robbie came home one evening and seriously assaulted Richard. Robbie went to jail for three years, and, for the duration of our study, Richard had no further contact with him. In August 1998, four months after he was assaulted, Richard decided to move back to Toronto. He sought out subsidized public housing only to discover the lengthy waiting lists and high rents due to recent policy changes. He said,

> There is no affordable housing. I wanted to see about getting in subsidized

housing, but there is a three- or four-year waiting list before I could get a place. I'll be dead before that happens. There are very few subsidies left, and I can only just barely afford to pay market rent. And, to top it all off, rents are going through the roof since the government got rid of rent control. Landlords can charge whatever they want now.

Despite these challenges, Richard found a bachelor apartment in the downtown area for $467 a month. He felt that with a monthly income of $930, he would be able to afford this apartment. Nevertheless, he still needed the first and last months' rent. His father paid for this, as well as his moving costs. With his sister's assistance, Richard moved into his new apartment. Once settled, he realized that his apartment was full of cockroaches. However, he concluded that the move was a positive step because he was closer to the services he needed, public transportation was more accessible and the geographic distance from his family had a positive effect on their relationship.

In November 1998, Richard's health status began to deteriorate rapidly. In particular, his mobility became severely impaired; this affected his ability to live on his own. He said,

Well, my doctors have discovered that I now have peripheral neuropathy of the right leg, foot and left arm. And, it's also starting in my hand. Peripheral neuropathy is the inception of AIDS. Basically, the virus has gotten into my central nervous system, which is terrible because it's going to be a lot of pain because your nervous system controls everything in your body. Mind you, the pain has already started, but it's going to get a lot worse. You know when you get a paper cut—that feeling you get—well, if you put vinegar on that open paper cut, then it stings like hell. I can't go anywhere without the cane. I just know that my mobility is going to become worse within the next six months. It's really scary.

To help alleviate some of the anxiety associated with losing his independence, Richard and his family agreed that he should no longer control his own finances. With his family now paying all of Richard's bills, he received a monthly allowance for spending money—$40 a week. Richard also felt that he was increasingly unable to undertake household chores. His family tried to fill the void, but given his father's age, the bulk of the work fell to Richard's sister. Also his apartment building was becoming physically inaccessible:

Now I know what my eighty-six-year-old father feels like when he gets so frustrated about not being able to get around. I don't like it at all. The future is really scaring me now. My AIDS counsellor suggested that I get a scooter to help me get around. I'm not going to get one.

By the end of 1998, Richard was in constant pain and having difficulty coping with his illness. Since moving to Toronto, he had found that the quality of the care he received by health care professionals was excellent. He began to frequent a pain control clinic at a local hospital for counselling and support. It was during one of these visits that Richard made public his intention—with the support of his father and sister—to kill himself at the point when the pain became too much to handle. By July 1999, however, Richard's situation had improved, and he was coping much better. In early 1999, he became romantically involved with another man who provided Richard with much-needed support. Paul was now able to help Richard with household chores, but the physical accessibility of his downtown apartment continued to present serious problems. Richard moved for the fourth time since 1997. Without his father's financial support, however, this move would have been impossible.

With Richard's deteriorating health, he had to find in-home supports. Since moving into his new apartment, with the help of his AIDS counsellor, Richard became a recipient of a home hospice program that was offered through the local AIDS organization. In addition, he received seven meals a week through the Meals on Wheels program. Given his low income, Richard did not have to pay for the food. Receiving good quality food was important for Richard's health; he now weighed only fifty-two kilograms. Because Richard was concerned that his declining health would scare Paul, causing him to move out, Richard tried to hide his pain from Paul, pretending that everything was fine, when, in reality, he was getting worse.

Throughout the period of our study, Richard consistently expressed frustration and confusion about the *Social Assistance Restructuring Act* (1998), which eliminated the General Welfare Assistance program, the Family Benefits program and the *Vocational Rehabilitation Services Act*. The replacement legislation was the *Ontario Works Act* (OWA) and the *Ontario Disability Support Plan Act* (ODSP). As an individual living with AIDS, Richard was legally disabled and therefore fell under the ODSP program, where his benefits began to flow to the new program. While he did not experience any interruption in his benefits, he often felt ill-informed and disliked the move from case workers to the team model. He said,

It makes me feel really insecure because I feel like there is nobody to help me. It used to be that you could go in and you knew your worker's number and they knew you and it was no problem. Now, you need to make an appointment way ahead of time and because they have teams now, you don't know who you are going to get, and they don't know you. They make you feel like a very low-class person.

The last time we spoke with Richard, he was feeling more secure; however, he worried that further changes to social assistance would negatively affect him. He concluded, however, that, perhaps, because he had a legal disability caused by a terminal illness, the government would continue to provide support:

> I'm really happy that I'm considered disabled because I think the government looks at you a bit differently. If you have AIDS, for instance, they know that you are going to die soon. Sooner or later you're going to die off, and then that will be one less person they have to look after.

The atmosphere of cutbacks caused him to feel like he was a drain on the public purse. He said,

> I sat down the other evening and figured out that it is costing taxpayers more than $30,000 a year in medication alone to keep me alive. I find it very depressing. I have this funny feeling that if people knew it was costing that much money to keep me alive, they would be really angry. I mean I'm going to die anyway, so why are we spending all that money to keep me alive a little bit longer? They just keep forking over all this money, and everyone is saying that we don't have any money anymore. Well, I'll be dead soon—then it won't cost anybody any more money.

Amy

At the time of the first interview Amy and her partner of seven years, Charles, resided with their children, Leon, Anthony and Mazi, in a low-rise apartment in Toronto. Amy and her spouse were originally from the Caribbean. The five-member household was cramped in a two-bedroom apartment. Amy was concerned for the health and welfare of her children; she worried particularly about Anthony, who had cerebral palsy and could not walk. She said, "I want to move, but I can't find a good, suitable place where my kids can be okay and I don't have to worry about Anthony crawling on the ground and picking up cockroaches." Amy also worried for the children's safety.

Charles worked full-time; Amy was enrolled in Ontario Basic Skills, an upgrading program for adult learners receiving social assistance. The family qualified for a welfare top-up to supplement Charles's earned income. The family's income, as Amy explained, had been reduced drastically with the 22-percent cut in social assistance benefit levels in October of 1995. Coupled with the uncertainty of the top-up amount, which varied depending on the hours her husband worked, budgeting became increasingly difficult. Amy and Charles were frustrated with the uncertainty of living from paycheque to paycheque. No matter how many hours Charles worked, they seemed no further ahead. Amy was tired of hearing disparaging welfare stereotypes and was frustrated by the lack of respect she was shown at the welfare office or the hospital, or when dealing with her landlord:

> I think they bash those on welfare. They think you're a bad parent, they think you're a drug addict, they think you're an alcoholic, they think you're an abusive parent, they just want to give you a bad name. When you go and rent a place, if you're on welfare, they're not going to give it to you. There are decent people on welfare, like me. Some low-income people are not on welfare; they refuse to go on welfare because it's degrading. They [social assistance workers] ask you so many questions.

Amy deliberated dropping out of the upgrading program and looking for a full-time job. The long-term benefits of a secondary education were hard to weigh against the immediate need to provide for her family. While a job would alleviate the financial pressure on the family, her limited education would mean she could only find an entry-level position paying minimum wage with little or no job security. Faced with an economic downturn, she figured she would once again find herself unemployed and receiving social assistance. However, her decision to remain in school, while a positive long-term strategy, took its toll on the immediate financial health of the household.

While Charles paid the rent, Amy was responsible for running the household, which included paying the household bills and buying groceries. Amy used local food banks three times a month. She admitted that she could not afford to purchase fresh produce and often cut back on food to manage other household expenses. "Sometimes the children miss a meal and it's not all the time that I cook healthy," she said. "To cook healthy, like a meal with vegetables, is expensive." Her concern for the well-being of her children prompted her to go to the doctor to get a prescription for a nutritional supplement. She said, "I went to the doctor to get Ensure for Anthony, and the doctor told me he couldn't prescribe it for me because Anthony is not malnourished." She went on to say, "But if anything happens to him, they will say that I am a bad mother, I didn't take care of him. Something is wrong here."

By the second interview Amy and her husband had separated. At the first interview, she foreshadowed the separation when she said that families were under a tremendous amount of financial strain:

> A lot of marriages break up because it's too much stress. Men run away from their responsibility, kids to be fed, kids who are crying, the wife is not working, he alone has all the pressure on him. He just steps out because he is always thinking there's a better way.

After the separation, Amy moved to a highrise in the west-end of the city, where she and the children shared a two-bedroom apartment. While their living quarters were cramped, she felt safe in the new neighbourhood. She continued to receive social assistance and attend upgrading. Even though the familial income dropped, Amy felt she could manage the household finances better. Amy's market rent was $975, more than she could afford on a $978 monthly social assistance benefit. She managed to juggle bills and other household expenses using the children's Child Tax Benefit and Anthony's Assistance for Children with Disabilities. Given that the entire social assistance cheque went to pay rent, welfare requested that she move. Amy refused. She accused welfare of wanting to ghettoize welfare recipients in low-income pockets, where housing was substandard, instead of assisting recipients to find decent housing. Amy had been on a waiting list for subsidized housing since 1991. All of the openings that had become available were very far away from schools and supports. She continued to apply pressure on her local and provincial politicians to do something about the lack of affordable housing in the city.

By the third interview, Amy had completed upgrading courses through Ontario Basic Skills and was enrolled in an early childhood assistant program at a local community college. Changes to social assistance disallowed post-secondary students from receiving welfare, so Amy had to take out a $16,500 Ontario Student Assistance Plan (OSAP) loan. Since the move to OSAP changed the nature of the support from a benefit to a loan, she and the two children were no longer covered under the Ontario Drug Plan. As a result, she and the children no longer went for dental check ups. Anthony, her son with cerebral palsy, continued to have his drug and dental benefits provided through the Ontario Disability Support Plan's Assistance for Children with Severe Disabilities. However, in trying to secure assistive devices for Anthony, Amy discovered that there were limits to so-called "extended" coverage programs:

His wheelchair is covered by Assistive Devices, but they cover only the wheelchair. He needs a walker, which I have to pay for. That's $200. He needs night splints to stretch his knees, but Assistive Devices won't cover them. They don't consider it necessary. That costs $400, and it's going to have to come out of my pocket. He needs a stroller, he's outgrown the one I have. The stroller is $2000 because it's customized especially for him. You have two choices. You get the wheelchair or the stroller. He needs the wheelchair for transportation, but on the bus, he needs the stroller.

Since Amy could not afford to purchase equipment, Anthony went without the equipment. Costs were not only escalating for extended coverage programs but also for services once covered under OHIP, such as ambulance service. From 1997 to 2000, Amy's expenses continued to escalate. In addition to health-related costs, her rent increased to $1004.

Expenses for her own education and her children's were starting to add up. She talked of not being able to afford to send her eldest son on any field trips and how she was hard-pressed to come up with costs associated with her own training program.

Amy articulated ongoing frustration with the lack of support she received not only financially, but emotionally, from formal service providers. She relied heavily on her eldest child Leon to assist her with household and child-care duties. Often, when the younger children were sick, the eldest child missed school to care for his siblings. Although she received calls about his absence from Leon's school, Amy reasoned that if she missed her classes she ran the risk of being ejected from her own program. In the meantime, Leon, who had a learning disability and required remedial help with homework, missed crucial classroom time. The lack of formal support also made it much more difficult to attend to the ongoing chronic health needs of her middle son. It was Amy's children who bore the brunt of poverty. Amy clearly felt overwhelmed and approached the Children's Aid Society (CAS) for assistance. However, they were reluctant to get involved, unless the situation escalated to a crisis or was potentially abusive:

Sometimes, like yesterday, I feel like I can't handle nothing. I'm in the store walking up and down. People are watching me because they probably think I'm going to steal or something. There are some days that my face looks so dreary. And there are other days when I know what I'm doing. And there are some days that like, "Who cares!" you know? I could go outside naked and don't care, that's how sometimes I feel. There are some times I can handle it, and there are other times that it's too much.

When we last spoke to Amy, she was preparing to move yet again. Her rent had increased to $1034. She had found a two-bedroom in a co-op for $812. She was on a waiting list for a three-bedroom, and she continued to wait for subsidized housing. Overcrowded living conditions contributed to an incredible amount of tension in the household. Amy felt uneasy about having her pre-teen son share a room with her daughter. Given her finances, it was all she could afford. She continued to take courses at the college level even though her debt load had burgeoned to $25,000. Since the separation from her husband, Amy had managed to single-handedly carry the family forward. However, she questioned how much longer she could continue to juggle financial demands, her son's health demands and her upgrading plans.

Antonio and Natalia

Antonio and Natalia live in a tiny two-bedroom apartment with their two children, Juan (aged thirteen) and Maria (aged nine). At the time of our last interview, Antonio and Natalia were both working for the same small family-run company, earning a little more than minimum wage. Both were desperately trying to supplement their small incomes in creative ways. In addition to his regular six-day work week, Antonio took a cleaning job on Sundays, while Natalia cooked food on weekends to sell.

Antonio and Natalia came to Canada as landed immigrants in 1992 from Latin America. They had both lived through civil war and had had family members disappear. Antonio was trained as an educator in his home country, had a master's degree; he worked in adult education before coming to Canada. Natalia trained at a college and had worked as a librarian and executive secretary. Antonio and Natalia brought with them Antonio's daughter, Lourdes, from a previous relationship, with whom Antonio has a strong bond. Antonio took over the custody and care of Lourdes when her mother was politically persecuted. Antonio and Natalia's hopes of finding economic stability in Canada had receded over the years, replaced by almost a decade of struggle and hardship.

When they arrived in Canada, Antonio enrolled in language and job-training courses. He worked part-time in a factory with his brother, who had also immigrated, and repaid the federal government his family's travel loan. With the help of social assistance, Antonio and his family rented a very modest three-bedroom house in Toronto. When their rent increased, social assistance would not contribute to the additional cost, and the family had to seek other housing. Antonio, Natalia, the two young children and Lourdes were crammed into their current two-bedroom apartment. Antonio was studying hard: he had returned to high school to take an Ontario equivalency, and he was taking training courses. He explained:

> I was already working hard on the land when I was six or seven years old with my parents... and even though I was in school, I was working. This is how my life was... this is what my story is about. Later, when I got here, I found myself surprised. I brought all of my degrees and my titles. I was a professional in my country, giving classes in schools and working in cultural institutions. I had a lot of experience. It was a surprise to find that I had to begin again. And so I began... but I did not think that I would have to begin again from so far below.

The family decided that the best way for them to get ahead in the long term was for Antonio to get Canadian college credentials. He enrolled at a local college in the social service field, received an OSAP loan and ceased receiving social assistance.

The household's main concern over the three years was always about income and housing. At the time of our first interview in early 1997, Lourdes, then almost eighteen, had moved out of the family home. This was a source of sadness to Antonio; he explained, in early 1998, that the cramped quarters were leading to more problems:

I am living in the same place, and things are a little worse because there are cockroaches and mice. Within the family, there have been some difficult situations. The boy and the girl are fighting because they have to share a room. This worries me because it was the same situation when my older daughter was sharing the room with my son. It became conflictual and Lourdes left.

Antonio's wife was embarrassed about their housing situation. A friend of theirs, who had come to Canada for a visit, called to say that she was coming to Toronto: "Our friend wanted to come to our house, and Natalia said to come to our work or somewhere else. She feels grief and does not want people to see where we are living." Antonio noted that there was a six-year wait for social housing in Toronto. He continued to search for other accommodation, as he did not want his kids to stay in the area they were in. The entrance to their apartment was at the back of a business parking lot. Young men gathered there to buy and sell drugs.

Antonio studied and worked in the social-service sector; he saw that his situation was part of a broader societal struggle to develop solutions to the kinds of poverty being faced by many. In 1997, when he was completing a placement with a social service agency, he explained:

I like my work very much because I am helping people. I have truly come to understand the really difficult situation that many people are going through. The majority of the people that I attend to are on Family Benefits. There are so many evictions now. This is where one has to keep fighting—to give people alternatives, an idea ... and sometimes to explain things to them. This is educational work, it is consciousness raising.

Antonio and Natalia's children's quality of life was deeply affected by their struggles to make ends meet and by changes in the education system. The children changed schools when they changed apartments; their son did not adjust well to the confines of the new home or to the new school:

I worry about the stability of my children's lives as they grow up.... Juan was student of the month many times in the school he was in previously, but when we moved to this area, his grades dropped.

Maria was experiencing severe stress about attending school, including nightmares, sleeplessness and a loss of appetite on school days. Antonio was closely in touch with the children's teachers; both parents helped with homework as best they could. The children's classes were large and the family's inability to pay new fees for school events meant that their children could not participate in certain activities. Antonio said, "In my home country, the teacher is much more concerned that a child learn. In Canada, they are more concerned with covering the program and meeting objectives, regardless of learning."

Antonio's health was poor. In addition to a bone problem, he had high cholesterol and two bleeding ulcers. "Most of the population in my home country have ulcers," he said. "It is a consequence of war." Since 1997, he had two bouts of illness that kept him from working. Because he no longer has a drug plan because the family was no longer receiving social assistance, he often could not afford to fill prescriptions. His condition worsened over the three years of the study.

Antonio's work history was peppered with short-term contracts, wage cuts and insecurity. When we first met, he was working at a job placement for his college course. He was receiving minimum wage, but counted it as experience in the field. During school, he worked at many contract positions in the social-service sector and after graduation, took contracts in his field. In 1999, when a job opportunity arose at another agency, Antonio approached the agency for which he was working and asked if he might be made permanent. They told him that there was little hope of that; the position he had occupied was replaced by a volunteer. He said,

Most of the jobs out there are temporary. All of the ones I have had are temporary. I haven't had a permanent job. That doesn't stop affecting you because if you are let go after three or four months, you don't have the hours required to apply for unemployment.

Antonio's written English was fine for contract jobs, "but when it is a permanent position, it becomes a problem. When it is temporary, I'm in. The permanent position is for the Canadian who speaks English as a first language and not for immigrants."

By the end of the study, Antonio was no longer working in the field in which he trained. He explained that, after graduation, he became ill and ended up taking the first job he could get after a period of unemployment. In the year 2000, he was still working at this retail job, trying to get enough to make ends meet. Antonio then owed $50,000 in OSAP loans, which were a source of unending struggle for the household. "Repaying my OSAP loan gives me a lot of stress," he said. "I do not sleep trying to think up a solution. I try to negotiate to pay less over more time. I cannot pay the monthly payment. Is my only alternative bankruptcy?" His boss offered to help him repay his student loan; at first Antonio refused because he felt it would oblige him to stay in a job unrelated to his interests in order to repay a student loan which had trained him to do work he loved. He also attempted to help Lourdes with her application to college by paying $10 at a time for the fees.

Antonio remained as politically active as he could during the time of the study, even though he felt exhausted just managing day to day: "The division becomes more rigid.... This government is not creating more rich people, it is creating more wealth, which is something different. It's making the top and the bottom well-defined." When asked where he saw himself in the future, he replied,

> I want to cover my necessities. I have never wished for wealth because it is on the backs of the poor. I want enough for my rent, my food, my children and to live. I do not really care about taking vacations. I just want a peaceful life.

Discussion

- What factors contribute to social exclusion?
- Does this concept help in understanding the experiences of participants?
- How do social science terms such as "at-risk youth" shape both our understanding of what's happening and policy responses?
- If the stories in this chapter are those of exclusion, what would be a story of inclusion?

In the experiences of many of the participants, but particularly so for those households portrayed in this chapter, the intense involvement of the state as an agent in the manufacturing of exclusion is visible. Racist, age-based, gendered and homophobic structures that permeate Canadian society are revealed in these household stories, which suggest that participation in some state programs triggers a classification process that places individuals into rigid categories defined by their dissimilarity to an idealized citizen-worker (Aronson and Neysmith 2001; Castells 1996; Dominelli 1999; Jordan 1996).

While often unnamed, unacknowledged or denied in Canadian society, racism is pervasive. Racism operates in multiple ways, including through the content and enforcement of immigration policies, in policies surrounding multiculturalism and in the historical and present treatment of Aboriginal peoples. James's story is that of government action which violently remapped the family and community life of a First Nations people. The history of the forced removal of children from their home communities is repeated today in his sister's attempts to keep her own family together. The history of colonization in Canada is now well-documented; its legacy affects the daily lives of people like James. Mainstream programs developed to assist people are rooted in ideas and assumptions that obscure the issues facing First Nations peoples. A pathway through this morass was opened for James only when he entered a socio-cultural space that recognized and worked with this legacy.

Antonio and Natalia came to Canada seeking a better life. Like the participants in other households in the study, Antonio struggled year after year to meet the costs of shelter. The lack of affordable housing, a direct result of federal and provincial government decisions to halt social housing and rely on the market for housing provision, guarantees the disappearance of lower-cost rental units. The visibility of the housing crisis in this story overshadows what was happening to Antonia and Natalia as immigrants. Social exclusion is manifested in their lives in multiple ways. Antonio encounters barriers, ostensibly based on language skills. However, as he notes, his skills are sufficient for contract work but not for a permanent position.

In this chapter, the stories of three young adults are highlighted. Samantha, Nathan and Brad are trying to achieve educational goals while managing living situations and responsibilities that are not considered by those who formulate education policies. Samantha, while caring for two children, attends high school. However, child-rearing responsibilities are generally not factored into educational programs. Students are assumed to be free of responsibilities to care for others and/or to earn money; they are expected to be protected and supported by their parents. Samantha found that even regular support from various family members is not sufficient to manage school and young children. Brad's story is permeated with signals of deepening marginalization. His addiction problem is exacerbated by education, criminal justice and workfare policies that view youth, particularly unemployed young males, as needing controls. The *Safe Streets Act,* which criminalized "squeegee kids," was at the time of the study only the most recent anti-street-youth piece of legislation. Despite the assumption in political discourse that youth is merely a stage on the way to adulthood, Samantha's and Brad's stories suggest that youth are regulated and shaped by the state in a way that views them as "problems" (Mizen 2002). Young people, such as Brad, Samantha and Nathan are often described as being "at-risk." Such a demarcation is rooted in social science research, which has associated characteristics such as age, race, employment status, the existence of a police record and so on with social problems such as truancy, youth crime and drug use. At issue here is not the existence of such correlations but the discourse that surrounds such findings and the resultant focus on the individuals who bear such markers. Less scrutinized is what might be called "risky public policies," such as legislation like the *Safe Streets Act*, the lack of youth employment programs, policing practices and other public regulations that increase the risks faced by youth (Bessant, Hil and Watts 2003).

In both Samantha's and Amy's cases social institutions that embody the welfare state are the conduits to marginalization. Amy questions the many contradictions in her life: poverty threatens her marriage; not receiving social assistance makes accessing the health benefits she needs more difficult; meeting the needs of one child costs another child his education; and she is unable to pursue training programs (needed for a better job) because adequate health and education programs are not in place for her children. The only services she can access are designed for crises; only when the situation reaches that point does she qualify for help. In the end, her efforts to get ahead work against her.

A consideration of these stories would not be complete without reflecting on the violence that permeates the lives of participants in these households. It operates in different forms for James, Richard, Brad, Amy, Antonio and Natalia, both in their own lives and in the lives of those around them. Although each of these participants deals with violence in their personal lives, they also endure the violence wielded by social institutions. Their experiences of violence also shape the response protocols of the Children's Aid Society, when women like Amy approach them for help. The violence that is part of the Canadian police and criminal justice system surfaces when those viewed as "other" enter their jurisdiction, whether because of criminal offences or because proper legal representation is not affordable. Experiences such as these need to be juxtaposed to professional discourses about the importance of promoting agency and of building empowerment strategies when working with marginalized populations. The data emerging from this study suggest that policies and programs must be scrutinized for the ways in which they disempower people, whether as individuals or members of communities, and negate their efforts to exercise agency. Marginal social location and attendant lack of power are regulated and maintained by the state, market and informal social institutions. Such forces of social exclusion are powerful protectors of privilege. Calls for exercising agency ring hollow when its presence, as shown in these stories, is interpreted as criminal behaviour. Similarly, empowerment strategies seem a weak form of resistance against such institutional violence.

Notes

1. There is a good deal of debate in policy circles about the concepts "social exclusion," "social inclusion" and "social cohesion." While the concept "exclusion" is perhaps the most descriptively negative, it circumvents important critiques about the homogenizing assumptions built into "inclusion" and "cohesion." For a review of these debates, see Saloojee 2003 and Mitchell and Shillington 2002.

2. Policy changes in a range of areas related to housing were significant in the late 1990s. In 1997, the provincial government passed a new landlord-tenant act that decreased protections for tenants (*Tenant Protection Act*, S.O. Chapter 24). In addition, the redesign of social assistance legislation and regulations

increased the housing vulnerability of social assistance recipients (see especially the *Social Assistance Reform Act 1997,* S.O. Chapter 25).

3. The passage of a law against panhandling in 1999 (Statutes of Ontario 1999, Chapter 8), called *An Act to promote safety in Ontario by prohibiting aggressive solicitation, solicitation of persons in certain places and disposal of dangerous things in certain places, and to amend the Highway Traffic Act to regulate certain activities on roadways* or the *Safe Streets Act,* enabled police to remove squeegeers and charge people asking for money on the street. In July 2000, Peter Rosenthal—a University of Toronto mathematician and lawyer—initiated a constitutional challenge to the *Ontario Safe Streets Act*, which failed.

Chapter Seven

The Myth of Community, Family and Friends

This chapter considers the idea that community, family and friends should provide supports to absorb or offset income insecurity. As federal and provincial governments across Canada have cut social spending, downloaded services to municipalities and weakened labour-market protections, the sites of community, family and friends have been foregrounded as the arenas where responsibility lies for meeting the needs of those facing income crises, health- or day-care shortages or housing problems. What really constitutes "community" is a complex question. Participants in our study pointed to important underlying assumptions about collectivities that exist in the work place, in the provision of public services, in neighbourhoods and among particular ethnic and racial associations; these assumptions affect the multiple ways people claim, or are compelled to claim, specific "identities." For example, in Chapter Two, Teresa talks about her participation in the labour market, the education sector, the health care sector and in various social settings. Her experiences in these environments are structured by her sexuality and disability. As a lesbian, the loss of her familiar health care team makes her feel particularly vulnerable. Furthermore, while she is keen to work, it is more urgent that she be defined as "unemployable." In many situations, definitions and categories created by the state force people to embrace an identity that contrasts with and affects their view of themselves.

Individuals, communities and populations take on multiple and overlapping roles simultaneously. The formation of communities changes over time; communities have vastly different connections, choices, rights and power within our body politic. Those communities embedded favourably in the power structure are often less visible, yet at the same time their power to determine the terms through which community-naming, recognition and subsequent funding possibilities occur is enormous. Given the disparity of resources that exist within and between communities, and the specific targeting of cutbacks, the doctrine of relying on community support has put some groups under serious and debilitating strain. Notably, the promotion of "community" as a policy shift occurs alongside the ongoing reduction of funding to equity programs and issues (for example, cuts to Employment Equity, Ontario Disabilities Support Program (ODSP), cuts to services for immigrants and refugees and equity programs in the education system). People with disabilities, Aboriginal peoples and people of colour—all defined as specific communities—have been disproportionately hit by reductions to public services in the face of government demands for increased community responsibility. The reflections of participants on these issues highlight how the varied and political notion of "community," whether it denotes a cultural group, a racial category or a neighbourhood, gets played out day to day.

While family and friends provide critical assistance in the lives of most people, household stories reveal that there are dangers and limits to straining these relationships. All the stories profiled here indicate that people can cope with the myriad challenges they face if there are sufficient appropriate resources available. Provincial government policy saw "the family" as a coffer for the provision of supports and services. This policy direction was reinforced by a conviction that tax breaks could offset the use of their own labour by citizens or facilitate the purchasing of services no longer available to them in the public sector. Although all participants received support from family, friends and community groups, these could not substitute for social programs or a steady income. Although informal resources are important to well-being, they are easily exhausted in conditions of poverty. Furthermore, this policy orientation relies on an extremely narrow, unchanging and homogenous concept of the family; at the same time, it posits this "ideal" as the natural site within which caring labour should occur. The unnamed candidate for fulfilling this caretaking role is often a gendered one: women are expected to take on the lion's share of unpaid work, both at home and in the community, as volunteers.

Ray lives in a northern Ontario community, with his partner and two teenage sons. He describes some of the complexities of what community means to him. As an Aboriginal man, he disapproves of some of his own community's policies, yet he also struggles with living in a larger racist environment. He feels that the changes introduced by the Ontario government are putting the poor "against the wall": they are also considered, by him, as a direct threat to the health, safety, and survival of the First Nations peoples. *Olivia*, her husband *Gary* and daughter *Gina*, who live in the greater Toronto area, explain how changes to the health care system have an impact on the treatment Olivia receives for breast cancer. Olivia articulates how disruptions in these complex and delicate "professional" relationships undermine her ability to ask for help from those closest to her. Reliance on friends, family and insufficient home-care services compromise her efforts to hold onto her dignity. *Rosa*, Rosa's mother *Ashley* and Rosa's infant daughter moved in together out of necessity. They pool their incomes and try to maintain the public face of a household that is managing well. However, a racially stratified labour market, along with cuts to the community sector and to social assistance, combine to make reliance on community, family and friends a damaging strategy for this household. The dearth of external supports undermines their relationship: they bitterly part ways. *Kate* and her children try a variety of housing strategies to stretch an inadequate income. Although her partner, *Carl*, is employed full-time, his income cannot cover all of their expenses. Kate receives some moneys from social assistance, which she supplements with a series of short-term, part-time jobs. This family also attempts to keep their financial struggles hidden, yet the increasing isolation leads to familial breakdown. *Jackie* turns to community and to family to assist her in managing on a part-time income with her children, one of whom lives with a disability. She works at maintaining a good relationship with her mother, in whose home she lived, and between her mother and her children. Her employment at a community non-profit agency means her home life mirrors and supports much of her work life. She notices, however, that other people "are too stressed to participate in neighbourhood or community life." Getting enough income and sufficient services for her daughter and ensuring that her mother's increasing health needs are met, along with contributing as much as possible to household costs, are struggles for Jackie.

Ray

Ray, a forty-four-year-old Native man, lived in a rented house in a northern city, with his spouse Lisa and their two sons, who were fourteen and eleven years old. All of the interviews were with Ray. English was spoken in the home; Ojibwa was used occasionally. This household received many visitors, primarily family members, who needed a place to stay. For instance, at the time of one interview, Ray's oldest son, his partner and his new baby were visiting; another friend, with her ten-year-old daughter, had stayed for two months. An older daughter was in college in the southern part of the province.

Since 1991, Ray had been employed full-time at a community-based agency that worked with low-income families. Ray had worked in the restaurant and hotel industry; earlier in his life, he had received social assistance. As part of his current job, he was developing cultural programs and teaching Native history, crafts and language in schools. He had recently introduced an Ojibwa language program in one school for Native and non-Native kids that was quite successful. He was also on the boards of a number agencies in the voluntary sector. His income was $30,000 a year. Lisa earned money sporadically, selling crafts. Finances were very tight for this family. Their major expense was rent, which was over $700 per month. Finding affordable housing was a constant source of stress for this family, along with ongoing experiences of racism when attempting to find and sustain rental housing. Although the household was struggling, they still felt they were in a position to help people in need.

Ray noticed that a number of pawn shops had opened up in the city just before the study began; he himself had visited the shops once in a while, to take something in when he was short of cash. His family had also cut TV cable in order to make ends meet, but they tried to give their boys the things that they deserved:

> I'm not saying that they deserve stereo systems and Nikes. What they deserve is one of those $5.99 pizzas from the grocery store. It's just as good as a $12 pizza. They deserve snacks in their lunches. Thank God there is all this grunge stuff around—so it's easy to shop for clothes for them.

Ray described his experience of, and belief in, "community." Through sharing with others, buying in bulk, providing mutual favours and swapping clothes, he felt he could rely on and be a support to those around him. Ray said that these coping devices reflected the spiritual part of him; he believed that we are all responsible for one another. When his car broke down, he just left it on the street, unable to pay for fixing it. "It is an annoyance not having transportation right now, but my sister-in-law is very supportive if you need a ride somewhere," he said. "If my boys have a dental appointment, she takes them over." One of the reasons Ray chose to live where he did was that he could get credit at a local store. He commented,

> We go there to charge stuff. [It is] not a lot. [We use it] if [we're] out of milk or groceries. Every two weeks we pay it back. It's amazing what a difference that makes because we don't have credit cards.

Ray was critical of what he deemed the "scarcity of adequate, fair living." He noted that cuts to welfare, in particular, and the lack of decent jobs are all the more harsh when placed alongside the myth of what he called "the big dream." In his work, with his friends and in his own life, he saw people bombarded with images of opulence and quick money:

> The poor have choices they can make. I guess we are dragged into this big dream. There's a hell of a lot of gambling going on now. A lot of scratch tickets, bingos, charity casinos. People are using that to make money. I did get caught up in that for while. I got into it. I'm not being a hypocrite here. I finally opened my eyes and said "Shit, I'm out of control!" But there are a lot of people I know that are into it still.

Ray was chiefly concerned about his children, like other parents. However, the changes in federal policies affecting Native peoples, along with the everyday racism they experience and his critique of his own community complicated these concerns. He wondered what the future held for Native youth:

I'm just worried about the opportunities for my kids, and, as a Native person, I'm concerned about their identity, their rights. All of these are slowly being lost I would say. Potentially they could be lost just like that. The federal government is transferring a lot of responsibility to the provinces. You get somebody like Harris who is somewhere down the line going to say, "The heck with them."

Ray struggled to give his kids a sense of community and connection, while balancing very real problems facing reserves and Native peoples in urban settings. Ray was critical of how reserves were run and preferred to live off-reserve. While he had family on-reserve, he said:

I've got to stick around the city. I have a lot of family back home but I can't move there because of the politics. I don't agree with my band. I don't agree with the politics there. There is a definite mark of who the haves and the have-nots are. The haves are the ones who have accessed the economic development dollars, and people who work for the band. They are focusing so much on making money that they've totally left the kids out of the picture. And the kids are starting to be very violent down there, starting drinking, drugs and disrespect for parents and elders. And those are the have-nots and that's their only outlook. I can't take my kids into that environment.

He still had his children spend their summers there, however, "so they would know where they were from and who their family was."

Ray worked in the broader educational sector. He was also on the parent council of his own children's school. The erosion of this system had occurred on a number of fronts: the effects included lack of materials and poor conditions in which kids had to learn. With major legislative changes to the sector and the number of changes to curriculum, Ray noted:

The provincial government, number one, has cut back on all the education stuff. Number two, they're trying to standardize all kinds of things with the kids. How are you going to do that when you don't supply the funding? They're basically saying our kids are dumb. Let's measure them and to make sure they are at this level. If they're not, something is wrong with the kid.

These changes were evident in terms of materials and infrastructure, but also in terms of the attention and priority given to issues of culture, equity and diversity. While funding, infrastructure and teaching loads were central to the education debate, the loss of equity programming and the ongoing problem of racism and discrimination within the system took a back seat in the struggle. Raising small amounts of money for cultural programming became a trial, resulting in a reliance on fundraising from casino nights and lotteries. Ray noted how issues of discrimination in the school system are always present, even though little public fuss is made about them. He had to keep on top of the kinds of texts his own children were reading, as many perpetuated false and negative stereotypes about Native people:

It's amazing to me some of the things they are taking. I guess it goes back to seeing my own kids' English assignment and it talked about the savages or wild Indians that attacked this fort. You know, I have to explain to them when they're reading something about history that there's another side to this too. I'm trying to not make them angry. I want them to be able to question our role in history, because we shouldn't be left out of these history books.

Ray explained that the task is to see structures of oppression and challenge them: "Every opportunity we get we try and educate the kids. What we try and do is say, 'Don't be angry at cultures, be angry at systems.'" In his view, government funding was more easily available for Francophone programming in his community—a policy that pitted groups against one another.

Ray articulated multiple notions of community that extended to himself, his family, his work and society as a whole. When discussing who he thought had been harmed by provincial policies, Ray concluded that it would be those who were on social assistance. He commented, "Thank God these people have not turned to violence. But I know more and more who are turning to trafficking and they say we have to. And I agree with them. The poor are being put against the wall." In response to government policy, his work place, in coalition with other community groups, had rallied to get rid of the local welfare "snitch" line. Bartering systems and events that pulled the community together were numerous. Ray also got his kids involved in some of the marches that were occurring:

I told them I don't care what you are learning in school, you've got to learn about how to stand up for yourself. I don't care if you're a scientist or a doctor or anything like that, you've got to look out for yourself, your family, your community. And I think my boys [pause]—I'm really proud of them. They've got values and you've got to have those first.

While other participants criticized the government for various policies, from Ray's perspective, the Ontario government under Mike Harris represented a real and immediate threat to Native peoples. "That whole Ipperwash thing—he's wiped his hands of that," he said. "You see when I say he's a racist I mean that he's scary to the Native community." Ray was referring her to the killing of Dudley George. This issue has been kept in the public realm by members of George's family, who have doggedly pursued every avenue possible to make the government accountable. Premier Dalton McGuinty called a judicial inquiry for 2004, to explain why

Ontario Provincial Police (OPP) snipers with automatic machine-guns opened fire on unarmed Native protesters.[1]

Over the course of the interviews, Ray had taken on more work; he became concerned about his eldest son. His son's marks were not very good and, for the first time, he had not come home one night. To deal with work and home stress, Ray took some time on his own to listen to music or do some woodworking. He said, "I'm afraid of getting behind, but there are some mornings where I just don't want to go in." Having people visit and come to him for advice was comfort:

> I think I'm lucky in my situation. I see our place as a safe place or a gathering place. There's quite a few people in the community who come over for dinner or they come and talk things over with my wife and I. And I appreciate someone coming to us or even just sitting there. They don't have to say anything. I guess it helps me to see I have some sort of purpose or I've made it to that next step in what I believe is a life cycle. I'm at that age where I'm not the confused one.

Although Ray's work was about making positive changes in communities, as the interviews progressed he expressed a more fatalistic view about the future. His conversations with friends had become ceaseless tales about looking for work and moving to different parts of the province to find work. He questioned why it was that we think things are going to change:

> We're sitting around and thinking something's going to change, but we're not doing anything about it. We just think something is going to change for the better but we don't know when. I've got to battle with myself about what does change mean. I'm really not of the belief that a good job or good money is going to make lives better for people.

He thought that, when change doesn't happen, people begin to cope with things, and the danger in that is that people begin to accept what's around them. He noted, "Five years of this punishment by the government for being poor; you know, people are accepting it now—that's what I see. I don't see any fighting back like there was in the first two years." Ray noticed how other people who did have money, including other Native people, seemed to think they couldn't deal with poorer people. His own income remained the same and met his needs; however, he was clear that it did not meet his family's needs. He exclaimed, "My kids, they need stuff!" In the last interview, he reflected that things were much better five years ago, nevertheless, he would continue, in his work and as a leader in his community, to fight for causes that he saw as critical for upholding important community values.

Olivia, Gary and Gina

When we first spoke with Olivia in the winter of 1996, she and her husband, Gary, and her teenage daughter, Gina, had moved from Metro Toronto to the surrounding area. Olivia was a white woman born in Canada: she described her ethnicity as "Canadian," while Gary had immigrated fifteen years ago from Greece. The high cost of living in the city coupled with a slowdown in their own business meant they could no longer afford Toronto rents. The move left them with an unsettled feeling of being precariously housed:

> You really need stability, you need to know that you have a home to live in. I've been driving with Gary a lot now, since I've been having to go to the hospital so frequently, and the route is always the same. And there's a lot of motels that run along there. Invariably the thought that goes through my mind is, we could have, and still can, end up in a motel along with other families that live there. That threat was a very real one not too long ago.

While their move was meant to offset the high cost of living in Toronto, the disruption of adjusting to a new neighbourhood presented other obstacles in the areas of work, school and family relations. For Gary, a self-employed painter, the already tenuous nature of self-employment was made worse by the loss of his customer base. Coupled with the seasonal nature of his work, the family's income had fallen substantially since the 1980s, when the business was booming. Olivia, who quit her job as a bookkeeper seven years ago to help her husband manage their business, was finding it difficult to solicit business in their new neighbourhood. Gina's competitive swimming, always a priority for the family, was threatened by the strained finances. The family was frustrated that their quality of life had not improved. Indeed, they commented that it had deteriorated, as they spent more time commuting and less time together. Olivia commented on how isolated and lonely they felt leaving behind both family and friends. Contacting their support network was more expensive because of long-distance telephone charges:

> So what I started doing when I moved here was calling strangers. I started calling all kinds of people. I just went through the phone book and called organizations and groups, and agencies and stuff, wanting false information. Sometimes the information was valid, you know, I needed it, but often, more often than not I didn't, I just wanted to talk to people.

The family was confronted with a more profound crisis in May of 1997. Olivia was diagnosed with breast cancer. Despite her illness, Olivia wanted to continue to participate in the study, seeing it as an opportunity to contribute to the ongoing dialogue about change in the province. Olivia was outraged at the slow response of the health care system. Even with an acute diagnosis, she waited longer than three weeks between her diagnosis and treatment: "It actually was a question of time," she explained. "The oncologist didn't have any other openings for me. I had to wait three weeks after the suggestion that I might have a tumour." Olivia's husband, Gary, expressed the fear of other household participants who were also waiting for specialized care: "Would the time spent waiting have made all the difference?" Both laid blame for the crisis in health care at the feet of the provincial government:

It has been proven that stress causes cancer growth, causes tumour growth. Well, I attribute my cancer to my living conditions over the past two months. Without a doubt, that's what it is. I blame the Harris government for what has happened to me, I really do, because no family and no human being deserves to suffer, to have to struggle every single day, only to survive. That is absolutely inhuman and unacceptable.

While undergoing treatment, Olivia described how hospital understaffing undermined the quality of care she received:

Initially, I was confident that the support system that I was establishing outside of family and friends was going to work very, very well. After two and a half weeks with the Oncology Clinic, I discovered that it didn't work well. The reason is that there is definitely not enough staff to take care of the needs of cancer patients. There's not enough time for staff to provide the services that they would like to provide and that we, as cancer patients, require.

Olivia explained that the needs of cancer patients are complex, extending beyond medical procedures such as radiation and chemotherapy. With higher demands being placed on specialists and nurses, the dignity of the patient is often replaced with an assembly line approach to health care:

My last visit at the hospital was a very, very traumatic one. I saw rows of patients waiting to get their blood test done. The waiting period was far too long, the conditions under which we were waiting were very claustrophobic and oppressive.

In October of 1998, Olivia's struggle to get the kind of care and relationships she needed was dealt another blow as a result of the Health Services Restructuring Commission's recommendation to merge her oncology unit with another hospital. Olivia's biggest fear was about the continuity of her care:

I've experienced compassion and care and attentiveness these past couple of months from doctors and nurses here, and I expect that to continue. I don't want to lose that. I don't want to have to fight for something that I believe a person in my position deserves. A right to choose where and with whom I get my treatment. Everybody should have the right to choose, but in daily life we struggle for it.

Olivia questioned whether the increased patient loads would be met with growth in the number of health care professionals. In a follow-up telephone conversation in January of 1999 regarding the impact of hospital mergers, she spoke of longer waits for treatment and her fears of understaffing. Olivia's concerns at that time extended beyond the issue of quality of care to her loss of control over that care. In between hospital treatments, a nurse and physiotherapist visited Olivia once a week. The at-home nursing care was disrupted by a labour dispute between the home care nurses and the province. The loss of the home-care support had implications for Olivia's health and for the well-being of her family, who were providing care in place of the nurse. Olivia explained:

It's obvious that care has shifted, more towards home care than hospital care. And there are advantages and disadvantages to that. Sick people like myself do need to have a professional who can do home visits. I also need to feel as though it's a giving thing, more than me taking. If I feel like I am only taking, then I feel humiliated. When someone is in the hospital, they don't feel humiliated like that because, there, staff are obligated to give you care, and that's exactly how it is perceived. But at home it is different.

For Olivia, the reliance on friends and family members to provide care was a mixed blessing: The comfort of home was accompanied by the fear that her family members lacked the skills or capacity to provide care and that the caring work burdened her family members. Moreover, emotional support could not substitute for the care received from health care professionals:

Friends are supports, they're emotional support. I guess what my thought is that the real heavy duty emotional stuff that occurs doesn't happen when friends are around, it happens in the home, in private. It also happens at odd times when you least expect it, but it's not planned. So it's great to have friends, and it's great to have family members around. People have been calling me constantly and have volunteered help, and of course I accept, I just don't know how to interpret that emotionally. On an emotional level I don't know how to interpret that, I'm kind of disconnected from it. These people are there, but they've got their own lives too. At the same time, it's not a cure for cancer.

Battling cancer provided Olivia with insights into how she would have liked to be treated, not only as a patient but also as a citizen:

> It's not the way a human being should have to live, in substandards conditions. That perspective has been born out of my prognosis and diagnosis, but I do believe and I know that Gary does too, that all people should be taken care of and basic needs should be met, always, without question, in our society. So just being alive is not enough, it's like saying, just because a homeless person is alive that's sufficient. No way. Everybody deserves to have a home to live in, deserves to have, quality food to eat.

Sadly Olivia lost her battle with cancer and died after the third interview. Gary and Gina slowly continued to piece together their lives after Olivia's death. The household's finances had been severely strained as a result of Gary having to take time away from work to care for Olivia. As a self-employed worker, Gary had no benefits, nor was he eligible for Employment Insurance. He resumed working after Olivia's death. At the time of our last contact Gina was completing her senior year in high school while continuing to swim competitively. Soon after father and daughter moved and were hoping to rebuild their lives in a new location.

Ashley and Rosa

Ashley, an African-Canadian women in her mid fifties, and Rosa her thirty-three-year-old daughter, who identified as African, took up residence together after they found themselves in financial straits. While not well-off, both Ashley and Rosa had managed to secure full-time jobs in Toronto, after moving there from a southeastern Ontario town. Their situation deteriorated after Rosa became pregnant and, because of complications with her pregnancy, could no longer hold down her job. Ashley also lost her job due to funding cutbacks at a community agency. Rosa applied for social assistance and was enrolled in a full-time upgrading program while Ashley continued to look for full-time employment. Although Ashley believed that the financial crises faced by the non-profit sector made employment opportunities more scarce, she still occupied her time with activities such as volunteering for a seniors group, for a community association of low-income people and for various arts organizations in the area.

Out of financial necessity Ashley and Rosa decided to pool resources and move in together. Both tried to keep the financial status of their household to themselves. However, isolating themselves from others, including other family members, made them more dependent on each other. The lack of understanding by family members was compounded by their feeling that they were victimized by a scornful public that demonized the poor and those on social assistance. The labour market was not any better.

Ashley attributed her difficulty in securing full-time employment to her age, race and hearing disability. Ashley and Rosa talked of having their utilities cut off, of buying cheaper cuts of meat and produce, and of "going without" to make ends meet. As their financial situation worsened, mother and daughter began to share personal belongings, such as winter boots. While they were each other's primary source of support, they also had other supports they could draw on. Ashley's partner of more than ten years, who did not live with her, extended his employer's medical and dental coverage to include her. While proud of their family's professional accomplishments, both Ashley and Rosa were reluctant to seek out their support.

Mother and daughter talked of feeling indebted and ashamed at having to accept the family's charity; at times they felt resentful of the undertones that accompanied this support. Being on the receiving end of help elicited a complicated series of responses on their part. On top of this, both sensed that the mood of the province was changing to one of less compassion for those who fell on hard times, Rosa commented:

> During the day I won't listen to [radio stations] 640 or 1010. Why should I listen to something that's going to be bashing me? It's like buying the *Sun* paper. Why am I going to buy a paper that's going to give me more concern, anxiety? I just don't. Things that drive me nuts, I just try and cut myself off from.

Ashley and Rosa were heavily indebted; they found the household carrying costs were becoming impossible to maintain. Rosa was still trying to pay off outstanding student loans, and Ashley's run-down home in south-eastern Ontario was at risk of being repossessed by the city because of overdue property taxes. At home in Toronto, they were preoccupied with household utility bills; second and third notices had gone unpaid. Changes to social assistance and health care confused Ashley and Rosa and made it more difficult to access support. Both believed they had sunk as low, financially and emotionally, as they possibly could. Rosa commented,

> You always have this feeling of anxiety, of some type of doom and gloom going to happen immediately. You can see yourself being okay in the future, but the immediate thing is just waiting for something to fall apart. Every time somebody rings that doorbell, what next?

Frustrated with their financial situation and overwhelmed by their debt load, Ashley and Rosa's relationship began to fray. The mutual support they provided to one another began to unravel. By the third interview, Ashley and Rosa were no longer living together, and each was accusing the other of not carrying their own weight. The financial hardship that brought them together ultimately drove them apart. Ashley described the final days of their shared living arrangement as strained:

I told Rosa, I said, "I just, I can't take it any longer," and I couldn't. We were just arguing and it was like very tense. She wasn't paying her fair share. All of my money was going, all of the food I was buying. I ended up paying most of the hydro bill and the cable bill. I didn't have the money and I was getting the money from Keith all the time, right. I just said, this is ridiculous. From about the sixth of the month, I would pay all the food from there. Where the heck was her money? I don't know, I was paying all of it, and I'm not going to not buy food. I spoke to my eldest daughter. I said "I'm going to move and I want you"—because she wanted to go away for the summer and they were looking for someone, their roomer had just left downstairs—so I said, "Why don't you just take Rosa and Mary?" And she said, "I'll think about it."

Rosa also attributed their break-up to strained finances:

It's almost like a married couple. When money and stuff comes into play, that's the big, that's one big argument. Do you know what I mean? And it gets worse, money always gets worse. The payments, it was just like trying to dodge, and trying not to get caught—give them a rubber cheque. I think that was the proverbial straw.

After a bitter parting of ways, Rosa rented the basement of her sister's home. While the arrangement proved to be mutually beneficial in terms of reciprocal child care, Rosa was unhappy. She continued to pay market rent and hide her financial situation from her sister. Her sister was oblivious to Rosa's frequent use of local food banks or her strategy of pawning personal possessions to make the rent. Her sister was so unaware of Rosa's financial situation that she asked Rosa to act as co-signer for a mortgage. Rosa also tried to shield her poverty from her daughter. However, Rosa was less successful in hiding it from her daughter than her sister. Rosa talked of how difficult it was trying to maintain a facade that everything is fine: "Something [my daughter] said just totally broke my heart, 'Mommy, how come you never have any money?' And I was just like, oh God, it's the last thing you want to put your kid through."

Now on their own, mother and daughter felt increasingly less able to cope with daily pressures. For Rosa this meant she stopped taking an interest in herself:

If I could see my way out, then [it's worth it] but it's when you have no light some days. Like I said, I don't care. Like going to the doctor and stuff, and just looking normal. I don't care if I have dandruff anymore, it's good enough— you don't have to sit beside me, you don't have to talk to me. That's how I feel about this.

The daily grind of poverty continued to wear them down, and it seemed as though things would continue to get worse:

> I feel like I'm going to explode walking around with ten cents in my pocket, but I just do it, I do it because I have to do it. It's my job to do it. If I was by myself I could do crazy things, but I don't, I can't do that to my daughter.

Ashley moved back to her home town and applied for social assistance. Income security continued to be her biggest preoccupations. Despite the fact that her partner and her own mother had paid off the property tax arrears, she feared her home would be taken away from her if her period on assistance exceeded the allotted time period. Ashley understood the changes to welfare as yet another hurdle put in the way of the poor. She felt victimized by what she saw as punitive measures that did little to give welfare recipients help in improving their circumstances. Indeed she felt that there were fewer options for those with the greatest need. She lamented that her expectations as a low-income woman were being transformed: "I think that because of the way things have gone I've gotten to expect less and not really my due. If you're on welfare you can't expect to have this or that, or your expectations are lower."

The collapse of her familial network and the scope of change to social programs such as social assistance undermined her confidence and her ability to make positive changes in her life. Ashley believed she was able to make some headway in spite of, not because of, the assistance from family or from government sources. Since her falling-out with Rosa, her contact with her other children had been minimal. Familial relations were fraught with conflict and, for a period of months, Ashley did not have any contact with her children. Her house was in disrepair due to years of neglect; she felt cut off from her community network in Toronto because she couldn't afford to have telephone service. Having few resources at her disposal, she applied for social assistance: she received welfare until her Employment Insurance benefits commenced. At this time she began rebuilding her support network and joined an anti-poverty organization that raised awareness of poverty issues in her community.

Ashley enrolled in an Employment-Insurance-funded business program and began a plan to start her own business. While she doubted that she would be able to earn a decent living from the business, she enjoyed what she was doing and felt she was making a worthwhile contribution to her community. She continued to look for full-time work. Her long-time partner resided with her on the weekends, and her children resumed contact through phone calls and visits. Ashley gets by day by day:

> One of my biggest fears is I cannot go on social assistance now, I would have to sell my house in order to go on there. And if I was on, they would have a lien

against the house by now, because it started in June. So what can I say about social assistance, it's just a crock of shit. It's for the PC [Progressive Conservative] government to get in bed with the banks so the banks can take over your house, that's what it is about. So you can sell your house for next to nothing and then...?

Since separating from her mother, Rosa was determined to become more financially independent. She successfully sought child support payments from her daughter's father and dropped out of the upgrading courses offered through social services. She voluntarily signed up to participate in Ontario Works. Given that her daughter was still under the age of six, her participation was not mandatory. Rosa had grown disillusioned with the upgrading program and saw the Ontario Works training as an opportunity to enhance her skill set. After completing the training session, the placement phase of Ontario Works failed to yield any employment opportunities. Rosa then took it upon herself to approach a temporary agency and was soon working short administrative stints in offices across Toronto. Luckily, one of these short-term placements became a full-time job. Rosa was able to move off of assistance and out of her sister's home. By the end of the study she and her daughter were living in a one-bedroom apartment in Toronto. She remained hopeful that her job and housing situation would remain stable.

Kate and Carl

When we first met Kate and Carl they were living together in the greater Toronto area with their two children, Kyle and Karrie. Kate was working as a telemarketer and Carl worked part-time as a community health worker. Kate was a white woman who described her ethnicity as Canadian; Carl identified as a Native Canadian. During the study, social policies affected their decisions about family composition, whether to have a "public" relationship and how to cope with family tragedy and relationship breakdown. Although both were employed, their jobs offered little, if any, job security. Paid barely above minimum wage, thirty-year-old Kate was often sent home if she was unable to fill her daily quota of sales. Instead of waiting to be called back, she found herself replacing one telemarketing position for another. Although the companies and products changed, the insecure nature of the job did not. She felt trapped in a wash of dead-end jobs. Her Grade Nine education, coupled with her sporadic work history, gave her little hope of advancing out of these entry-level positions. Carl worked with a community health agency for five years as an AIDS educator. Although he made a decent wage, he was only working twenty-four hours a week (due to agency funding cutbacks) at the time of the study. While he seemed to get personal satisfaction from the work, he explained that in the current era of fiscal restraint, governments and charitable organizations were having to make difficult choices over which social causes to fund. AIDS was slowly falling out of favour. Although Carl was actively looking for other work, he feared that his lack of post-secondary education blocked him from advancing into higher-paid positions.

In this household, employment income was supplemented with social assistance. Both hid their relationship from welfare, fearful that their benefits would be terminated under the recently revised eligibility criteria that no longer allowed persons of the opposite sex to co-reside for a period of three years before deeming their relationship spousal. Having to apply as a family would result in termination of benefits or a welfare top-up, which would reduce the household's overall income. Carl explained:

> If it was out that [we were living together] it would have great impact on what this family was able to do and provide. The quality of life would drastically go down. [Kate:] Without Carl here I wouldn't have any choice. I wouldn't have a TV, I certainly wouldn't have cable. I wouldn't be living here. I'd be in a one-bedroom, squished.

Carl and Kate were adamant that as soon as they found better employment they would move off assistance. They were weary of living their lives looking over their shoulder in fear of being found out. Carl was fearful of disclosing his relationship to people, including friends, for fear that welfare would get wind of their situation. Kate talked of having to warn the children not to tell anyone that their father was living with them. She also felt the need to hide other forms of support. She said, "If you have a support network, and if you get any money from them, if you get anything from them, you have to tell social services, and then usually there's something that's taken off your cheque." Their inability to fully live out their lives as a couple strained their relations at time and made corresponding with welfare, health and education officials difficult.

Money was always a concern for Kate; it became more so with the reduction in the social assistance benefit level in October of 1995. At that time, Kate resided with her three children. Her eldest daughter, from a previous relationship, was born with a congenital birth defect and required full-time care. At that time, Kate had chosen to stay home and care for her children. However, the reduction rendered her decision to be a full-time caregiver impossible:

> I couldn't stay home. I was getting a little over $1100 for three kids, and with rent at $750 I couldn't do it. I think the kids do more suffering from the cuts. Number one, because it's stress on me; number two, because I was, like, constantly on them; number three, they weren't getting what they were used to.

After careful consideration, she asked her eldest daughter's father to take custody of their child:

> The twenty-two or twenty-one, whatever percentage that [welfare] took off, that divided my family. It took away a part of my family.... I had to give up Chantelle because of [the welfare cut], because I couldn't [afford] to take her to the hospital, back and forth. I mean for me to actually sit there and tell her own father I can't financially take care of our daughter, I can't take her to the hospital.... It took away things, money that I used to use for my kids and for myself.

This decision left Kate and the other children heart-broken. She felt that she had failed as a mother to provide for her daughter, but, given her dire financial circumstances and Chantelle's high needs, she felt she had little choice. Kate began to look for employment to make up the shortfall in assistance. Up until this point, Kate's relationship with Carl was on and off again. It became more secure at that time. Carl gave up his separate residence and moved in with Kate and their two children: he explained that the decision to do so was as motivated by financial necessity as it was by emotional attachment.

> Eventually it just became too much money to have two different residences, so we moved in together. It made more sense for me to [give her] my rent money. I was spending most of my time with her anyway. So we moved in, it was more out of necessity of money rather than true, honest, down to earth, thought-out, talked-out, emotioned-out, kind of thing. It was more, you know, we need to do this, it's a hard choice, let's do it. Anyhow, that's one perspective on how we got together. There's all kinds of other issues. We certainly loved each other, you know—we were happy; it was good for the kids.

Still, the cut in assistance put additional pressure on their relationship and intensified the pressure on Carl to find better employment to assist the household.

Things appeared to improve marginally for Kate and Carl at the time of the second interview. Carl picked up an additional contract and Kate continued to work as a telemarketer while collecting social assistance benefits. They were able to purchase a microwave oven: for Kate, this was an important symbol of improved finances. However, just as things started to look better, Kate and the family suffered a setback. Kate's brother died suddenly: the unexpected expense of having to fly to British Columbia to attend the funeral threw the household into financial and emotional disarray. In a later interview, Kate disclosed that she had an emotional collapse after her brother's death and was in the hospital for a month, recovering. In the meantime, the Children's Aid Society had threatened to take custody of her children. She asked her sister in British Columbia to move to Toronto during this time to help her through this hardship.

Debts continued to overwhelm the household. Household purchases were minimized as Kate attempted to regain control of spiralling costs. Carl had outstanding student loans, while Kate had amassed a huge credit card debt. While making rent payments was always a priority, other utilities were cut, as were clothing and food expenses. Both Kate and Carl talked about how unexpected expenses had the potential of throwing off their monthly budget. Something as simple as one of the children developing a fever and requiring over-the-counter medication, not covered under their drug plan, was enough to set them back. Despite marginal improvements, they still did not feel they were financially sound enough to plan for their future, or for a rainy day.

By the third round of interviews, Carl had found a new job as an outreach worker for a community health agency. His employment was full-time, with benefits, and his income climbed to $40,000. It appeared as though Carl's permanent job was the break Carl and Kate needed. They were ready to leave welfare and to declare themselves a family, openly living together as a couple without fear of being discovered by welfare agencies. They moved into a small house in a mainly low-income area.

They were thrilled that their children had a yard to play in. Kate, Carl and their two children shared the house with Kate's sister, who moved to Toronto from British Columbia. They divided expenses among them and shared in household responsibilities. They continued to grapple with the overwhelming debt load they had accumulated, although it was clear that the debt load was not seen as a family responsibility. Kate was solely responsible for the debt load: she fretted about how it would be paid; Carl no longer worried about money. The strain of the financial hardship finally took its toll on the couple. As Carl recounts,

I was definitely angry at her for running up all the debt. I had no idea what she was doing, and I don't even know how much is out there. I think she gave me a rough estimate. I would say to her, well, whatever debts you're piling up is my debt too, because, one way or another, I'm going to have to pay for that, and the kids pay for that as well.

By the final interview Carl and Kate had separated. While there were no formalized custody arrangements, Kate retained full custody of the children while Carl, who paid child support, saw the children every other weekend. Kate hadn't fully come to terms with the separation and still held out hope that they would reunite. Carl's departure had a tremendous impact not only emotionally but also financially. Household expenses remained the same even though Carl was no longer residing in the house. With less income, Kate wondered whether she and her sister would be able to afford to continue living where they were. Kate continued to work odd jobs as a waitress, receptionist and as a telemarketer. However, these jobs failed to become permanent full-time positions. Kate was unemployed at the time and had no idea how she was going to pay her share of the rent that month. Although she had always talked of upgrading her education and one day becoming a nurse, she felt this goal was even more unattainable now. As she struggled to find a way out of her predicament, Kate described her conflicted feelings about asking for support:

> I couldn't phone my ex and ask him for money. That's something I don't do. I can't even phone Carl. Like, I know I can, but I won't ever phone Carl and talk to him about money, like, give me more money, that's not in me. It's something I've never done. I had a hard time just bringing a bill to him, saying this is your part to pay. I just, well, it's something I don't do.

Carl, on the other hand, moved into his own apartment, which he shared with his brother. He felt that the strain of the debts, as well as personal differences, had led to the separation. He continued to work full-time; he felt he was prepared to start saving for his future as well as the children's education fund. He also planned to enrol in a post-secondary institution to pursue a degree.

Jackie

Jackie was in her mid-thirties and lived in a medium-sized city in southeastern Ontario. She worked half-time for a small not-for-profit agency and shared a home with her three children and her mother, Edith. She immigrated from England twenty years ago. Jackie was a white woman, who stated that her ethnicity was "Anglo-Canadian." When we first met in 1997, Jackie's son Angus was not yet a toddler. Her daughter, Kerry, was fourteen years old. Jackie and Kerry's father divorced many years before. Jackie characterized him as violent and angry. She refused to have her daughter grow up in that environment; she raised Kerry mostly on her own after her separation. Jackie was able to manage on her part-time income because she received a partial day-care subsidy, and she shared costs with her mother. Her household tells another story about the strains placed on families who are forced to rely extensively on one another.

Jackie had a B.A. and much labour-market experience. In 1991, she got a job working for the not-for-profit organization who currently employed her; the job consisted of sporadic contracts. When she went on maternity leave in early 1996, she did not know if there would be a job to which to return. Finally, after years of insecure short-term contracts with the same agency, a multi-year grant was received. Jackie's position was split, however, between two agencies, so she was dropped down to part-time hours.

She thought her wage of $15 an hour was quite good, but it was not enough because she only worked twenty hours per week.

Although family connections were key to maintaining a home for her children, keeping a good relationship with her mother, and between her mother and her children, was a constant struggle for Jackie. Although her financial situation made her feel that she and her children were a burden to her mother, they had few other housing options. In 1997, Jackie and her mother were trying to maintain separate residences and lives while living in the same house. Although they shared the kitchen, the laundry facilities and the yard, they had separate telephone lines, and Jackie, Angus and Kerry were living in the basement; her mother used the rest of the house. In early 1998, when Angus was diagnosed with asthma and allergies and could not be in the basement, the space-sharing arrangements had to be changed. For both Jackie and Edith, this meant significantly less personal space and time, and increased unpaid work for Jackie, who was attempting to make up in household labour for the expenses that she could not share in the house. Jackie said,

> My mother complains about the house, that the roof needs doing, it needs painting, the furnace is old, the windows need to be replaced, the rug needs replacing. It just gets right on top of me, and I have no escape. I don't know where to channel it. I have no money or time to go work out at a gym. But I have to manage. I have to be healthy for Kerry and Angus. I have to [provide a good home].

At various points, Jackie had considered co-op housing as an option for her family. However, when they moved in together, Jackie and her mother bought a used car. Edith had increasingly severe arthritis, and Jackie's eldest child, Kerry, had a genetic growth condition that meant that the bones in her legs had developed improperly. Jackie contributed to paying off the loan they got for the car, but Edith paid the insurance and maintenance. Kerry would not have been able to get around the city if they had moved, because Edith would keep the car, and Jackie could not afford to buy and maintain one on her own.

One of the constant battles in Jackie's life over the last decade had been trying to get adequate and consistent child support payments for Kerry from her ex-husband. In early 1998, when she felt she had exhausted her capacities to bargain with Kerry's father for payments, Jackie retained a lawyer. Kerry's medical costs were high, and Jackie did not have a plan to cover her prescriptions or equipment. "We could really use the money, especially since I have to take Kerry to another city to see a specialist," Jackie explained. "It costs $250 by the time you pay for a hotel, for gas, food—that's coming out of my pocket, and I am losing work time." In addition, as Kerry got older, she was increasingly self-conscious about both her height and her inability, as a result of her illness, to participate in activities like gym or dances at school. Kerry's father had agreed to pay for horseback riding lessons for Kerry, as it was one activity that she could do. Jackie had to cancel the lessons because, after only a few monthly payments, Kerry's father stopped sending money to cover the classes:

> The last conversation I ever had with him was about him not paying on time. I was very nicely trying to ask him to keep on top of his payments, and he ended up insulting Kerry. At the beginning of the conversation, I opened by telling him that Kerry had come in second in Public Speaking. I was trying to be really positive, and I hoped that would soften it to ask for the money that he was in arrears on, especially the portion for horseback riding, which I could not cover on my salary. It wasn't like I was asking for anything more than he's supposed to pay. He said, "Tell Kerry to call me and ask me for that money." I said, "It's not her place. If you offer to pay for riding lessons for her, then you should just pay it." He replied, "Oh, she hasn't got the gall to phone and ask me for that money, no wonder she only came second in Public Speaking." He is so abusive. I don't want to go through him anymore. I'm just trying to do it all through my lawyer now.

Covering the cost of a lawyer, however, was a challenge. In late 1998, Jackie tried mediation: for a period of time this resulted in a more consistent and higher flow of money to Kerry. By 1999, however, the struggle was beginning again, with Kerry's father "forgetting" or claiming that he had sent money that he had not. Jackie said,

> He's in arrears again. It's $175, it's not a lot, but when you don't have much of a margin of error each month in your budget, you can't be behind $175 at any point in the month. It just wears you down. It's been fourteen years. He sees it as giving me money, and I see it as supporting his child.

To make matters worse, the Ontario government sent Jackie a letter in 1998 stating that, when she had received social assistance in the late 1980s and early 1990s, she was overpaid. They sent a collection agency after her for $1400; however, they had no proof of such an overpayment.

In our second interview in early 1998, Jackie was overwhelmed by the number of demands on her. Her son's asthma, her inability to contribute more to rent and household costs, her daughter's upcoming major leg surgery and the insecurity of her work and her child support caused her to feel that she had no escape to have a few minutes to herself. "I am feeling like I just can't take too much more of this, getting knocked down," she said. She and Angus' father were trying to bridge the distance between them, but were not having good success. One of her biggest challenges was trying to accommodate her son's health needs while holding down her job.

On a number of occasions, she ended up spending $30 on a sitter for one day of child care so that she could go to work. Despite all of these demands and her sense of being overwhelmed, Jackie said that she loved her life and her children were an unending source of joy for her. Jackie confided that she had never expected to have any more children after Kerry; she was thrilled to have a second child later in her life.

Jackie was committed to and involved in the community in which she lived. Because she worked for a not-for-profit agency that dealt with poverty and social justice issues, she confronted many of the difficulties faced by residents of her city on a daily basis. She saw herself, like many others, as participating in what she termed "the new insecure economy." In this economy, she thought, people expend all of their energy to manage day to day and "are too stressed to participate in neighbourhood or community life." Jackie pointed out the irony that she worked for a progressive organization that paid her part-time and hired students at "poverty wages."

Between our second and third interviews, Jackie reconciled with Angus' father. She became pregnant with her third child and gave birth to a baby girl in 1999. Several weeks later, Kerry went into the hospital to have surgery on her other leg. Jackie's mother accompanied Kerry, taking her holidays to care for the child. However, as Jackie explained,

> The baby was born in March and, when she was three weeks old, we went to the hospital for Kerry's surgery. Mom took a week off work to stay with Kerry in the hospital and they were there for five days. She got out of the hospital, mom went back to work for one day and fell off a chair and broke her arm. I was looking after a newborn baby, a three-year-old, a daughter with a broken leg and a mother with a broken arm, and it was her right arm and it was in a cast. Mom couldn't do a thing, she couldn't put her bra on, she couldn't cook, she couldn't wash herself, she couldn't do anything. There was one moment I had a cry. I'd been doing something for everybody for the last three days, and I hadn't gotten anything done for myself. I didn't bathe for several days, but yet I was running baths for my mom, running baths for Kerry and I was washing the baby, giving Angus baths.

Jackie had applied, but was not accepted, to teachers' college for 1999. She thought that it was just as well in the short-term as she felt she had "a lot on her plate." Jackie's biggest fear was of returning to social assistance. She did not even apply for top-up medical benefits for Kerry, because she could not face being part of "the system." She had been working with social assistance recipients and noted the escalating requirements and rigidities of the new workfare program. Jackie noted that those earning marginally more than minimum wage were being pitted against those receiving social assistance, resulting in a climate of resentment and hatred:

I think it is just the nature of the way employment is changing. There are so many jobs that are just above minimum wage, like $7 or $8 an hour. They are one paycheque away from welfare but manage to stay in these jobs. Mike Harris is playing to those people because their lives are so hard, they're not making much more than welfare people, but yet they have this pride in what they're doing. They see people coming through on their taxes, so they think they're welfare bums, sitting at home, not working. It just creates a [culture of] hatred. I don't know why we don't all try to pull each other up instead of pulling each other down.

Despite the stresses of raising small children, a teenaged daughter and caring for her mother while trying to maintain paid work, Jackie was optimistic about the future. She had moments where she felt overwhelmed by the demands in her life, but, on the whole, she found great comfort and energy in the people who surrounded her. "How can you be depressed when you have such wonderful children in your life?" she asked.

Discussion

- Given that people often turn to family and friends as sources of support, what was the purpose of making these relationships so prominent in policy statements during the nineties?
- Which groups of citizens are going to be particularly advantaged or disadvantaged when programs assume family and friends have primary responsibility for providing the resources and labour for those needing ongoing help with the activities of daily living?
- What kind of supportive roles should be played by community, family and friends, in relation to the state and the provisions of public services?

The participants profiled in this chapter lived in very different types of households but all relied on help from, and gave help to, communities, family and friends as they struggled to meet the responsibilities they were carrying. These patterns of support are endangered by a policy discourse which invokes a vision of strong communities, families and extended kinship ties as the ideal source and form of support. The experiences of these household members reveal some of the costs of such policies. Relationships are being taxed and familial tensions exacerbated by changes that, separately and together, have been downloading responsibilities to the family. Not a single household spoke about the benefit of tax cuts as a buffer or replacement for needed services and employment opportunities. Indeed, Kate discovered that her only way to cope with the welfare cut was to give up custody of her eldest child. Instead of the stated aim of promoting family responsibility, the stories detail family breakdown and, paradoxically, punitive state measures when people do turn to relationships for help. As a result, many hide the supports they receive from their families or hide their situations from family members, while trying to conceal their most important relationships from public officials. As we witnessed, Kate and Carl coached their children to deny that their parents lived together. Their relationship eventually failed as a result of these pressures. Policies that do not work can be redesigned, but broken relationships and ruptured communities are not so easily mended.

Policies can help those who are advantaged and increase the vulnerability of others. Offering tax breaks as a way to supplement family incomes or to help pay for services was ineffectual at best, and, in many cases, it exacerbated family tensions. As many household experiences illustrate, unequal power dynamics determine who is in a position to "hear" the requests of those asking for help and how those transactions may transpire. For some, the situation makes it impossible to ask for help in the first place. Olivia, Rose and Kate describe how asking for help is fraught with complications. All three attempt to negotiate these power dynamics in ways that help them retain some personal control and dignity. For Olivia, this means attempting to manage her own health care, while, for Rosa, it means hiding her financial situation from her family. The relationship breakdown between Rosa and Ashley must be understood in the context of the isolation they experienced from the rest of the family and the stigma they felt in a labour market that marginalizes people by race, class and gender. Ashley adopted an exit strategy, distancing herself from family connections and from relying on social assistance.

Asking for support was a significant risk for Jackie. Although she turns to family for help, the demands on her energy and resources are substantial. While there are points of stress in sharing a house with her mother, there is some reciprocity in the work, help and resources they pool. Her ex-husband has resources; however, he uses them to wield power. The costs to her young daughter would have been much higher if Jackie had used this route to obtain money. Women who bear the responsibility for supporting their families are placed in a position in which financial requests or legally sanctioned rights are transformed into "asking" for child support. Even when arrangements are accepted by both parties, the caring labour and the opportunities are not evenly shared. While Kate knew that her dreams of being a nurse would not be fulfilled, Carl was looking forward to pursuing his post-secondary education. These "personal" dynamics are organized by public policies and exist within the public domain.

Health care policies are a crucial ingredient if people, young and old, are to remain integrated members of their communities. Olivia's experience with hospitals and home care reflect changes in staffing, funding and infrastructure that affect the quality of care. Placing a few tax dollars into Olivia's pocket could not replace the deterioration of the system that she experiences. Moving quickly from hospital to community-based care, without adequate planning and coordination, undermines the quality of health care she receives and puts added pressures on her already worried family. Her experiences and insights expose the human costs of the well-known crisis in health and home care in the province. Families and friends can give support but they cannot provide home health care. At a more fundamental level, Olivia describes the complex dynamics at work in any helping relationship. She articulates how notions of dignity and reciprocity are as important to the health care system as they are to someone who is homeless and in need of support. To her, these notions are fundamental to citizenship.

Ray and his family live in and between many communities that are in conflict. Their story reflects changes and adjustments in society as a whole, among the First Nations and at the household level. Similar to Ray, Jackie and Ashley draw strength from community organizing, while they continue on with their own struggles. Both view the low-income community and their respective neighbourhoods as sites of resistance. Yet, they notice that people are too tired to access these places of support. From Ray's perspective, a downward spiral for the Native community (in health care, reserve life, the increase in casinos, the Ipperwash incident and the downloading of Native issues to the province) and for low-income people are at play. In the last decade, governments across the country have turned to lotteries as a way of raising money for social programs. Lotteries, however, are played disproportionately by low-income people, transferring further the burden of paying for social programs onto the poor. Ray is disconcerted that casinos are also favoured by the First Nations as an approach to raising revenue, while gambling is presented as a "way out" for those with few supports.

Communities are constructed and identified in different ways. They also have differential access to power and funding and are positioned differently within the nation-state. When education cuts are made and communities become more vulnerable, Ray notes that this simply adds to the ways in which Aboriginal peoples' lives are already absent from the curriculum. He must re-educate his sons, who are part of a system that often rejects or ignores Native history and contemporary issues. Where each community lies in the larger power structure is central to its survival and success. Ray argues that in his region, certain "minority groups" like the Francophone community, receive preferential treatment and more access to public funds. The notion of "cultures" competing for resources has long been part of government policy. Policy changes in Ray's view, however, are not simply about access to resources. As Ipperwash shows, government decision making can be a distinct threat to certain communities. These larger political forces infiltrate Ray's family dynamics, as he worries about the future of his children and struggles to keep the household afloat. As all the households profiled here show, the political world of personal relationships can only sustain so many pressures.

Notes

1. Acting-Sergeant Kenneth Deane was found guilty of criminal negligence for knowingly shooting an unarmed man, causing the death of Dudley George on Sept. 6, 1995. The judge found that the protesters were all unarmed. The George family launched a wrongful death lawsuit that alleged senior provincial officials, including former premier Mike Harris, had pressured the OPP to end the occupation by force, which has since been dropped due to the inquiry. The protesters claimed the park was on a sacred burial ground. Their claims were later supported by documents released by the federal government (Edwards and Levy 2004a). For eight years the provincial government has misused freedom of information to block records concerning Ipperwash. It took almost eight years for the government to admit it had film of the occupation, including the day of the fatal shooting (Edwards and Levy 2004b).

Chapter Eight

Interpreting Experience, Attributing Cause and Considering Options

What kind of analysis or narrative(s) did households employ to help organize and explain the series of events that occurred in their lives? Unlike previous chapters, which have concentrated on the effects of reduced social programs, this chapter focuses on how participants: (1) explain their own experiences in relation to the cutbacks; (2) attribute cause or motive for the political shift to the right in the province; and (3) see these experiences and opinions shaping their life options. Here, we explore the discursive strategies participants in our study utilize when it comes to understanding their experiences. When problems arise, do participants view them as personal issues and/or do they point to the influence of social, economic and political forces? How do people place their specific stories in a larger context for meaning? Does social location affect how interpretations transpire?

Analyzing language for its social meaning rather than its linguistic properties shows us how discourses and disciplines are put together. Not simply a reductive exercise, understanding terms and language should be viewed as a way "of categorizing and limiting, but also producing, the objects of which it speaks" (Foucault cf. Threadgold 1997: 59). As participants draw on available discourses to make sense of the world around them (media, government messages, texts and images), they are, at the same time, challenging and producing them. All of the stories rely on the ways in which people "make meaning" and on our capacities, as researchers, for hearing these practices at work. While experiences have a material reality, once they are communicated and continue to be retold, they take on a new shape. Discourses also operate at an institutional level. The meanings and values of an institution are expressed in systematically organized sets of statements. These are also picked up by participants. The notion of a "discursive field" is helpful here because it seeks to understand the relationship between language, social institutions, subjectivity and power. Discursive fields "consist of competing ways of giving meaning to the world and/or organizing social institutions and processes" (Threadgold 1997: 60).

Social location, with subjectivity being one of its aspects, determines the multiple ways people are positioned in society and their strategies for resisting or ignoring exploitation by race, gender, sexuality, disability and class. As people describe their experiences, they are telling us about their particular identity and subject position. For example, only participants of colour name racism as a central feature of Canadian society. In this way, race and concerns about racism are attached to people of colour, while white privilege disappears from view. Many households in our study felt targeted by a relentless stream of disparaging attitudes that view their presence in society as a drain on the economy. The damaging associations attached to being labeled a welfare recipient, a new immigrant or refugee, or a sole-support mother cause some to work against and within these stereotypes in order to resist and/or manipulate policy regulations or public opinion. As mentioned previously, Teresa adopts the "unemployable" label for financial security while rejecting its meaning and connotations. Sadly, however, during the time of this study, many participants felt the need to withdraw, no longer reading newspapers, listening to the radio, opening mail or applying for supports to which they were entitled in the first place. For others, these same "figures" are invoked in order to assign blame and help make sense of a changing world.

What becomes clear in these interviews is that few linear strands tied "experience" to a corresponding "worldview" or "opinion." For example, Rick, who experienced a decrease in income due to changes in employment insurance policies, still applauds the get-tough approach of the Conservative government. Christine, who fought for pay equity, simultaneously holds racist views in relation to new immigrants, while a participant who lamented the dangers of racism was particularly sexist. The forms of experience, subjectivity and opinion in relation to public policy are complex and often contradictory. Exploring and mapping these relationships remains an important project for investigating how power, exploitation and resistance filters through people's stories, institutions and government policy.

Denise's and *Rick's* daily lives are tumultuous, filled with ongoing conflict between the children from their respective families. Money and work are a constant source of frustration. They portray their household as an isolated unit struggling against a government that favours "immigrants" and that betrays its white citizens. *Pam* and *Bert*, a white middle-class family, closely follow social issues and are surrounded by a large network of friends and family. Living in northern Ontario, disparities between the north and south are central to their experiences. An analysis of their fledgling local economy exists in relation to the "wealth" in southern Ontario. *Christine* and *Dwight*, a couple in their thirties, live with their teenage son in a small rural community. Both are employed but have significant financial concerns. At the time of the interviews, Christine was involved in a pay-equity legal fight, while her husband found himself competing with "immigrants" for training opportunities. *Jessie* and *Mark* rely on her income and received considerable support from family and friends. The Conservative government's cuts to social spending galvanized

171

this low-income household which, ironically, has built Jesse's career and identity as a community advocate. *Aida* and *Xavier* fled to Canada because of political violence and persecution. As refugees, they describe how racism in Ontario has deepened in the nineties, for themselves and the Spanish speaking community. Although they are targeted by citizens such as Christine and Dwight, or Rick and Denise, Aida and Xavier's analysis of discrimination concentrates on systemic forces rather than the actions or opinions of individuals.

Rick and Denise

Rick was a forty-three-year-old father of three teenagers and Denise was a thirty-nine-year-old mother of two teenage girls. Two of Rick's children, Johnny and Victoria (aged sixteen and fourteen years old) lived with Rick and Denise; the eldest son ran away from home and had been in and out of jail. Denise's two daughters, Kelly and Carol, were sixteen and thirteen years old. She won custody of her eldest daughter a year earlier, after the father had been negligent. Her ex-husband fled to British Columbia to avoid paying $400 of child support per month. All were white, of Scottish descent, and were born in Canada. Rick and Denise met in a subsidized apartment building and moved in together two years before the study started. The following year, they found a rented home around the corner. It was a small bungalow with a finished basement and a yard that housed their two dogs. Throughout the study, daily life was tumultuous for this family; neither Rick nor Denise was able to say if they would be together by the next round of interviews. The task of merging two families was a considerable strain, given that the mother of Rick's children had died only a few years previously and given that all the children were teenagers who wanted their own space. Rick worked in a unionized job in the transportation sector making $18.05 per hour. Denise had been working full-time as a support worker for a municipally funded community organization. Due to cutbacks and the restructuring of this sector her hours were cut from thirty-five to four hours a week.

At the time of the first interview, Rick worked six days a week to keep up with the bills, but he never earned enough. He brought home $500 per week, which covered some bills and groceries, but "by the time I get home I'm lucky to have $50 in my pocket." Denise's earnings covered her cigarette money. Rick described how this reality diverged from what he expected in life:

We don't drink. This just goes towards bills, the house, maintenance, food, the kids. We struggle. We're supposed to be a middle-class society here. I'm supposed to be a middle-class citizen but I feel more like a pauper than anything.

Rick's and Denise's jobs and income level had been directly affected by provincial policies. Both criticized how government and corporate interests were acting in concert, making things better for those who were already rich. At the same time, the "tough love" approach of the government policies appealed to them. Denise and Rick applauded welfare cutbacks, streamlining government and getting rid of the "fat cats," like teachers and school-board officials. Still, Rick was annoyed by governments that asked the public to tighten their belts, while businesses, such as Nike, bombarded kids through advertisements to buy $100 running shoes. In order to alleviate life stresses, this couple attempted to go out once a week, usually to see a movie on half-price Tuesdays. Many items were bought on sale, in bulk, and all their furniture was second-hand. To go out for a nice dinner downtown, Rick said he would have to save for a couple of months.

Rick had been at his job for eleven years and offered an informed analysis of how unions can protect workers' rights. He observed that if his work place had not been unionized the entire place would be staffed by part-time workers:

> With our union we have a stipulation that only so many part-time workers are allowed there. And after so many hours they are supposed to go on full-time. But that's all changed. By getting rid of Bill 40,[1] these part-timers that make $10 an hour have no chance of getting hired on full-time. Before, we were able to strike and they were not allowed to bring in scab labourers. Now they've wiped that out. The company can turn around and bring in labourers—it causes a fight between two people who shouldn't be fighting against each other. By eliminating Bill 40, the government puts them against each other.

At the time of the first interview Rick had two years left in his contract. In future contracts he did not think the union should ask for more money, but rather improve an already decent benefit package. He considered himself lucky. However, because of their up-and-down relationship, his benefits applied only to his own children, while Denise's children had no coverage. This arrangement remained the same throughout the course of the interviews: "One minute I'm leaving him, the next minute I'm staying," said Denise. Nevertheless, both saw themselves as relying solely on one another—"facing the world together." As Rick put it: "We don't get support from anyone and we don't give no support." This presentation of household isolation stood in contradiction to the new car Denise's parents had bought her and other forms of substantial outside support.

Rick expressed a great deal of anger about the world around him: student welfare, the *Young Offenders Act*, immigration policies, social assistance and the education system—all discriminated against the working poor—who, in his view, were white families. Student welfare was too easy to get and represented the excessive rights bestowed on children to the disadvantage of their parents. Rick and Denise had wanted to move north out of the city; however, the kids refused to go:

> The kids turn around (they know their rights), and say, "We'll leave home!" "Well, what are you going to do when you leave home?" "Don't worry about it—I'll just go and live with a friend. As long as I'm going to school the government will support me."

From Rick's perspective, the system discriminated against parents who were trying to discipline unruly kids. Based on his experience with his eldest son, he felt that kids knew exactly what they were up to; they needed to be punished as adults.

Denise and Rick were concerned for their children and their future job opportunities once they finished school. In their view, their children's vulnerabilities were due to the fact that

> A white Canadian male has less chance of getting a job no matter what kind of education he's got than anybody that walks into this country right now. The white Canadian male has a major problem. And that is not a racist statement, that is a fact.

The root of these problems, according to Rick, came from policies like pay and employment equity that discriminated against white males. A sense that things were going wrong and that he had little control underlaid much of his commentary.

At one moment, Rick would claim that he worried about everything; a few seconds later he would assert that he tried not to worry: "If I worry about all the things I have to do just to make this household exist from day to day, I'd have no hair on my head at all and I'd probably be a total nervous wreck." Rick was unable to save any money and felt that he needed to come to terms with the fact that he might never be able to. In attempting to understand his situation, Rick blamed immigrants and refugees:

> We have so many people out of work and yet they're [the immigration department] so free and so open to allow a 100,000 or 200,000 refugees or any kind of immigrant to come over to this country. To do what? Collect welfare. To stand in line for government to give them a house, to teach their kids English while our kids are not being taught properly. The welfare scam is so bad and it's happening with people who are coming from other countries. They have to stop the fraud. If you've got the right resources, you can make fortunes.

Rick believed that food banks should be closed. No one required them and no one should receive free food. Denise added that, "Young girls get pregnant for the sole purpose of being able to collect welfare some day. Some families should think about paying welfare back." This sentiment, however, did not seem to apply to her. Denise had collected welfare in the past when she had left an abusive relationship. For Rick, abused women were the only category of people who should be allowed to get any social assistance. The disabled had been living off the system for too long when they could easily work. It wasn't the poor or those on assistance who had been "squeezed," but rather working people like himself who were paying for government "over-spending."

At the time of the second interview tension was high. Rick's second son had just run away from home. A couple of weeks earlier, Denise had to have surgery for pre-cancerous cells. They were thinking seriously about living apart due to difficulties with the children; Rick's eldest son was encouraging his siblings to reject Denise. She wanted to go into counselling with Rick and the kids but he was steadfast against it. Denise had become discouraged about finding a better job. The children had also been looking for part-time jobs since the last interview. Rick went to working five days a week; however, the drop in income made things too financially tight and he returned to six days a week. At his work place, the number of part-time workers increased at a steady rate.

The education system did not escape their disapproval. The number of high-school expenses bothered both parents. When asked, Denise and Rick could not think of a single positive attribute of the public education system. Teachers were lazy and school board officials were overpaid. In fact, Denise recited a comment made earlier that week by Premier Harris that most teachers operated businesses on the side. Yet, later on, in the same interview, both described how every single teacher they had encountered thus far was dedicated, approachable and helpful to their own children. Denise said, "We've never had any problems communicating with teachers. They're great, they really are. And that's going down to kindergarten right up through. They're people, they're down-to-earth people, even the principals." Still Rick worried about the school's lack of accountability to parents and taxpayers generally and the possibility that his children might end up on welfare. Schools did not inform the parents enough about attendance and achievement. As Denise described,

I phoned up the other day to find out the attendance of my daughter, only to find out if she was skipping. Do you know they wouldn't give me that information because my daughter is sixteen.

Again, in the labour market, with social assistance and with the education system, Denise and Rick felt that white families were at a disadvantage. Indeed, according to Rick, the lack of discipline was found disproportionately in white families: he felt that immigrant families could still demand respect from their children.

By the third interview Rick's son had permanently moved out, refusing to follow the rules of the house. Denise went to write a test to get her general level English (Grade Twelve) so she could continue on with formal support worker training:

> They said I would have to take an exam and there was a $20 fee. I paid my $20 and failed. That was a disappointment, a big disappointment. I figure I'm forty now. By the time I'm going to get anything good, My God, I'll be ready to retire.

Soon after, however, Denise managed to get a part-time job, twenty hours a week, for $7.50 per hour under the table. For her it meant that "I'm buying groceries now and I'm paying the girls their allowance. Which means they have to get their chores done. I'm not daddy. I don't let things slide." Denise was quite excited by this change; yet, at the same time, she observed how she was competing with her own teenage daughters for the same kinds of jobs. At this time Rick was getting ready for a strike vote at work.

The final interview seemed to find Denise and Rick the most relaxed. Two daughters had found summer jobs, and, as Denise noted, "They're working as much as I am and they're making the same wage." The family was living in the same rented house, having failed to find new accommodation or to qualify for a mortgage. Some contact with the son who had moved out had begun. At Rick's place of work, they were locked out. The final contract banned overtime, included more part-time workers and a move to keep the company running twenty-four hours a day. He said, "There was a 100 percent strike vote, and then we were locked out. We lost so much, we might as well not have a union at all. They folded. They went and made a private deal on their own." With more part-time workers, Rick said he has trained more staff in the last few months than in the ten years of working there. In addition, the contract used to have a clause stipulating that if the owner hired anyone from part-time to full-time, or if he replaces a retired full-time worker, it must be at the full-time worker rate of $18 per hour. That wage rate was dropped to $15 an hour.

At the beginning of the interviews the children in this household were threatening to leave. By the end, they were threatening to stay:

> [Rick:] Your feelings are more important than anything. How stable you are in your life with your spouse. I never realized that until the last few years. [Denise:] Even the kids now are more secure. When I worked for the last three days, the three girls really missed me a lot. And they let me know that. They like me being here but I go, "Yeah, but nobody pays me."

Pam and Bert

Pam and Bert lived in northern Ontario with two sons, Steven and Michael (twenty-six and sixteen years old). The parents of this white middle-income family had Scottish ancestors; both children were born in Ontario. All members of the family participated in the interviews. They also shared chores, activities and decision making, which were parcelled out in a democratic fashion, with Pam as the driving force. Bert worked in the resource industry, making $50,000 per year, maintained their cars and had completely rebuilt their house. He had a thirty-two-year history at the company; over the course of the project, he was considering retirement. He was busy either helping friends and neighbours or having them return the favour. Bert did the plumbing for an elderly woman next door; in return, he said, "I usually get garden produce all summer long." Another member of the family was an elderly grandfather; they worked to make sure that he continued to be able to live on his own. Bert said, "We take him an extra meal every day, do maintenance on his house." After he had an eye operation, Pam and Bert's eldest son lived with him for six weeks.

Although this family experienced financial security, they kept abreast of, and were deeply affected by, provincial policy changes that targeted the poor, the health and education systems and the environment; provincial policy also created taxation increases. Pam had worked for a number of years as an assistant director of a community agency. Few policy changes occurred in her community that she did not notice and about which she did not notify others. In our first interview, she had been laid off due to provincial cutbacks and was collecting Employment Insurance benefits:

> We were getting budget cuts for the programs that I supplied, which meant that I would be telling staff that they would be laid off or have their hours cut. I went to the board. I wasn't feeling well. I really didn't feel that I should come back to work and they couldn't afford to pay me anyway, so why didn't they lay me off?

In the third interview Pam admitted that the pressure related to the first round of cuts in 1996 had affected her health. With the 22 percent cut to welfare in 1995, she saw, for the first time, that no amount of training, clever planning or cooking could sustain a family's health. Pam remained on a committee in town that examined issues of poverty in the area and kept busy running the household and doing volunteer work.

Bert, Steven and Michael played an array of sports; Bert also volunteered as a coach. As the study began, Steven was completing his second undergraduate degree in science, working hard to keep his marks up in the hopes of scholarships to graduate school. Michael, who was enrolled in French immersion and qualifying for a special applied science program, was finishing Grade Ten; he also played piano. The family had a camp outside the city and an income property. At the first interview, they confided that they did not keep a tight budget but were still able to buy what was needed. Before purchasing major items, they would sit down, discuss and decide on each one. A family clothing exchange with relatives enabled them to switch clothes and equipment for hockey and other sports back and forth.

The main concern for Bert at the time of the first interview, as he said, was whether "I was going to get back to work when I was on strike." Most of the first interview focused on his concerns about the labour market and the deteriorating conditions at work. A recent strike was affected by the changes to labour legislation that repealed Bill 7, a law that banned the use of strikebreakers and made it easier for unions to organize:

> The strike would still be going on if it wasn't for the company going over our heads for a court order and bringing in scab labour—the same thing that they did with another company I know. They had an employee list of 9,000 people and they replaced them in two years with scab labour. So that's what's going through our minds. We're on strike. Do we vote to get what we think we should get, or do we take a little bit and say we'd better not push any more because he's got Harris on his side. The government's sitting in his corner.

Bert noted how policies in relation to injured workers had also changed. After a serious neck injury at work, Bert decided to pay a chiropractor out of his own pocket every month rather than deal with Workers' Compensation: "It's a lot of hassles you know," he said. "The Board goes out of their way to discourage people from ever applying." Bert stated that the closer ties between business and government permeated all sectors of society.

He pondered the possibility of retiring once the strike was settled. Pam had serious concerns about their community, its fledgling economy and high unemployment rate:

> I would like to make a firm decision about where we are going to retire. Michael wants to stay another two years, and then he wants to leave. Steven may well be gone. We may be wiser to sell whatever we own, go rent and be ready to move.

Pam wanted some decisions to be made and long-term planning to be done, yet she recognized that

> Bert will continue to go around and talk to all the people. Like you know how he deals with a car issue. I have this problem with the car? Well he's doing that with retirement. He's talking to all the people that have retired—"How do you like it? How are things going?"

Both Pam and Bert listed the number of user fees that had been introduced at the municipal level: a new fee for taking things to the dump, increased sewer fees and water bills, ice fees at recreation centres, fees at the YMCA, and costs for playing hockey. Adult education classes were cut for those who most needed them. Cuts to the Ministry of Natural Resources meant that garbage was often left behind by people who fished and hunted in the area. Waste dumping by large companies was increasing in their community, because fewer inspections occurred. New assessments on properties in their region increased property taxes; however, the plummeting economy meant the market value of homes would drop below recent assessments. By increasing the value, "local government got around having a tax increase." At the time of the first interview, the idea of municipal amalgamations had been introduced. At the same time, Ontario Northern Grants were significantly cut. (Ontario Northern Grants are one of the ways northern communities are compensated for the extraction of resources and wealth that comes from these communities.)

These policy changes, specific to Northern communities, had major effects on people's everyday lives. A family friend on welfare had asked to borrow their wheelbarrow one day. Bert asked his son Michael why it was needed:

> He said, "They're moving." The mother and son moved everything they could possibly move with a wheelbarrow. I mean how much more humiliating can you get. So I said to Michael, "You tell her I will take one day and move all their big furniture."

By the second interview, the eldest son, Steven, had completed applications for graduate school. He lamented the rising costs of post-secondary tuition, which were exacerbated by living in northern Ontario:

> We have the highest tuition in the country, which is shocking because we live in the north. Only the middle class and the upper class now have the ability to send their children to school because of the cost. I couldn't believe the amount of monthly repayments.

Since his parents had put him through his first degree, Steven applied for one year of an Ontario student loan. Michael was in Grade Eleven at the time of the second interview; he complained about the student class sizes (forty or more), deteriorating equipment, fewer subject choices, the loss of teachers, due to cutbacks and an early retirement package, new school fees, less cleaning in the schools and a drop in extracurricular activities. The search for standards by the provincial government was viewed by Pam as a way to stream children and to bring in methods for saving money in the system. Pam explained, "There's more payment of fees for everything, for example, field trips. My sister had to send Kleenex, and you get your name off the list once you bring a box of Kleenex in." The cuts to education and the vilification of teachers angered members of this household. Pam decided to quit the parents' council at her son's school because,

> I didn't like their rules in Bill 160, where you aren't allowed to complain—you can complain in the system but not outside, in the public or tell your neighbours, go on TV or take a news piece to the newspaper.

At the second interview Bert was still working, although he was waiting for a possible buy-out as his company was going through another series of layoffs, while posting low profits. His fears about surviving financially after retirement seemed confirmed with more user fees and high local taxes. Pam was no longer receiving EI; she had picked up a few contracts. She said, "There are not a lot of jobs here and I would have to do computer training."

By the third interview, Steven had moved to southern Ontario to pursue graduate studies; his studies were funded by a scholarship, covering most of his costs. His parents moved him and paid for all the start-up costs of living in a new place. Bert had finally retired. This decision meant the household income dropped from $52,000 to $32,000. Bert's "retirement" resulted in a busier schedule for both parents. Because some unanticipated expenses arose, budgeting had to be more rigorous. Despite their meticulous calculations and "middle income," this household was not insulated from policy changes. Yet, at the same time, due to their investments and pension, options in relation to work and future projects were open to them. A future business with other relatives was in the early planning stage—"nothing too taxing but something that could keep interest alive and bring in a little more spending money."

By the final interview, Michael had found a summer job in a field in which he was interested. Bert claimed he would "like to go back to work to get a rest. I've reconditioned all my vehicles, I worked at camp and rebuilt this basement—insulated the walls and ceiling." Poppa (the grandfather) had broken some vertebrae in a fall since the last interview. Bert described this:

> Everybody gave him up for dead. He had about two months where he didn't do anything. I just went over and got him out of bed and fed him and got him up and bathed him and he'd sit and wait for the next meal. I spent two months doing that every day. We're retired and we've got a lot more time. Most people who are working two jobs with an elderly person, that elderly person might as well call the undertaker.

Although Poppa had home care, the hours the home care offered were of little help. Bert noted how his situation as a retired person allowed him to contribute in this way: however, this was also part of his family's commitment to the local community.

Jesse and Mark

Jesse and Mark were thirty-one and thirty years old and had been married for five years. Mark described himself as a mix of Native Canadian and French, and Jesse had a Scottish and Irish background. Both were born in Ontario. They lived in a house in northern Ontario that was formally owned by her parents, although they paid the "mortgage" and taxes and were responsible for the upkeep. Jesse's parents lived in another province; this arrangement made good financial sense for Jesse and Mark, who would not have be able to afford a house on their own. Mark's family lived close by. Jesse worked just short of full-time, while Mark ran a small business. Their combined annual income was around $25,000, which put them in the low-middle income category. This was a significantly better income than they had earned in earlier years when they were receiving social assistance and Jesse was a waitress: at that time they made $12,000 to $14,000 a year. Mark explained, "I started working and then she got full-time work; we got this house—her parents helped us with that big time—and, with the business taking an upswing, we've had this gradual movement up." The main issues in their interviews were about striving for income security and the stress of dealing with bills and creditors.

Mark was responsible for the majority of domestic duties: although he was happy to take on that role, it upset other family members. Their biggest expenses were the mortgage and insurance for the house and the car. The rest of their bills filled a file folder: most were final notices. They sometimes obtained goods through a barter-and-exchange system or through the generosity of family members. Because Mark had carpentry skills, they saved a lot of money by doing their own plumbing and renovations. Mark was a studious shopper who bought in bulk and kept a close eye on upcoming specials. He did most of the cooking, laundry, dishes and cleaning of the house, while Jesse, who worked outside of the home, helped out a little. She said, "I think that was one of the first things I told him on our first date, "I don't do housework, this will never change, don't get together expecting it to change."

While the cutbacks had a negative impact on this couple, they also significantly altered Jesse's personal identity and success. Ironically, she counted the election of the Conservative government as the main reason for her success. At the start of the study, Jesse had become a spokesperson for low-income issues. Yet, as she became a more forceful public figure, better employment opportunities came her way. She grappled with feeling both inside and outside of the low-income community, because her own situation had actually improved. Phone calls reached her home from people who had been cut off social assistance or who were having problems with their social workers or with filing citizenship claims. Being able to access support was the main factor that helped these people handle the stress of such situations. Jesse said, "That is one of the things we are really aware of, that as much as we're low-income, we have good family support, we don't have kids, so we were in the easiest position to go through hard times." Both called their parents if something good or bad happened in their lives. Jesse said, "I realized I was calling them only when something bad was happening, so I changed that." Their Christian faith, which was part of their daily lives, also pulled them through difficult times.

Jesse was galvanized into action in 1995 before the Harris government came to power when she first saw him on TV:

> After struggling to get work, he [Premier Harris] was saying, "We'll put those lazy bums to work," and we started talking to people about what he was saying, and I just got terrified. So we were talking to everybody, and then he came in, and the first thing he did was that 21.6 percent [social assistance] cut. And a bunch of low-income people got together because we noticed there were people fighting for us, there were people fighting against us, but nobody was really hearing from us. The women's march on poverty wanted someone who would be willing to be identified as low-income and most people weren't. I went ahead and did an interview, and they took my picture.

In the meantime, Mark struggled with his small craft business. He started up a support group for people who run businesses to exchange ideas and experiences.

One of the daily worries for Jesse was the depression of people targeted by the above social assistance cut and the constantly growing host of regulations:

> They look at me and say, now they want to fingerprint me, and now they want to take my house, and the worst thing than any of the cuts is that they are excusing the cuts by calling people down, calling them lazy. I tell them it's a lie, and they are lying for a reason.

The idea of putting a lien on homes was just another punishing move that made no sense to Jesse:

> I really don't understand this. How is this incentive to get off welfare? You've lost your home or you are going to have to pay back any assistance you get. I mean a lot of people end up on assistance because of debt load.

Mark noted that these policies were joined by a rise in racism, especially between older immigrants and new immigrants in his community. Cuts to Northern Grants was another major local issue:

> A lot of the resources are taken out of this area and a lot of the wealth for Ontario comes from this area. And so one of the ways they compensated for this was through Northern Grants. We need them for health care, we have to go to Toronto sometimes, then there is our weather and the shape of our roads.

After the first interview, Jesse decided to run for municipal office. At the second interview, she talked about the campaign. She did not win and was disappointed that people she met through door-to-door canvassing did not come out to vote. Mark commented,

> When you're low-income for a long time you already have a sense of powerlessness. You already feel like, "I can't do anything, how am I going to change anything by going out to vote?" [Jesse:] I try and tell people they have polls, they know you don't vote. They don't consider you. They look at polls and say better watch that public housing issue, they show up to vote. Better watch that women's issue, they show up to vote!

Jesse picked up another contract. With the two part-time jobs, she was working forty-nine hours a week. Both jobs were flexible; one of them allowed her to work at home on a computer that had been recently purchased through a work budget and with help from Mark's parents. Mark decided to close his business: he decided there was no market for his product. He became preoccupied with getting out of debt. At home every day, he was harassed by creditors calling about their student loans ($6,000 each). The phone calls continued, along with threats to take their house and vehicle. When Jesse got the second contract, they hoped to be able to start paying some bills. Mark said, "Thank god she got that other contract, without that other contract.... It's just been day to day. With her income we can start trying to pay some of the bills, we're just squeaking by as it is." Both resented the fact that their post-secondary education had done so little to help them secure well-paid jobs.

The main focus of the third interview was Mark's health crisis. Mark had found a job in the service sector. After a week of training he experienced severe pains in his leg as a result of blood clots. Mark had to be taken to the emergency department of a hospital; he was released on a regime of needles and medication to control the problem. However, the drugs cost $150 per month. Although Jesse's income with the two jobs brought in over $40,000, she had no benefits. Their own research, however, brought the costs down to $50 per month. Given the shortage of doctors in the north, dissatisfaction with any health care providers is difficult to resolve. Mark suggested that

You've got to be more pro-active. Don't just take the word of one doctor, insist on care, and, if you are not getting a response from your doctor or your hospital, call your MP, start talking to people, let people know what is going on.

Debt, student loans, the health care system and the environment remained areas of concern. Jesse warned, "And, with the cuts, we have one government official to monitor our air, our water, all of our environment stuff. We used to have twenty-six. We now have one that monitors everything."

By the fourth interview Mark no longer needed to take his medication, and Jesse's jobs continued to bring in a fair income. They had concentrated on paying bills; however, because of the student debt, Jesse's wages had been garnisheed. Their plan was to be debt-free in eighteen months so they would only be left with paying the mortgage. Mark continued to produce art, while managing the household. Jesse contributed $300 every two weeks for the running of the household and the car:

In this way it does not become about Mark asking me for money, because before he didn't know where he stood with bills and stuff, so in splitting it this way he has control over the amount of budgeting, and, if he has extra, he would know it. He makes his choices, and then it also prioritized putting money aside for us to live.

The house remained in Jesse's parents' name as a precaution in a community where unemployment was high and investigations into the past of applicants for welfare assistance continued. In the past, Mark had received social assistance; after they graduated from school, both had received Employment Insurance and then social assistance. If Jesse lost her jobs or Mark became seriously ill, they wondered how soon it would be before their house was taken from them?

Jesse talked about a number of new projects at work, which were taking up more time. Although her income had significantly increased, she felt that she still had legitimacy in speaking on issues of poverty and marginalization. As the "breadwinner," she instituted mechanisms so that Mark would feel more independent and productive. Both continued to be their own best support. Jessie explained, "A couple of years ago we made a conscious choice that when things are tight financially, we're not picking at each other and that's it." Their spirituality remained a source of support when things got tough.

Christine and Dwight

Dwight worked for a local community newspaper; at the time of the first interview, he had recently opened a small business on the side. Christine ran a day-care centre out of their modest home on a quiet street. She had a certificate in early childhood education; when we first spoke in 1997, she was in the second year of a part-time university degree. While Christine and Dwight were taking steps to improve their financial situation over the long term, their incomes were rarely enough to meet their current expenses.

Christine grew up in the Toronto area. She and her husband moved to their current home in the early 1990s. The location and size of their community was central to how they organized and described their daily activities. An injury caused Dwight to switch careers from one involving heavy lifting to journalism. Christine began working as a day-care provider when her son was very small. When they moved, she had to work hard to gain the trust of local residents as a child-care provider. Nevertheless, the town soon became home to Christine and Dwight, and both were actively involved in local volunteer initiatives. Eli, their teenage son, volunteered as well. Christine explained that "Eli needs to learn early that when you live in a community, you give back to your community." Dwight and Christine's family was a white middle-income one: Dwight earned about $20,000 a year and had benefits, while Christine averaged about $28,000 a year and was considered self-employed. Christine managed household finances and kept to a tight budget. Because day-care children came to her home, she prioritized their food costs. Christine routinely exchanged goods and services for child care as a way to make ends meet. She explained that her veterinary care came in exchange for child care: "Sometimes the vet would pick up an extra day at work, so rather than charge her extra for the extra day of child care, she would owe me for rabies vaccines for the dogs."

Christine was able to use interpersonal relations in a small community to ease some of the burden of her living expenses. Her van was an expensive but crucial part of her job. Living in a small town that had no public transportation, while caring for young children who must travel together, meant that maintaining a vehicle was a necessity. She explained that her mechanic was allowing her to pay in installments for van repairs:

> This is the advantage of living in a small town. Our mechanic has been letting me make payments. So $500 a month has been going to him, which has meant that I haven't been able to pay some of my other bills.

Christine and Dwight received some financial support from their parents. Over the three years of the study, Christine's mother helped her to pay her tuition and contributed to school trips for Eli. Dwight's mother bought most of Eli's clothes and covered some major purchases for the household.

Since the first interview, Christine had been concerned about education and services related to education in her region. Eli started high school in 2000. While she worried that Eli would not get a quality education,

Christine's response to the changes in public education was mixed. She supported the teachers' work stoppage in 1998, but told us in the first round of interviews that she agreed with cutting the bureaucracy in education and in standardizing curriculums across the province. "If our previous governments weren't handing out money like water, we maybe wouldn't be as badly off as we are now," she said. Christine was alarmed at the size of her son's classes, the lack of resources, such as textbooks, and the poor infrastructure at his school. In 1998 Eli was selling chocolate bars in order to buy music books. Eli was in cadets and in French Immersion. Because Christine was herself pursuing a post-secondary degree, she knew how much a university education costs. Her hope was that, if Eli were to continue in the military, his education costs would be met. Christine was angry about the rising costs of tuition and the effect this had on her own education. In 1997 she was told she could no longer receive student assistance (OSAP) and could only get Canada Student Loans. Her debt load continued to mount as tuition escalated each year. Yet, throughout the time of the study, she remained convinced that completing a university degree would afford her new opportunities and improve her financial future.

Both personally and professionally, Christine was concerned about directions in child-care services in the province. At the time of the first interview, she had been working as a child-care provider for twelve years:

I started when Eli was a year old, initially so I could be at home with him. There were times, when I have needed money, that I started work Monday morning at 7:00 a.m. and finished Friday night at 9:00 p.m. I did overnight care. I had to do that to pay the bills. Currently, I start work at 7:00 a.m. and finish at 6:00 p.m.

Her pay scale did not increase over time. In a later interview Christine argued that she was not recognized as a professional, even though she was trained to educate young children:

If you look at the hierarchy, we have university professors, high-school teachers, elementary school teachers, day-care centre workers and then there's the lowly day-care provider. I'm an ECE [Early Childhood Educator] but nobody would recognize that if I wanted a job as a supervisor in a day care. I have done fourteen years of quality programmed day care, and I am [seen] as a babysitter.

Christine viewed this as a blatant example of gender discrimination.

When it came to the issue of social assistance, Christine's gender analysis took a different turn. She compared her "middle-class" decision to have one child to the choices made by women on welfare:

So we stopped at one because we thought, you know, we couldn't afford it.

People who don't have a job, and there's nothing out there, why are you having another four kids. You know, I appreciate just because you're on welfare doesn't mean you shouldn't have a cigarette or a drink every now and then or you shouldn't have a child.

Her opinions about children in society generally shifted from discussions about sexuality to foreign aid. While Christine would be comfortable with a friend of Eli's who was the child of a same-sex couple, she stated, however, that "Our society isn't quite ready for same-sex marriage or same-sex adoption." As in most of her interview, Christine described the benefits of living in a small community, yet continually referred to "the many rednecks we have here." Christine felt that the problem of poverty in Ontario stems from policies that do not prioritize our "own children," but give money to "foreign causes," such as Save the Children, instead.

Christine took the matter of day care to her MPP. When the provincial government announced that it was including single mothers receiving social assistance into the Ontario Works program, the need for provincially funded child care became apparent. Christine had many concerns about the further deregulation of child care and what it would mean both for women who were providing care and the quality of care for children:

I went to my MPP, and I told him about the people who come to see me who say, "We like what you're offering, but we can't afford your price. Would you charge us less if we didn't get a receipt?" Of course I tell them no, because I don't operate without receipts. But where are they going? If they can't afford what I'm charging, they are forced to go to somebody else. There are people out there with ten, fifteen kids in their homes.

Since 1994, Christine had been embroiled in a pay equity case with a regional day-care placement agency. In 1996, a judgement was made in her favour. The region appealed it. By the time of the last interview, a decision was still pending, and Christine's financial resources were depleted. Her hope for equity for child-care workers was dwindling.[2] Christine explained:

We're currently involved in hearings which I felt were going very well, when the Minister snuck her legislation in denying home child-care providers rights for pay equity. She introduced the legislation on a Tuesday. On Wednesday I show up for my hearing, and lo, to my bewildered ears, do I hear the county went and asked for the case to be quashed because there was a clause in Bill 136 that denied home child-care providers the right to even inquire into pay equity, back-dated to 1988.

She explained that the cards were stacked against her, and she felt that she had no voice as a citizen:

It's never been a level playing field and it never will be. But I thought that I was at least going to get my right to due process and justice, and the government has pulled that.... I figured I was going to have the right to finish my case and see it through. You can't win fair because the people with power just change the rules. I have no power, I'm one lousy little day-care provider so what do they care if I'm not happy?

Bill 136 was a substantial and controversial piece of legislation. Public sector unions threatened a walkout and demanded consultations on the bill. Christine managed to rally a number of forces together and insisted on being part of the expanded consultations on Bill 136:

I wrote to the Minister of Labour.... I put a complaint in with the ombudsman office, I wrote to the Lieutenant Governor.... No one called me.... I find out in the *Toronto Star* that there are consultations.... That was the first time I ever got nasty. I said to my MPP: "I don't [care] how many people want input, I wrote to the Minister back in June demanding consultation. I want to be part of these hearings."

The clause about pay equity for day-care workers in Bill 136 was eventually taken out. Christine reflected on her role in effecting this change:

I felt really good about it after because I really do think that if nobody had noticed that [part of the] legislation, it would have gone through. Bill 136 was so huge, and people were reacting to so many things in it. That's the biggest thing I am finding: I'm having trouble getting help and support because there's just so much crap happening that people can only do so much at one time.

Christine switched parties in the next election, deciding to support the NDP instead of the Conservatives, while her husband remained an avid Reform Party supporter.

Despite her victories over the years, Christine was not optimistic. In our last interview she despaired, "Whether I win or lose, they will appeal. There's no way I can hope to pay a lawyer. I'm just tired of fighting." Her hope was that her attempt for equity would be picked up by others and that it would change the provision of child-care services in the province. She remarked,

There is something fundamentally wrong when you live in a country that allows child-care providers to make less than $2 an hour. I'm just hopeful that should my son have a daughter some day and should she decide to do this, she will at least be compensated a fair wage.

The strain of insufficient income, no holidays, court cases, long hours and increasingly differing priorities brought on a bout of depression and a dramatic weight loss for Christine, and ultimately caused a breakdown in her marriage. In 1999, Christine and Dwight separated for several months. Christine stopped most of her volunteer work because she was overwhelmed with trying to pay for and manage school, work her job, fight her court case and find energy for her family. During their separation, Christine left the small community in which they lived. Reflecting on what had happened she observed, "I think we were just too busy trying to have the middle-class dream. We wanted to own a house, have this and that, and we never took any time." Christine has since returned to Dwight; they are trying to work through their differences and rebuild her day-care business and their future as a family.

Aida and Xavier

Aida and Xavier came to Canada with their three children as refugees from Latin America. Xavier worked in construction and Aida was in the social service field. They owned a small home in the greater Toronto area and earned about $35,000 a year. When the study ended, their eldest daughter had recently married; the younger daughter had finished university and was working and living with them; and their son was in jail serving the last part of an almost two-year sentence. Jorge Luís, their son, was diagnosed with a life-threatening health condition which resulted in erratic and destructive behaviour.

When we first met, Aida's main concern was getting enough income from jobs. Upon her arrival in Canada, she took a small job at a local school and cleaned churches. She enrolled in college to gain Canadian credentials and, because of her background in social services, trained as a community worker. She was hired with a not-for-profit agency in the mid-1990s, right before many of the cuts to the sector came into effect. By 1997, her hours had been reduced at both her school and agency jobs. She explained that she felt that her employers had taken advantage of her:

> One year ago, [at the school] they simply took two days off of my work. I went from twelve hours a week, to eight hours a week, to four hours a week, two hours per shift. This is sixteen hours per month.... At my job as a community worker, I feel that they are taking advantage of us. It is a program that has a high budget, where two or three people get a fabulous salary of over $50,000, and they contract with us—five women who speak different languages—so that we can give the service in our language. They only pay us for fourteen hours a week, but I work thirty.

Aida feared that, because she was outspoken, she would be targeted for further reductions. Aida's job extended far beyond home visits. She accompanied clients to the hospital and to visit doctors; she also translated for parents in schools. Aida continued to look for other work but explained that the positions that were available in her field offered the same working conditions and insecurity as her job with the not-for-profit. Aida wanted to train to do more specialized work. She said, "I would like to become more specialized in working with at-risk children so that I can have more secure work. The problem is financial. The course is expensive. I do not want to take on more debt." Aida's household struggled to meet its expenses, since debt level far outweighed income. The OSAP debt was of particular concern to Aida; her daughters were also in debt, and she worried that "children are born with debtload now." In 1998, she said:

> We always have tremendous concerns, both my daughter and I, about OSAP. My situation right now is really bad, I can only pay $100 a month. The interest rises, rises and rises, and so I still owe them $5,000 for my diploma in Community Work.

Despite her financial concerns, she was devoted to the clients with whom she worked. Over the three years of interviews, she explained that changes in provincial spending in social services had dramatically affected the poorest and most marginal people, many of whom were clients of hers:

> Many of the problems that we experience are because of racism. Especially in my work with Spanish-speaking peoples. I have to fight twice as hard to get them services which they are entitled to and worthy of. At first try, I always hear no.

In early 1998, she explained that the combined effects of cuts in social assistance payments and the *Tenant Protection Act* (1997) were having a brutal consequences on young mothers:

> You see the abuse. Especially of poor people who do not know where to complain. Every time the landlord decides to do repairs and it does not work, the people have to pay the consequences. Nobody stops paying their $714 of rent for a dirty place. $714 for one bedroom. It is abusive because they receive money and do not provide a good service. If a poor person does not pay, she is out. Before, the person could appeal and explain the situation or negotiate.

In 1999, Aida said that the situation for poor families, particularly for single mothers, was desperate:

> It is very bad. They are left with empty refrigerators. Nothing to eat. I have to look for food in the food banks for them or find coupons for baby formula for

them. What happens is that I work with mothers that don't have rights to baby bonus because they still haven't gotten their papers. I see many more people without a home. Young people and families that simply are evicted and I have to look for family motels.

Aida and Xavier's family experienced a major crisis in early 1998. Their son, Jorge Luís (age twenty), developed a severe and life-threatening thyroid disorder that manifested, before diagnosis, in extremely erratic behaviour. Aida explained: "The thyroid poisons the body and creates a psychotic state much like schizophrenia. He had paranoia. He had psychotic episodes. He would have delusions of persecution." Jorge committed vandalism and uttered threats, and was charged and sent to jail. Trying to help Jorge led to encounters with the health care and the judicial systems. The family spent large amounts of money on legal fees ($5000), psychiatric assessments ($3500) and Jorge's prescription drugs. Jorge was held in a placement centre for over a month, before he was placed in an appropriate facility. In response to her concerns about the length of time he was detained there, Aida was told, "Oh, there is a backlog," or "Oh, we are behind." She said, "His health deteriorated and I felt powerless to get him the care that he so badly needed." Aida fell into a deep depression while battling the health and criminal justice systems.

During his arrest, Jorge Luís was beaten up by the police. The family wanted to pursue the matter, but their lawyer, whom they subsequently fired, insisted that it would work against Jorge's case. He cited statistics that said that those who complain about the police serve longer sentences. Jorge had applied for legal aid but was turned down because he had worked for his father. Aida said:

When Xavier asked the lawyer to give him advice on how to denounce the police that beat him [Jorge Luís] he was told, "Oh, no, no, no don't do it." He [the lawyer] said it was going to slow down the process; he said he wanted to defend my son. He told us "If you don't want Jorge Luís to be in danger don't do it." We believed him.

The conditions in the classification facility were poor, and the backlog for processing cases was long. Despite all of her and Jorge's medical specialist's attempts to get Jorge proper care, his health deteriorated. Aida lamented that he was made to sleep on the floor:

With the thyroid problem it hurts him a lot. Well, the doctor recommended that we give him a bed so his muscles won't bother him. But they have him thrown on the floor like a dog. That is my impotence. We struggled a lot along with the doctors to keep him healthy, to come to this.

Aida tried to get the jail to understand his medical needs, as she believed that any further aggravation of his condition would kill him. Jorge Luís' health did not improve quickly. In late 1998, he had been on a waiting list for chemotherapy for six months. Aida had a very difficult time coping with these events in their lives. She spent most of her time seeking information, both about the disease and about the law and legal matters. She was unable to let others know that her son was in jail; her sense of belonging in her community would be compromised, she believed, if she told anyone. She said that they tell people that Jorge Luís has gotten a scholarship to Cuba. "It hurts me not being able to talk about it," she said. "The judge put the whole family in jail. He condemned us all." She explained that she isolated herself so as not to have to lie to people about her son.

The stress took a huge toll on her and her family. For almost a year, she did not tell her mother, who lived in Latin America, what was happening. Aida stopped sleeping and was prescribed antidepressants, which she only took for a brief period because she hated their effect on her. She began to see a counsellor in order to deal with the strain of working her way through the legal and medical systems:

Maybe all this we have gone through has helped me be stronger, because I know there are worse things than what is happening to me right now. You have to develop courage. The thing with the big challenges in life is that either you get through them or you go crazy. You have to overcome them in some way. It's important for me to have a healthy mental state so that I will overcome this because there are many who depend on me. You have to look for a balance. My life has never been very pleasant. It has been hard. It hasn't been easy. I've had to escape from criminals and move from country to country with little babies.

Aida said that the fact that the police in Canada beat Jorge Luís confirms her life's experience:

Now look what happened to Jorge. We have always told him that Canada is a civilized country and the police are here to safeguard public security. Not to torture, not to beat. And he turned himself in peacefully to the police. And look at what happened to him! There is repression but not the same degree as in our countries. But this happened to worst possible person. Imagine, for us to go through this with the hate we feel for people in uniform, to know how they act and it happens to our son. And that's why Jorge Luís is so scared. It's that these people live in a kingdom and no one can do anything. No one. That is the feeling Jorge has now.

By mid 1999, Jorge had spent several months in an approved facility. Aida was calmer, but was still trying to get Jorge out early. The crisis with

Jorge Luís overshadowed all else in their lives for 1998 and 1999. Aida mentioned in passing that her hours had increased to four days a week and that she was now receiving some minimal benefits at work. Education and health care were still serious concerns, but her energy remained focused on the judicial system. In 1999, Aida's eldest daughter got married. Since her mother came to the wedding, she was forced to tell her about Jorge Luís; this was an enormous relief. She said:

> It's been very hard for her to find out about Jorge Luís. I had lied to her. I told her Jorge Luís was abusing drugs and, because his problem was so serious, had to be put in rehabilitation. To make the thing softer. But, when she wanted to see him I told her it was more than that. Well, she went to see him. She is very good, very spiritual, a very intelligent woman, very incredible. She even taught Jorge Luís how to meditate. She said, "If you want to accelerate going back home, when you meditate try to transport yourself home. Imagine everything, the door, go in."

Discussion

- What kind of explanations do people employ to account for increasing pressures or demands on their households?
- When experiences and beliefs/opinions clash, what does this tell us about the significance of "public opinion" and the formation of subjectivity?
- While discriminatory views are rampant, how are racist, sexist and homophobic stereotypes reinforced by public policies?
- How can "experience" and its interpretation lead to social change?

As demonstrated in Chapter Seven, what happens to individuals is intertwined with events in the lives of other household members as well as those of extended family, friends and community. However, events do not just happen: their effects, meanings and significance get interpreted and evaluated by household members. Interpretations and explanations are built on ideas, discourses and images prevalent in a variety of "discursive fields." Contained in these fields are the operation and influence of language, social institutions, subjectivity and power.

    The household narrative of Rick and Denise presents an important challenge to theories about the relationship between experience and opinions/beliefs. Although their income level decreased and Rick lamented the loss of union power, racist sentiments about immigrants and welfare recipients frame their concerns. "Outsiders" accessing public provisions are felt to be the source of many of the problems this household faced. Denise and Rick believe that cuts to social assistance and social housing are necessary, in spite of their own reliance on both. Razack describes how during the 1990s many Canadians, considering themselves as the "original citizens," adopted the racial "story of a nation besieged and betrayed" (2000). The loss of the white, middle-class dream for many households and a growing sense of isolation (as is the case for Rick and Denise) become linked to the arrival and presence of new immigrants and refugees in the community. Rick and Denise's household embraces an identity of isolation, in order to portray themselves as "victims" of racism, surrounded by people of colour who are fraudulently benefiting from public provisions. The immigrant narrative continues to disavow the presence and labour of First Nations people and people of colour whose labour contributed significantly to the development of Canada.

Rick's class analysis of the labour market and the role of unions is underpinned by racist views. The change from full-time to part-time work and the consequences for wages and hours at his work place are quite evident to him. He describes how the increased power of business is supported by a political rhetoric of "restructuring" in a globalized economy. Still, according to him, it is primarily the white male who is disadvantaged in these new arrangements. Denise is outraged about a factory job she started through a temporary agency. She is shocked to find that she is the only white worker in the entire place. While recognizing that it is a terrible job (she left after two days), she is unable to see how immigrants of colour are being exploited. Instead, she sees the injustice as the racial isolation she feels in a "Canadian work place."

Unlike Rick and Denise, Bert and Pam do not see themselves as an isolated couple battling the world. They are engaged with others; they have integrated a range of experiences into their own analyses. Financially, they have options unavailable to Rick and Denise and a secure family life. The discursive field that provides meaning for their experiences and identity comes out of where they are located—in northern Ontario. A weak regional resource-based economy with fewer health care options and serious environmental concerns affects their choices for the future.

Jesse and Mark live in a community feeling the effects of changing socio-economic policies; this leads to considerable activism on the part of Jesse. This couple makes informed choices about the organization of unpaid and paid labour in their lives. Nevertheless, the reversal of the breadwinner role is complex. Even though Mark says he is comfortable with staying at home, both go to great lengths to ensure that he does not feel powerless. While the disapproval they encounter from some family members is hurtful, they do not isolate themselves from the concerns of the larger community. They are aware of what is happening around them and try to get others to be proactive. At the same time, as a household, despite careful budgeting, the debt they carry causes considerable stress. Mark took up a small entrepreneurial endeavour, a model much encouraged in recent labour policy. Mark's experience raises questions about the feasibility of this model as a training route, in an economy where small businesses have a high failure rate. Jesse easily connects local issues to broader policy changes but finds that most of her neighbours remain disengaged. Her work allows her to develop these critical skills and perspectives. Thus, among the participants described in this chapter, it is Jesse who seems to be the exception. This gives rise to questions about the conditions necessary for people to engage in community issues and those that result in their inability to make connections (Reitsma-Street 2000). A great many participants in this study commented on the scope and speed of changes that quickly became too overwhelming to deal with.

Christine is consumed with her pay-equity fight. Her identity as child-care provider fuels her sense of outrage and her commitment to a long-term political battle. She views this issue as a critical example of how gender discrimination occurs in the province. Her location in a small town allows her to barter with neighbours and friends, making it, ostensibly, an easier place to live than in a large urban centre. Yet, when attempting to reconcile a number of political issues in her mind, whether welfare reform or same-sex marriage, Christine constantly refers to the "rednecks" or right-wing element in her same small town. In part, this is a strategy to help her find a way through her own conflicted location and beliefs on a number of issues. To her, having only one child was a middle-class decision that makes her more respectable than women with more children who are receiving social assistance. She replicates a discursive strategy in which judgements about women's reproduction and sexuality are made when discussions turn to social assistance benefits. At the same time, she complains that her child-care business garners little respect because of its gendered nature. Accumulated pressures eventually become too much for their marriage and the couple separate. Like Rick, Christine laments the loss of an identity—the white middle-class dream—while her husband feels displaced by new immigrants.

Aida describes the everyday racism that her Spanish-speaking clients face. In many ways, like Jesse, she is an advocate in the system, yet she does not receive the same kinds of rewards or recognition for this role. She speaks of having to work twice as hard to assist clients, in a work place that offers minimal contracts to her and the other women who together provide a service in five different languages! Aida notes how racism operates across policy areas, such as education, housing and social assistance. She is familiar with, and is targeted by, discourses of blame that view refugees and immigrants as perpetually problematic. And while she analyzes and critiques these views as systemic problems, it is not in a distant or removed fashion. Although a strong advocate, Aida's own identity as a refugee and survivor of political persecution incapacitates her when it comes to her son's experience with police brutality and the judicial system. Aida cannot face her own community, or family, and instead retreats and isolates herself, until her mother provides some much-needed comfort.

All of these households were in the same province, at the same moment in history and subject to the same range of social policies. However, there is a vast range of interpretations about what was happening to them and to those around them. Their stories suggest how experience is constructed, relying on numerous discursive fields that range from one's own identity and network to social policies and their accompanying discourses. Although one may experience the effects of changing labour-market policies, blaming immigrants and refugees reconfigures that event. Ideologies or discourses reorder experience in ways that may directly contradict the empirical outcome of any one policy. Because the way people interpret and then communicate any narrative is both complex and contradictory, documenting experience is much more than eliciting "evidence" from research participants.

Notes

1. In November 1995, Bill 7, the *Labour Relations and Employment Statute Amendment Act*, replaced Bill 40. It withdrew anti-scab provisions and altered the rules governing union certification and decertification.

2. In 1997, the provincial government introduced Bill 136, the *Public Sector Transition Stability Act* (see Ontario 1997, Public Sector Dispute Resolution Act and Ontario 1997, *Public Sector Labour Relations Transition Act*), which aimed to freeze collective bargaining for many public sector workers and enable the government to downsize and reorganize health, education and social service sectors. Part of this bill was a clause stating that day-care providers could not seek pay equity. Christine fought hard to have it removed.

Chapter Nine

Developing Methodology
that Can Deal with Complexity

What we cannot imagine, cannot come into being. (hooks 2000: 14)

The preceding chapters documented the differing ways that the inter related and cumulative effects of policies shaped options available to members of households. Understanding how policies affected people's daily lives meant seeing participants as individuals who were also members of households, who identified with diverse communities and who, as citizens, were engaged with a variety of social issues. Furthermore, participants were providers as well as users of services. They were taxpayers, as well as consumers, striving to acquire resources to sustain a meaningful quality of life for themselves and their dependents. This final chapter considers the implications of this research approach for the study of public policy.

Capturing the meaning of experiences to research participants is an undertaking riddled with questions about the validity of data interpretation. Since participants were chosen for their diversity, their social realities differed. Reflecting this diversity accurately was an ongoing challenge in the reports issued while the study was underway and during the writing of this book. In both fora, we have made extensive use of quotes to capture the language participants employed to describe and explain their experiences. This approach also gives readers the opportunity to make their assessments of participants' accounts.[1] We knew from casual conversation that participants talked with their families and friends about the research and their part in it. The narratives told in these settings undoubtedly differed from those they shared with us as researchers. We, in turn, heard and interpreted what was being spoken from the standpoint of policy analysts. All these narratives reflect aspects of participants' social reality; however, different audiences influence both the content of the story and the language used to convey it. Accordingly, it is as part of an audience of students of social policy that the authors of this book take up some of what was said and heard.

The first part of the chapter focuses on several aspects of the methodology used in the "Speaking Out" project, the research upon which the analysis in this book was built. In this section we argue that a concept of household defined by meaningful relationships, in-depth interviewing in areas determined by participants, a panel approach to data gathering and a sampling template reflecting social location were essential ingredients to a methodology that allowed us to gather the type of data that revealed how the cumulative and interactive dynamics of policy operate differentially within a society. Some aspects of these processes were highlighted in the policy reports released during the time of the study (1997 to 2000). In this book, the potential of this methodology is realized more fully than was possible in the periodic reports. The methodology enabled us to explore the themes in the preceding chapters. In the second part of the chapter, we argue that the types of data gathered by such a methodology opens up possibilities for policy analysts to explore questions emerging in current policy debates; namely, issues of identity, social exclusion, expanded understandings of work, changing patterns of employment in a globalized economy, caring responsibilities and changing rights and entitlements of citizenship.

A Research Strategy to Document Change

Traditional policy analysis ranges from focusing on predicting policy outcomes to assessing the ways in which institutions are responsible for certain policy outputs in particular policy sectors during specific temporal periods. Another approach focuses on the role of ideas: how they shape worldviews, articulate our interests, form associations and devise courses of political action (Manzer 1994: 6). How people experience policies in their everyday world often remains peripheral to these models. By beginning from the perspective of those who participated in our study, we were able to explore how people lived and how they interpreted their relationships to social policy. Tracking the cumulative and compounding impacts of multiple policy changes was built into the design of the study. In each interview, through a series of benchmark and specific policy questions, participants described how they were affected by policy changes, their interactions with a variety of government agencies and other institutions and the ideas that helped shape their worldviews. Our narrative-based approach permitted us to discern how policies operated within and across forty very diverse households, in a multiple, compounding and cumulative fashion. By "multiple," we mean the sheer volume of policies and policy changes that affected the daily lives of household members. "Compounding" refers to how these policies interact with one another, often cancelling out positive effects and unduly complicating the lives of participants. And finally, the "cumulative" effect speaks to the collective impact of cutbacks, policy and regulation changes and the speed of legislative change[2] over the three years of the project.

This documentation of change would not have been possible if data were collected at any one point rather than four times over three years. A cross-sectional study asking participants about past experiences would have resulted in a different set of narratives because people do reinterpret experience in the light of change. Documenting what changes and what does not is best revealed through data using a panel design. Charts 1, 2 and 3 in the Appendix capture this dynamic, showing that, although economic mobility for this sample was backward as well as forward, short-term ups and downs cancelled each other out. Indeed, it was the capacity to track change that allowed us to document just how little improvement there was over three years in the circumstances of most households. Apparent gains, such as getting a job, were often quite deceiving. Similarly, a constant focus on single policy areas would not have unveiled how each area operates within other policy jurisdictions. It would also have masked the resulting strain on households, and it would not have exposed the effects on participants of having to interact with a battery of professionals and bureaucrats.

Expanding the Concept of Household

The basic unit of analysis with which we worked was the household, the unit within which most Canadians live. Thinking of households as units for living, units that change and units where individuals mix with others is important in policy analysis. Studies frequently reproduce a category of family into which many people simply do not fit (Dua 1999; *Toronto Star* 2003).[3] In the 1996 census, family was defined as a married or common-law opposite-sex couple with or without children, or a lone-parent of any marital status with at least one child (Statistics Canada 1996: 119).[4] Our definition of household more accurately reflected how people live; we defined it as one or more people sharing living space on a regular basis, where adult members share some resources and some degree of commitment to the relationship.[5] Such a definition allowed us to include households of extended kin, three-generation households, single parents, individuals, two-parent households, same-sex partnerships and close friends. This approach made it essential to document household changes over time, as relationships began and ended or people moved or became ill. Whenever possible, we followed individuals like Ashley and Rosa through household changes.

Mapping the daily operations of relationships means challenging what constitutes categories of "household income," "family income," "household expenses," "caregiving" and the "division of household labour." Thus, the Statistics Canada definition of family income could not be applied to some participants in our sample, whereas the broader classification of household income could be applied (Statistics Canada 1996: 141). Nevertheless, the ongoing changes in households and the number of relationships upon which they depended and which they supported would have remained masked by these categories. While predetermined categories necessarily erase these fluid arrangements in order to aggregate information, our definition of household allowed us to explore how income, expenses and household labour rely on a variety of relationships. Grounding the definition of household in a nexus of relationships was important for understanding policy implications in new ways—an analytical dimension taken up later in the chapter. Given the longitudinal nature of our study we were privy to household changes, the effects of policy on household arrangements and survival and the multiple external relationships of family, friends and community that were part and parcel of household life. By retaining a flexible concept of household we were able to trace how relationships were altered alongside ongoing changes in the economy, the labour market and government programs.

Sampling for Social Location

The forty households were chosen to reflect some of the diversities in Ontario that we thought would be significant for understanding the differential impact of social policy; in other words, the sample was purposive. Such an approach to sampling ensured a range of income levels and sources and a variety of household structures and demographic characteristics (see Tables 1 and 3 in the Appendix). Furthermore, diversities intersect, so no household represented a single dimension. Of course, even though households might have been selected for specific characteristics, this selection did not predict or limit how household members discussed social policy. A household that was chosen for its income sources and regional location (for example, a household in a small urban setting whose members had social assistance as a primary income source) might have had members with much more to say about their experiences with Canadian immigration policies. Issues were illuminated in various ways, with participants emphasizing aspects of their lives we did not originally expect, adding new dimensions to the outcomes of policy changes.

In compiling our sample, we found it easier to access particular groups, such as sole-support mothers and those receiving social assistance, rather than others such as a two-parent working-class family or higher-income households. It became evident that a history of service use and of being studied as social problems makes some citizens far more visible than others. Higher-income groups often escape scrutiny and categorization in research, as do the effects they may experience due to policy changes. This study speaks to the importance of including such households in order to understand how social location cushions or exacerbates the effects of policies.

An analysis based on social location goes beyond organizing data around indicators such as income, race, gender, age or physical ability. It integrates these social dimensions; these then become a guide for understanding people's policy-related experiences. For example, people living with disabilities are often associated with health policy debates. Given the massive restructuring of health services at the time, participants in this study certainly experienced some of these debates. Just as pressing, however, were concerns about declining education and job possibilities and how they were exacerbated by changes to the rules for accessing transportation and social assistance programs, along with the more obvious changes to post-secondary education and student financial assistance programs. Similarly, universal access to health care was meaningless to a person who had no transportation for getting to the doctor's office, while access was enhanced for those with the expertise or time to navigate the health care system. In another case, concerns about changes in education policy were understood by an Aboriginal family in the context of how they had to constantly scrutinize their children's history texts for harmful depictions and/or invisibility of Aboriginal peoples. In sum, starting the original study with a sampling frame based on an understanding of social location made it possible to end with a book that draws a social map of a province at a particular moment in history.

Moving from Household Stories to Social Analysis

The intent of the interviews was to hear, in people's own words, how changes in government policy were affecting them. During the course of the study, however, the following question was often asked: "What can forty households tell you about an entire province?" In response we pointed to a research strategy that joined experiences over time with analysis in ways which allowed us to generalize beyond the specifics of the forty households that made up our sample. The design of the study was multi-method as well as longitudinal. It included not only data from in-depth interviews which are highlighted in this book, but also archival research, government documents, budgets, public accounts and a large body of statistical information. Together these various sources of data helped us to link particular household findings to broader policy effects reported by others. A multi-disciplinary research team ensured a number of perspectives were applied to the interpretation of these data.

The above notwithstanding, the richness of the data collected by using loosely structured, in-depth interviewing helped us to see the limitations of the conceptual tools policy researchers routinely use. The "forty household" question assumes that surveys with large samples are the "gold standard" for valid policy research. The data from this study challenges assumptions that "gold-standard" research designs exist. In the case of surveys, large numbers necessitate the use of predetermined response categories—and therein lies their weakness. These categories and their forced-choice options are determined by researchers, not participants.

Not surprisingly, they can miss as much as they reveal about how households manage financially or experience policy changes. Although the quantitative-qualitative debate is not new in the social sciences, the assumption that surveys tell a "truer" story remains the dominant paradigm in policy research, as well as amongst the media and the general public. They tell one story, not *the* story. Intensive and prolonged interviewing uncovered relationships and issues that would not have been found if we had limited our design to that of a longitudinal survey.

In each of the four rounds of data collecting, the interview was divided into two sections. First, we asked members of households a common set of benchmark questions that focused on demographic changes, daily routines, immediate and short-term concerns, coping strategies, the dynamics of household decision-making and community connections. The resulting data were used primarily to track households over time and to uncover the variety of forces that had an impact on the daily lives of participants. In the second section of each interview, we shifted our focus to consider household experiences in a particular policy area such as the labour market, education or health. The policy areas that became the focus of later research reports were identified during the first round of interviews, when households talked about the issues that were central to their daily lives. In the later rounds we allowed participants to direct the discussion about the policy area under consideration, raising issues that were relevant to them. This approach not only ensured that we did not impose priorities on households, it also helped confirm the subjects for discussion in subsequent interviews.

The dual aspect of the design (benchmark questions and policy area) helped ensure that connections between daily events and policy changes could be tracked and analyzed. It was also a strategy to circumvent the classic schism between private troubles and public issues. Although these may be distinct in much policy analysis, as well as the literature, they are not so clearly delineated in people's lives. Not surprisingly, some participants readily made connections between their experiences and the policy changes that were whirling around them, while others did not follow changes in government policies. The data-gathering approach ensured, however, that both types of information would be gathered so that analysis would not be abstract and severed from the events of daily life. At the same time, the dual approach of discussing benchmarks and new policy areas meant we were documenting household dynamics associated with the costs of "getting by" during a period of rapid social, political and economic change.

Once the narratives were collected, the next step was to take the forty stories and seek out common and disparate experiences for further analysis. The following box contains a step-by-step outline of the research process.

The "Speaking Out" Research Process

1. Interview forty households—benchmark and policy open-ended questions. Transcribe.
2. Establish themes across the forty households (first interview laid out topics for future interviews*).
3. With main report focus determined, do basic coding of interviews using NUD*IST.
4. In context of report focus, disaggregate interviews to produce more sub-coding on specific policy issues.
5. Sub-coding adds more detailed discoveries about policy across households and over time.**
6. Comparison is made with external studies, reports, statistics, seeking connections between household experiences and general data.
7. Begin draft of outline for report, basic areas, general sections.
8. In each section, researchers begin connecting specific household findings and stories to other data.
9. (A) Generalize from household findings to entire province when possible, (B) use stories to illustrate the findings of larger studies, (C) explore the multi-dimensional effect of policy on households.
10. Clearer themes of each section and overall picture emerge. Numerous drafts of sections, feedback from entire team.***
11. Hammer out final report, final agreement from households on quotes and descriptions.
12. Produce, release and distribute final report.

* First interview established more specific policy areas for subsequent interviews, i.e., interview two—education; interview three—health; interview four—income, jobs and social programs.
** This became more useful as rounds continued.
*** The entire team provided external research and support to the writing team.

With a complete set of forty interviews, plus earlier sets of interviews, the research team began the inductive process of reviewing transcripts and seeking out broad sets of themes. Our desire to keep households at the centre of our analysis meant that themes had to be considered while making sure that the specificity of people's experiences was not lost. These broad patterns directed the focus of each periodic report and its analysis.[6] Given that we could search our database over time and across a common set of issue areas, we were able to uncover associations not previously evident. The next step was to consider these linkages and themes, while reflecting on how they resonated (or not!) with debates in the wider policy landscape. When the focus of each report had been determined, we collected and considered external research. In particular, we considered polling data, surveys and other large-scale studies, related policy research and government reports and statistics relevant to our topic. From the inception of the project, the research team monitored and collected provincial (and relevant federal) news coverage in three newspapers. These varied data sources contributed to the emerging analysis of what was happening to participants and the relevance of such experiences to other households across the province. In other words, household experiences were located within the context of current policy changes, taking into consideration quantitative information about Ontarians generally; interview results did not remain isolated as narrative-based personal stories.[7]

Creating a balance between using narrative accounts and external data sources was an ongoing challenge. The speed of policy changes and lack of access to regulatory information also complicated the research process. One of the purposes of the "Speaking Out" project was to expand debate in specific policy areas through a conscious use of multiple modes of dissemination, especially the media. However, the particular policy area being investigated at each round of interviewing did not always coincide with the current hot topic that was of interest to the media. Furthermore, we often struggled with trying to concentrate on one policy area when participants described, not surprisingly, how multiple changes were happening at once. Interviewing people over time and mapping their relationships to social policies did allow us to gain insights into the tensions and contradictions between people's experiences and their worldviews. The data from this project suggests that these tensions need to be analyzed and theorized rather than edited out of policy reports. Although we attempted to do this in the reports at the time, our first priority in these reports was to tell the story of the effects that current policy changes were having on households. There was no room to explore in depth the broader dimensions of social policies that reverberated throughout the interviews.

The Importance of Intersectionality to Policy Analysis

A multi-method research strategy offered insights for research and policy analysis. This strategy revealed how the differential effects of policy changes occurred, depending upon the social location of participants. A flexible definition of the household uncovered the numerous relationships that make up people's experiences and showed how these are affected by social policies. Studies that can track the multiple, compounding and cumulative effects of policy changes on participants who are differentially located in Canadian society have a significant contribution to make to future policy analysis. The panel design of this study made complex accounting more viable. By starting with experience these connections could be drawn out, providing a picture of the everyday world where policy decisions have an impact.

Exploring participants' experiences and interpretations challenges and complicates the process of understanding people's responses to policy changes. As we sought to construct linkages between experience and areas of public policy, we were struck by how people managed the contradictions in their daily lives—not the least of which were tensions between their ideas of what constitutes a "good" policy and their actual experience of policy consequences (see Chapter Eight). People understand and interpret differently because they are differentially located in social space (Dhruvarajan and Vickers 2002). Contradictions regularly surfaced in our data. Documenting these gave us an opportunity to investigate how readily available discourses about the causes and consequences of social problems (as seen, for example, on TV or in newspapers) get picked up and used. On the one hand, people's stories can actually reproduce harmful stereotypes embedded in prevailing understandings of what is and what is not a "social problem." For example, policies related to child care, Ontario Works and the job market all too easily converge in ways that construct sole-support mothers as a "problem" for government. On the other hand, the specifics of a story can also be used to justify reducing social, political and economic issues to the problems of individuals. Steering an analytic course through these shoals demands vigilance and data-gathering instruments that are robust, but sensitive enough to document more then surface appearances.

Clarke and Neuman (1997) note that the combination of rising need and scarce resources is being redefined as a management problem, rather than being seen as a public issue about governance, policy priorities and the allocation of resources. One result has been a narrowing of program eligibility as agencies and governments attend to what the new market language calls their "core business." This process has meant that numerous issues that cross policy areas are defined as lying outside of the "core business" of more and more market, not-for-profit and public agencies. Community safety, dealing with poverty, child protection and care of children and elderly people are increasingly seen as the "core" business of families. Households have varied resources for dealing with the growing array of responsibilities assigned to them. Documenting this process of offloading and its effects on households is a critical part of policy analysis; it will affect future definitions of who is a citizen and, ultimately, which groups in society will be able to make claims as well as carry responsibility. Narratives such as Veronica's (Chapter Four) ground theoretical formulations by critical feminist and race analysts, such as Fraser (1997) and Williams (2000) who argue that social policy involves more than redistribution of resources. Unpaid work, and its companion, time, need to be redistributed. Veronica's life was measured out into five-minute teaspoons of time as she balanced her responsibilities: as a mother of young children who were also users of the health and education systems; as a part-time worker juggling split shifts; as the ex-wife of an abusive man; as a friend who needed to reciprocate help and support if she was to sustain valued relationships; and last, but not least, as a social assistance recipient who lived under increasing scrutiny and regulation.

Social policy as a subject matter has changed since the mid-seventies: the Keynesian economics that underpinned post-World-War-Two welfare-state policies was displaced by monetarism and a neoliberal social agenda in countries such as Canada. At the same time postmodern and post-structural theory has introduced alternative analytical approaches to the study of social policy. Policies are no longer seen as statements of intent, nor is language taken as a representation of experience. Both are considered as parts of discourses, to be understood and interpreted. While people experience policy differently, policies also construct groups in ways that entrench serious inequities.[8] Thus, the concept of need, for example, might be used as the basis for developing indicators for service priorities but it can also be examined as part of a discourse for controlling sectors of the population through categorizing some as in need of care, others as in need of surveillance and still others as in need of incentives to get off social assistance. These are struggles over meanings as much as they are struggles over resources. Thus, Canadian policy analysis, like its counterpart in the U.K., is facing the double challenge of focusing

> the analytic gaze of the discipline of social policy on the relations of meaning that are internal to the discourses embedded in policies themselves rather than to seek an objective truth "out there" which the policy documents then describe. The second is to insist that the study of social policy involves an identification and analysis of the forms of agency adopted by diverse welfare subjects. (Lewis, Gewirtz and Clarke 2000: 11)

To this we would add that the forms of agency of anyone, not just welfare subjects, should be considered.

Postmodern critiques created a crisis in policy analysis, in that the very idea of universalism seemed to deny that the roots of divisions were systemic and that they were actually reproduced in existent social policies. The challenge also undercut prevailing ideas of justice, truth and equality upon which post-World-War-Two social policy analysis rested (Lewis, Gerwitz and Clarke 2000; Twigg 2002). However, new understandings of social divisions, difference and identity are critical if social policy is to address new forms of local, national and international inequities. The boundaries of social policy are being questioned. Some are geographic and include the powers and limits of the nation-state. Others query social institutions, asking such questions as what constitutes family and community. The contested boundaries of public, voluntary and market sectors have been examined repeatedly over the last decade. Perhaps most challenging have been issues of identity and representation. Debates have revealed assumptions about who is imagined as the ideal citizen. In that regard, the data from this study also showed how these identities intersected in ways that might offset, but frequently exacerbate, disparities. Consequences of privilege occur whether a person chooses them or not. One cannot turn their effects on and off. The roots of privilege are often obscure and thus not recognized as such by those who bear them. Furthermore, the various dimensions of one's social location are not discrete entities; they intersect with others and are transformed into hierarchies of privilege, institutional structures and discourses that legitimate inequalities. These are routinely reproduced in daily life and become part of common sense knowledge[9] (Dhruvarajan and Vickers 2002: ix).

An important concern in research is the problem of "representation," sometimes discussed as an issue of voice. Our attempts to be mindful about issues of representation must also be considered alongside the interests of the research participants themselves. As active members in the study, many agreed to participate so they could be heard and influence the direction of government policies. In our final round of interviews we solicited responses from panel household members about their participation in this project. Their responses speak to the serious nature of sharing stories, the goals participants bring to the research process and what people learn about themselves (Kvale 1996; Ristock and Pennell 1996; Smith 1999). In some cases, participants became more engaged with public policy knowing the researcher was returning in a few months. Others saw it as an opportunity to track their own difficulties and accomplishments in life, with each round acting as a personal benchmark:

[Richard]: I have AIDS and I wanted those people who don't have it, or know someone with AIDS, to read and understand the kinds of problems that I face ... and how the government can affect my life, both good and bad.

[Angie]: My participation in this project gave me the opportunity to have a voice. I knew that my experience and opinions were going to be listened to, along with other people in the province, and then you were going to take all those experiences and opinions and put them into a report that would be read by people who were making decisions.

[Carl]: My participation in this project helped me articulate my feelings and thoughts around welfare in a more complete way. I was able to think about my experiences on welfare and think about other people and that definitely helped me articulate my thoughts a little better.

Policy researchers and analysts, like others working in the social sciences, are coming to terms with the implications for our discipline of situating ourselves in relationship to those we study. Understanding the effects of social policy is about understanding how power operates in hierarchical relationships. Thus, in order to understand poverty, we need to understand affluence; where white skin privilege exists, we need to understand how the dynamics of racism operate; in an able bodied society, we need to understand how the parameters of disability are determined.

The preceding chapters provide the type of data that can further our understanding of some of the "new social policy questions" facing individuals, communities, policy makers and analysts today. Questions such as: What differences and divisions matter? Why is it important to build into policies mechanisms that insure voice and situate people as citizens exercising agency, not merely as consumers of options defined by markets or states? These questions are important because they call attention to boundaries and definitions that affect the quality of life of individuals and collectives in local, national and international arenas. Throughout the study we struggled to articulate and operationalize the powerful and dominant images of consumer, citizen and community. We conclude, along with Hughes (1998), that these concepts are components of current social policy discourse that need to be interrogated rather than used as nouns that portray a meaningful subject. This powerful trinity guards the entrance to privilege, defending it against the rebellion of subversive discourses that present alternative ways of thinking about issues.

And What of the Future?

Gina and her father Gary portray some of the power of policy to affect the social conditions which frame the possibilities available to people:

[Gina]: Well, we're not on welfare anymore! Some people in my high school are incredibly harsh and very mean. They say, "Oh, you're on welfare, you stink, don't hang around with me."... It's hatred towards anybody that doesn't have money—just plain hatred.
[Gary]: That sort of attitude is the same as the government's towards people on welfare.... But it's not just welfare, it's those bad teachers, those bad students....
[Gina]: Those bad nurses, those bad ambulance drivers, bad everybody! The people that do the most for us, they hate. It's gross!
[Gary]: It's like, we should be extinct by now.

At sixteen years of age Gina has been thoroughly disciplined in the school of moral regulation. To belong means having income from sources that are not social assistance. The comments made by her peers draw on long-established dominant discourses about people on social assistance, but are silent about assumptions and values that underlie rhetoric about the market/consumer model of the responsible citizen. Incredibly this young, competitive swimmer whose body bore many marks of privilege, could not escape being defined as "dirty and stinky." The felt hatred for those in poverty was then extended by Gina and Gary to other sectors of the society, which seemed to be painted with the same brush—those who educated children, students and health care workers serving the ill. This devaluing goes beyond the common practice of drawing on readily available stereotypes about immigrants, racialized youth and sole-support mothers as the cause of social problems. Who escapes this expanding net of exclusion? Who is counted now as a legitimate citizen? Addressing such questions is pressing because the message being conveyed is that all who do not fit a narrow understanding of who can make claims as a citizen should be "extinct."

This study provided a unique data source. We had the opportunity to speak with and track the experiences of forty households across Ontario during one of the most widespread and contentious periods of policy change in that province. These changes shifted the relationship between the state and its citizens. Such a policy shift signals that the state is not an impartial arbitrator of competing interest groups but an active player in determining how privilege and oppression are distributed within and across different sectors of the population. The question of the meaning of citizenship has taken on urgency as nation-states grapple with the implications of globalized economies. Restructuring agendas, such as that developed in Ontario during the time of the study, do not flow automatically from changing world economies. Rather they reflect policy decisions made at the national, provincial and local levels. These "Made in Canada" policy responses will determine the meaning of citizenship to different sectors of the Canadian population. Thus, Canadian decision makers are responsible for the types of policies developed to regulate the influences of multilateral agreements; to recognize people as contributors to community, caregivers to family and friends, as well as consumers; to promote equity in a society where immigration policies, developed to meet labour force needs, instead leave newcomers without work. Under the rubric of "The Common Sense Revolution," social policy in Ontario was restructured in ways that supported already privileged sectors of society. While the government applauded its own actions, our study presents a very different version of what was happening in the province. The boundaries of the social map of Ontario were being redrawn, excluding those who were most vulnerable, while others teetered on its borders.

Notes

1. In Chapter One we discussed our rationale for using household voices as the conduit for conveying the effects of social policies, appreciating that participants' narratives were "reconstructed" to highlight aspects that addressed the

theme of the chapter into which we placed their story. Croft and Beresford (1998) observe that one of the paradoxes of the postmodernist turn in social policy is the way in which the experiences of service users are reinterpreted and restructured in academic debate, such that their voices are appropriated into another's privileged speech.

2. For information regarding the speed and scope of policy change see *Act in Haste ... The Style, Scope and Speed of Change in Ontario*, Kate Bezanson and Fraser Valentine (1998).

3. In Ontario, British Columbia and Quebec, superior courts have ruled that the current definition of marriage is discriminatory and unconstitutional. As of July 2003, the Supreme Court is being asked to examine a draft federal bill that would redefine marriage as "the lawful union of two persons to the exclusion of all others."

4. We refer here to the 1996 Census definition: this was the one in use as data was being collected and analyzed. The definition was modified in the 2001 Census.

5. Statistics Canada defines family income as the sum of the total incomes of all members fifteen years and over. We decided to not use family; instead we used household as the unit of analysis in our study.

6. A qualitative coding structure was developed to systemically classify the interview data. Using a computer software package, *Non-numerical Unstructured Data: Indexing, Searching and Theorizing* (NUD*IST), facilitated the indexing and comparison of our interviews in a variety of ways: (1) individual households at one time; (2) individual households over time; (3) groups of households at one time; and (4) groups of households over time.

7. Many of the themes we discovered from household experiences were supported by external research and quantitative studies and, in turn, informed other research and studies. The rise in non-standard work in our participants' lives was also evident in labour-market statistics (Noce and O'Connell 1998). The zeal for student testing and curriculum changes, while supported in principle by some parents, went hand-in-hand with the myth of the average student. Our identification of this theme was supported by other studies tracking the impact of education changes and was exemplified by a funding model that reduces supports to students with special needs (O'Connell and Valentine 1998). In the health report, we found caregiving was moving from hospitals to homes and increasing the unpaid work of women. This outcome was verified through examination of long-term care and hospital funding, along with research on changing policy directions in the health sector (Bezanson and Noce 1999).

The findings in *Booming For Whom: People in Ontario Talk About Incomes, Jobs and Social Programs* (Bezanson and McMurray 2000) are supported by Statistics Canada data, indicating that the booming Ontario economy is not benefitting everyone equally (Statistics Canada 2000). In fact, not only were we able to extrapolate our findings beyond our panel study, but we were able to provide data that in turn could situate and provide meaning to the results from large quantitative studies.

During the 1999 Ontario election, the government often celebrated statistics that reported a significant drop in the number of individuals on social assistance. The numbers have certainly decreased, but we challenge the interpretation that, while no longer receiving social assistance or welfare, these individuals have found good jobs. As we reported in *Take It or Leave It: The Ontario Government's Approach to Job Insecurity* (Noce and O'Connell 1998) and in *Booming For Whom* (Bezanson and McMurray 2000), an "improved" economy, public and nonprofit sector cutbacks and changes in labour legislation and income support programs work together to increase employment insecurity in Ontario.

8. For a recent discussion of how social location is connected to social policies and the welfare state, see Anderson, Eisenberg et al. 1998 and Dua and Robertson 1999.

9. The data from this study offers indirect evidence that the slogan of the Conservative government, "The Common Sense Revolution," was quite successful in fuelling and creating divisions amongst the electorate between 1995 and 2000.

References

Abu-Laban, Yasmeen. 2002. "Liberalism, Multiculturalism and the Problem of Essentialism." *Citizenship Studies* 6 (4):459–82.

Anderson, J., A. Eisenberg, S. Grace and V. Boag-Strong (eds.). 1998. *Painting the Maple: Essays on Race, Gender, and the Construction of Canada.* Vancouver: University of British Colombia.

Armstrong, L. 1993. *And They Call it Help: The Psychiatric Policing of America's Children.* Reading, MA: Addison-Wesley.

Armstrong, P., and H. Armstrong. 1996. *Wasting Away: The Undermining of Canadian Health Care.* Toronto, Oxford University Press.

Aronson, J. 1993. "Giving Consumers a Say in Policy Development: Influencing Policy or Just Being Heard?" *Canadian Public Policy* 19(4): 367–78.

Aronson, J., and S. Neysmith. 2001. "Manufacturing Social Exclusion in the Home Care Market." *Canadian Public Policy* 27(2): 151–65.

Baines, C., P. Evans and S. Neysmith. 1998. *Women's Caring: Feminist Perspectives on Social Welfare.* Toronto: Oxford University Press.

Bakker, I. 1996. *Rethinking Restructuring: Gender and Change in Canada.* Toronto: University of Toronto Press.

Bannerji, H. 1997. "Geography Lessons: On Being an Outsider/Outsider to the Canadian Nation. In L. G. Norman and L. Eyre (eds.), *Dangerous Territories: Struggles for Difference and Equality in Education.* New York: Routledge.

———. 2000. *The Dark Side of the Nation: Essays on Multiculturalism, Nationalism and Gender.* Toronto: Canadian Scholars Press.

Beiner, R. 1995. "Why Citizenship Constitutes a Theoretical Problem in the Last Decade of the Twentieth Century." In R. Beiner, *Theorizing Citizenship.* Albany: State University of New York Press.

Berthoud, R., and J. Gershuny (eds.). 2000. *Seven Years in the Lives of British Families: Evidence on the Dynamics of Social Change from the British Household Panel Survey.* Bristol: Policy Press.

Bessant, J., R. Hill, and R. Watts. 2003. *"Discovering" Risk: Social Research and Policy Making.* New York: Peter Lang.

Bezanson K., and S. McMurray. 2000. *Booming for Whom? People in Ontario Talk About Incomes, Jobs and Social Programs.* Speaking Out Project. Periodic Report #5. Ottawa: Caledon Institute of Social Policy.

Bezanson, K., and M.L. Noce. 1999. *Costs, Closures and Confusion: People in Ontario Talk about Health Care.* Ottawa: Caledon Institute of Social Policy.

Bezanson, K., and F. Valentine. 1998. *Act in Haste... The Style, Scope and Speed of Change in Ontario.* Speaking Out Project. Periodic Report #2. Ottawa: Caledon Institute of Social Policy.

Bongers, A., and D. Palmer. 1997. "At attention: Critics worry Ritalin is being used as sit down and shut up drug in classrooms." *Calgary Herald*, 30 June.

Boris, E. 1995. "The Racialized Gendered State: Constructions of Citizenship in the United States." *Social Politics* 2(2): 160–80.

Bryne, D. 1999. *Social Exclusion.* Buckingham: Open University.

Castells, M. 1996. *The Rise of the Network Society.* Oxford, U.K.: Blackwell.

Castles, S., and A. Davidson. 2000. *Citizenship and Migration: Globalization and the Politics of Belonging.* Houndsmill and London: MacMillan Press.

Clandinin, D.J., and F.M. Connelly. 1994. "Personal Experience Methods." In N.K.

Denzin and Y. Lincoln, *Handbook of Qualitative Research*. Thousand Oaks, CA: Sage.

Clarke, J., and J. Newman. 1997. *The Managerial State: Power, Politics and Ideology in the Remaking of Social Welfare*. London: Sage.

Coburn, D. 2000. "Income Inequality, Social Cohesion and the Health Status of Populations: The Role of Neoliberalism." *Social Science and Medicine* 51: 135–46.

Croft, S., and P. Beresford. 1998. "Postmodernity and the Future of Welfare: Whose Critiques; Whose Social Policies?" In J. Carter (ed.), *Postmodernity and the Fragmentation of Welfare*. London: Routledge.

Darville, R. 1995. "Literacy, Experience, Power." In M. Campbell and A. Manicom (eds.), *Knowledge, Experience and Ruling Relations*. Toronto: University of Toronto Press.

Dery, D. 2000. "Agenda Setting and Program Definition." *Policy Studies* 21 (1), 37–47.

Dhruvarajan, V., and J. Vickers. 2002. *Gender, Race and Nation*. Toronto, University of Toronto Press.

Dobuzinskis, L., M. Howlett, and D. Laycock (eds.). 1996. *Policy Studies in Canada: The State of the Art*. Toronto, University of Toronto Press.

Dominelli, L. 1999. "Neo-liberalism, Social Exclusion and Welfare Clients in a Global Economy." *International Journal of Social Welfare* 8: 14–22.

Drache, D., and T. Sullivan (eds.). 1999. *Health Reform: Public Success, Private Failure*. London and New York: Routledge.

Drover, G. 2000. "Redefining Social Citizenship in a Global Era." *Canadian Social Work. Special Issue on Social Work and Globalization* 2(1): 29–49.

Dua, E. 1999. "Beyond Diversity: Exploring the Ways in Which the Discourse of Race has Shaped the Institution of the Nuclear Family." In E. Dua and A. Robertson (eds.), *Scratching the Surface: Canadian Anti-Racist Feminist Thought*. Toronto: Women's Press.

Edwards, Peter, and Harold Levy. 2004a. "OPP secretly filmed woman." *Toronto Star*, March 27, Saturday Ontario Edition: A10

——. 2004b. "Long-awaited probe gearing up." *Toronto Star*, January 3, Saturday Ontario Edition: A15.

Elson, D. 1995. "Gender Awareness in Modeling Structural Adjustment." *World Development* 23 (11): 1851–68.

——. 1998. "The Economic, the Political and the Domestic: Businesses, States and Households in the Ogranisation of Production." *New Political Economy* 3(2).

Evans, R., K.M. McGrail, S.G. Morgan, M.L. Barer, and C. Hertzman. 2001. "APOCALYPSE NO: Population Aging and the Future of Health Care Systems." *Canadian Journal on Aging* 20 (suppl. 1): 160–91.

Fischer, F. 1990. *Technology and the Politics of Expertise*. Newbury Park, CA: Sage.

Fraser, N. 1989. *Unruly Practices: Power, Discourse and Gender in Contemporary Social Theory*. Minneapolis: University of Minnesota Press.

——. 1997. *Justice Interruptus: Critical Reflections on the "Postsocialist" Condition*. New York and London: Routledge.

Fudge, J., E. Tucker, and L. Vosko. 2002. *The Legal Concept of Employment: Marginalizing Workers*. Ottawa: Law Commission of Canada.

Gilbert, N. (ed.). 2001. *Targeting Social Benefits: International Perspectives and Trends*. International Social Security Series. New Brunswick, NJ, and London, U.K.: Transaction Publishers.

Glazer, N.Y. 1993. *Women's Paid and Unpaid Labour: The Work Transfer in Health Care and Retailing*. Philadelphia: Temple University Press.

Goldberg, D., and P. Essed. 2002. "Introduction: From Racial Demarcations to Multiple Identifications." In P. Essed and D.T. Goldberg, *Race Critical Theories: Text and Context*. Malden, MA, and Oxford: Blackwell.

Gustafson, D.L. (ed.). 2000. *Care and Consequences: The Impact of Health Care Reform*. Halifax: Fernwood.

Henderson, James Youngblood. 2002. "Sui Generis and Treaty Citizenship." *Citizenship Studies* 6 (4): 418–40.

Henretta, J., E. Grundy, and S. Harris. 2002. "The Influence of Socio-economic and Health Differences on Parents' Provision of Help to Adult Children: A British-United States Comparison." *Ageing and Society* 22(4): 441–58.

Herd, D., and A. Mitchell. 2002. *Discouraged, Diverted and Disentitled: Ontario Works New Service Delivery Model*. Toronto: Community Social Planning Council of Toronto.

Hill Collins, P. 1998. *Fighting Words: Black Women and the Search for Justice*. Minneapolis and London: University of Minneapolis Press.

hooks, b. 1989. *Talking Back: Thinking Feminist, Thinking Black*. Toronto: Between the Lines.

———. 2000. *All About Love, New Visions*. New York: Harper-Collins.

Howlett, M.I., and M. Ramesh. 1995. *Studying Public Policy: Policy Cycles and Policy Subsystems*. Toronto: Oxford University Press.

Hudson, H. 1998. "A Feminist Reading of Security in Africa." *Caring Security in Africa*. Cape Town: Institute for Security Studies.

Hughes, G. (ed.). 1998. *Imagining Welfare Futures*. London: Routledge and Open University.

Huntington, Samuel. 1993. "The Clash of Civilizations." *Foreign Affairs* (Summer) 72 (3): 22–28.

Jordan, B. 1996. *A Theory of Poverty and Social Exclusion*. Cambridge, MA: Polity.

———. 1998. *The New Politics of Welfare*. London: Sage.

Knijn, T., and M. Kremer. 1997. "Gender and the Caring Dimension of Welfare States: Towards Inclusive Citizenship." *Social Politics* 4(3): 328–61.

Kvale, S. 1996. *InterViews: An Introduction to Qualitative Research Interviewing*. Thousand Oaks, London and New Dehli: Sage.

Lewis, G., S. Gewirtz, and J. Clarke (eds.). 2000. *Rethinking Social Policy*. London: Open University and Sage.

Lewis, J. 2001. "Decline of the Male Breadwinner Model: Implications for Work and Care." *Social Politics* 8 (2): 151–69.

Littlewood, P., and S. Herkommer. 1999. "Identifying Social Exclusion: Some Problems of Meaning." In P. Littlewood, *Social Exclusion in Europe: Problems and Paradigms*. Aldershot, U.K.: Ashgate.

Luxton, M. (ed.). 1997. *Feminism and Families: Critical Policies and Changing Practices*. Halifax: Fernwood.

Luxton, M., and L.F. Vosko. 1998. "Where Women's Efforts Count: The 1996 Census Campaign and 'Family Politics' in Canada." *Studies in Political Economy* 56: 49–81.

Madanipour, A., G. Cars, and J. Allen (eds.). 1998. *Social Exclusion in European Cities*. London: Jessica Kingsley.

Malacrida, C. 2002. "Alternative Therapies and Attention Deficit Disorder: Discourses of Maternal Responsibility and Risk." *Gender and Society* 16 (3): 366–85.

Manzer, R. 1994. *Public Schools and Political Ideas: Canadian Education Policy in Historical Perspective*. Toronto: University of Toronto Press.

References

Marshall, T.H. 1965. *Class, Citizenship and Social Development.* New York: Anchor.

McMurray, S. 1997. *"Speaking Out" Project Description, Research Strategy and Methodology.* Ottawa: Caledon Institute of Social Policy.

Mitchell, A., and R. Shillington. 2002. *Poverty, Inequality and Social Inclusion.* Toronto: Laidlaw Foundation.

Mizen, P. 2002. "Putting the Politics Back into Youth Studies: Keynesianism, Monetarism and the Changing State of Youth." *Journal of Youth Studies* 5(1): 5–20.

Morris, J. 1993. "Feminism and Disability." *Feminist Review* 43: 57–70.

Mulinari, D., and K. Sandell. 1999. "Exploring the Notion of Experience in Feminist Thought." *Acta Sociologica* 42: 287–97.

Navarro, V. 1999. "Health and Equity in the World in the Era of 'Globalization.'" *International Journal of Health Services* 29 (2): 215–26.

Neysmith, S., and M. Reitsma-Steet. 2000. "Valuing Unpaid Work in the Third Sector: The Case of Community resource Centres." *Canadian Public Policy* 26 (3): 331–46.

Noce, L., and A. O'Connell. 1998. *Take it or Leave it: The Ontario Government's Response to Job Insecurity.* Speaking Out Project. Periodic Report #1. Ottawa: Caledon Institute of Social Policy.

NUD*IST. 1996. *Non-numerical Unstructured Data: Indexing, Searching and Theorizing.* Release #4. Victoria, AU: QSR International Pty Ltd.

O'Connell, A., and F. Valentine. 1998. *Centralizing Power, Decentralizing Blame: What Ontarians Say about Education Reform.* Speaking Out Project. Periodic Report #3. Ottawa: Caledon Institute of Social Policy.

O'Connor, J., A.S. Orloff, et al. 1999. *States, Markets, Families: Gender, Liberalism and Social Policy in Australia, Canada, Great Britain and the United States.* Cambridge: Cambridge University Press.

Oliverio, A. 1998. *Rationalizing a Social Problem: Mental Health and the Case of Attention Deficit Hyperactivity Disorder.* Paper presented at the annual meetings of the American Sociological Association.

Ontario 1994. "Long Term Care Act." *Statutes of Ontario,* Chapter 26.

Ontario 1995. "Job Quotas Repeal Act." *Statutes of Ontario,* Chapter 4.

Ontario 1995. "Labour Relations and Employment Statute Amendment Act." *Statutes of Ontario,* Chapter 1, Schedule A.

Ontario 1995. O. Reg.179/95.

Ontario 1995. O. Reg. 409/95 s.1 (1)(d), S. 1(3).

Ontario 1995. "Workers' Compensation and Occupational Health and Safety Amendment Act." *Statutes of Ontario,* Chapter 5.

Ontario 1996. "Employment Standards Improvement Act." *Statutes of Ontario,* Chapter 23.

Ontario 1996. "Family Responsibility and Support Arrears Enforcement Act." *Statutes of Ontario,* Chapter 21.

Ontario 1996. "Healthcare Consent Act." *Statutes of Ontario,* Chapter 2, Schedule A.

Ontario 1996. "Savings and Restructuring Act." *Statutes of Ontario,* Chapter 1.

Ontario 1997. "City of Toronto Act." *Statutes of Ontario,* Chapter 2.

Ontario 1997. "Education Quality Improvement Act." *Statutes of Ontario,* Chapter 3.

Ontario 1997. "Fair Municipal Finance Act." *Statutes of Ontario,* Chapter 5.

Ontario 1997. "Fairness for Parents and Employees Act." *Statutes of Ontario,* Chapter 32.

Ontario 1997. "Fewer Schools Boards Act." *Statues of Ontario,* Chapter 3.

Ontario 1997. "Government Process Simplification Act (Ministries of the Solicitor General and Correctional Services)." *Statutes of Ontario,* Chapter 39.

Ontario 1997. "Government Process Simplification Act (Ministry of the Economic Development, Trade and Tourism)." *Statutes of Ontario,* Chapter 36.

Ontario 1997. "Ontario Property Tax Assessment Corporation Act." *Statutes of Ontario,* Chapter 43.

Ontario 1997. "Ontario Works Act, 1997." *Ontario Regulations,* Chapter 134.

Ontario 1997. "Police Service Amendment Act." *Statutes of Ontario,* Chapter 8.

Ontario 1997. "Public Sector Dispute Resolution Act." *Statutes of Ontario,* Chapter 21, Schedule A.

Ontario 1997. "Public Sector Labour Relations Transition Act." *Statutes of Ontario,* Chapter 21, Schedule B.

Ontario 1997. "Red Tape Reduction Act (Ministry of Finance)." *Statutes of Ontario,* Chapter 19.

Ontario 1997. "Red Tape Reduction Act (Ministry of Northern Development and Mines)." *Statutes of Ontario,* Chapter 40.

Ontario 1997. "Social Assistance Reform Act." *Statutes of Ontario,* Chapter 25.

Ontario 1997. "Tenant Protection Act." *Statutes of Ontario,* Chapter 24.

Ontario 1997. "Water and Sewage Services Improvement Act." *Statutes of Ontario,* Chapter 6.

Ontario 1997 "Workplace Safety and Insurance Act." *Statutes of Ontario,* Chapter 16, Schedule A.

Ontario 1998. "Back to School Act." *Statutes of Ontario,* Chapter 13.

Ontario 1998. "Economic Development and Workplace Democracy Act." *Statues of Ontario,* Chapter 8.

Ontario 1998. "Energy Competition Act." *Statutes of Ontario,* Chapter 15.

Ontario 1998. O. Reg 134/98.

Ontario 1998. "Prevention of Unionisation Act (Ontario Works)." *Statutes of Ontario,* Chapter 17.

Ontario 1998. "Red Tape Reduction Act." *Statutes of Ontario.* Chapter 18.

Ontario 1998. "Statutes and Regulations Revision Act." *Statutes of Ontario.* Chapter 18, Schedule C.

Ontario 1998. "Tax Credit and Revenue Protection Act." *Statutes of Ontario* Chapter 34.

Ontario 1998. "Tax Cuts for People and Small Business Act." *Statutes of Ontario* Chapter 5.

Ontario 1999. "Balanced Budget Act." *Statutes of Ontario* Chapter 7, Schedule B.

Ontario 1999. "Ministry of Health and Long Term Care Statute Law Amendment Act." *Statutes of Ontario* Chapter 10.

Ontario 1998. "Tax Credit and Revenue Protection Act." *Statutes of Ontario* Chapter 34.

Ontario 1999. "Ministry of Health and Long Term Care Statute Law Amendment Act." *Statutes of Ontario* Chapter 10.

Ontario 1999. O. Reg. 386/99.

Ontario 1999. "Red Tape Reduction Act." *Statutes of Ontario* Chapter 12.

Ontario 1999. "Safe Streets Act." *Statutes of Ontario* Chapter 8.

Ontario 1999. "Taxpayer Protection Act." *Statutes of Ontario,* Chapter 7, Schedule A.

Ontario 2000. "Balanced Budgets for Brighter Futures Act." *Statutes of Ontario,* Chapter 42.

Ontario 2000. "Education Accountability Act." *Statutes of Ontario,* Chapter 11.

Ontario 2000. "Employment Standards Act." *Statutes of Ontario,* Chapter 4.

Ontario 2000. "Ministry of Training, Colleges and University Statutes Law Amendment Act."*Statutes of Ontario,* Chapter 36.

Ontario 2000. "Family Responsibility Act." *Statutes of Ontario,* Chapter 4.

Ontario 2000. O. Reg. 494/00.

Ontario 2000. O. Reg. 677/00.

Ontario 2000. "Post Secondary Choice and Excellence Act." *Statutes of Ontario,* Chapter 36.

Ontario 2000. "Red Tape Reduction Act." *Statutes of Ontario,* Chapter 26.

Ontario 2000. "Safe Schools Act." *Statutes of Ontario,* Chapter 12.

Ontario 2000. "Social Housing Reform Act." *Statutes of Ontario,* Chapter 27.

Ontario 2000. "Taxpayer Dividend Act." *Statutes of Ontario,* Chapter 10.

Ontario 2001. "Government Efficiency Act." *Statutes of Ontario,* Chapter 9.

Ontario 2001. O. Reg. 364/01.

Ontario 2001. "Responsible Choices for Growth and Accountability Act (2001 Budget)." *Statutes of Ontario,* Chapter 8.

Ontario Federation of Labour. 1998. "The Common Sense Revolution: 1184 Days of Destruction." <http://www.ofl-fto.on.ca/publications/daysofdestruction/> (retrieved March 2004).

Ornstein, Micheal D. 1995. *A Pofile of Social Assistance Recipients in Ontario.* Toronto: Institute for Social Research, York University.

———. 2000. *Race and Income Splits.* City of Toronto Access and Equity Office. Toronto: City of Toronto.

Perrons, D. 2000. "Care, Paid Work, and Leisure: Rounding the Triangle." *Feminist Economics* 6 (1): 105–14.

Razack, S. 2000. "'Simple Logic': Race, The Identity Documents Rule and the Story of a Nation Beseiged and Betrayed." *Journal of Law and Social Policy* 15: 181–209.

Reitsma-Street, M., and S. Neysmith. 2000. "Restructuring and Community Work: The Case of Community Resource Centres for Families in Poor Urban Neighbourhoods." In S. Neysmith, *Restructuring Caring Labour: Discourse, State Practice, and Everyday Life.* Toronto: Oxford University Press.

Ristock, J., and J. Pennel. 1996. *Comunity Research as Empowerment: Feminist Links, Post-modern Interruptions.* Toronto, Oxford.

Room, G.J. 1995. "Poverty and Social Exclusion: The New European Agenda for Policy and Research." In G. Room, *Beyond the Threshold: The Measurement and Analysis of Social Exclusion.* Bristol: Policy Press.

Saloojee, A. 2003. *Social Inclusion, Anti-Racism and Democratic Citizenship.* Toronto: Laidlaw Foundation.

Scott, J.W. 1992. "Experience." In J. Butler and J. W. Scott (eds.), *Feminists Theorize the Political.* New York and London: Routledge.

Sevenhuijsen, S. 1997. "Feminist Ethics and Public Health Care Policies." In P. DiQuinzo and I. M. Young, *Feminist Ethics and Social Policy.* Bloomington: University of Indiana Press.

Smith, D. 1987. *The Everyday World as Problematic: A Feminist Sociology.* Toronto: University of Toronto Press.

Smith, L.T. 1999. *Decolonizing Methodologies: Research and Indigenous Peoples.* London: Zed Books.

Statistics Canada. 1995. *Household's Unpaid Work: Measurement and Valuation.* Ottawa,

Supply and Services Canada.

_____. 1996. *Census Dictionary—Final Edition*. Cat. No. 92-351-UIE. Ottawa: Statistics Canada.

_____. 2000. *Income Trends in Canada 1980–1997*. Ottawa: Statistics Canada.

_____. 2003. "Census of Population: Income of Individuals, Families and Households." *The Daily* Tuesday May 13.

Threadgold, Terry. 1997. *Feminist Poetics: Poiesis, Performance, Histories*. New York: Routledge.

Torgerson, D. 1996. "Power and Insight in Policy Discourse: Post-Postivism and Problem Definition." In L. Doubuzinskis, M. Howlett and D. Laycock, *Policy Studies in Canada: The State of the Art*. Toronto: University of Toronto Press.

Toronto Star. 2002. Editorial. July 18: A24.

Toronto Star. 2003. "Cauchon unveils marriage bill." Friday July 18: A7.

Trickey, J. 1995. "The Racist Face of 'Common Sense.'" In D. Ralph, A. Regimbald and N. St.-Amand (eds.), *Open for Business, Closed to People: Mike Harris's Ontario*. Halifax: Fernwood.

Tronto, J. 1993. *Moral Boundaries: A Political Argument for the Ethic of Care*. New York and London: Routledge.

Twigg, J. 2002. "The Body in Social Policy: Mapping a Territory." *Journal of Social Policy* 31(3): 421–39.

Ungerson, C. 1987. *Policy is Personal*. London and New York: Tavistock.

Vandenberg, A. (ed.). 2000. *Citizenship and Democracy in a Global Era*. Houndsmill and London: MacMillan Press.

Vobruba, G. 2001. "Actors in processes of Inclusion and Exclusion: Toward a Dynamic Approach." *Social Policy and Administration* 34 (1): 601–513.

Vosko, L. 2000. *Temporary Work: The Gendered Rise of a Temporary Employment Relationship*. Toronto: University of Toronto Press.

Wacquant, L. 1996. "The Rise of Advanced Marginality." *Acta Sociologia* 39.

Waring, M. 1988. *Counting for Nothing: What Men Value and What Women are Worth*. Wellington: Allen and Unwin.

Williams, A.P., R. Deber, et al. 2001. "From Medicare to Home Care: Globalization, State Retrenchment, and the Profitization of Canada's Home Care System." In P. Armstrong, H. Armstrong and D. Coburn, *Unhealthy Times: Political Economy Perspectives on Health and Care*. New York: Oxford: 7–30.

Williams, Fiona. 2000. "Principles of Recognition and Respect in Welfare." In G. Lewis, Sharon Gewirtz and John Clarke (eds.), *Rethinking Social Policy*. London: Open University and Sage.

World Bank. 1998. *The Initiative on Defining, Monitoring and Measuring Social Capital*. Washington, DC: World Bank.

_____. 2000. *Entering the 21st Century: World Development Report 1999/2000*. New York: Oxford University Press.

Yalnizyan, A. 2000. *Canada's Great Divide: The Politics of the Growing Gap between Rich and Poor in the 1990s*. Toronto: Centre for Social Justice.

Appendix

Identifying and Selecting Households

Because of the project's emphasis on people with low incomes, the majority of participating households were low-income, with different sources for that income. Our financial constraints dictated that at least half would be from the Metropolitan Toronto or greater Toronto area, while the remaining households would be split among different regions in Ontario. The proportion of other characteristics was finalized during the selection process.

The template then was used to determine the types of contacts we needed to find potential household leads. We returned to the template over time to check our success in achieving a diverse sample of households but recognized that the template served as a starting point, to guide us in our recruitment and selection, and not as the final determinant in our selection.

We asked selected community organizations to identify potential participants. We felt that people might be more willing to reveal personal details and make a commitment to participate in a three-year study if they were introduced to the project by someone they knew.

Our primary criteria for selection were that households meet some mix of the template characteristics and that participants be able to communicate their day-to-day experiences. We were primarily seeking experiences, not opinions. To determine whether our criteria were met, we collected initial demographic information and then followed up with a face-to-face or telephone screening interview with at least one household member.

Households were selected on a rolling basis. We examined each household's characteristics to see the match with those we were seeking, explored the characteristics for variety (in occupations, for example) and compared households with similar characteristics with one another. The selection process evolved as more households were selected, and we became more specific about the desired proportion of other characteristics, such as sources of income and household structures. At the same time, we remained flexible about exact proportions, given that those proportions would change anyway as household situations changed.

Organizations with which we had spoken passed along information about our project to other contacts; as well, potential households passed along our brochures to people they knew. All of this had a snowball effect. We received calls directly from interested people as well as referrals from community organizations. We continued to make decisions as new screen leads became available.

A strict guarantee of confidentiality was critical in finding households who would be willing to reveal personal information and who would commit to three years of participation. The steps we took to provide this guarantee are described under "ethical considerations." We provided each household with an honorarium following each interview, to acknowledge their contribution to the project and to compensate them for their time during the interview as well the time spent reviewing written materials or providing additional information in follow-up contacts. Finally, so that households would incur no cost as a result of their participation, we paid for expenses such as child care or transportation.

Our search for households began in March 1997 and was completed in December 1997. The careful and detailed search for representative households enhanced the quality of our research.

Ethical considerations

Each household was given a copy of the ethics protocol it signed, which described the project, promised that no reports would contain identifying information, outlined household participation and identified any anticipated risks and benefits. To ensure that these ethical guidelines were followed the following steps were taken:

- We described the project and its objectives thoroughly to each household and answered questions they had regarding the project.
- We clearly indicated that households could withdraw at any time for any reason and that they could ask for the tape recorder to be turned off.
- We guaranteed confidentiality to all participating households. Even the contacts who provided potential household leads did not know whether those people were participating, unless contacts were told directly by participants.
- Pseudonyms were used in our reports. Our database did not include identifying information, such as real names and addresses, names of children's schools or child-care centers. With the exception of Metropolitan Toronto, the names of communities were not used.
- At an administrative level, we were careful with even minor details, such as not identifying the honorarium receipts that households signed.
- We taped the interviews to build up a computer database over time: we included transcriptions of each interview, to the ensure accuracy of our data and to permit the interviewers to pay full attention to the discussion. However, after the project was completed, the tapes and transcripts were destroyed. Only team members, the transcribers and the translator (for interviews not conducted in English) heard the tapes. Each of these people had signed a confidentiality declaration.

- Finally, since there was a possibility that the project might be perceived as a resource to households in times of crisis, team members prepared themselves to play a limited role by identifying actual resources, such as food banks and shelters, to which we could refer people if necessary. (Adapted from McMurray 1997: 4–5)

Table 1: Income Levels

Level	# of households
Low	25
Middle	13
Mixed	1
High	11

Table 2: Primary Sources of Income

Source	# of households
Employment	24
Social assistance	10
Other (e.g., OSAP)	6

Table 3: Other Characteristics of Individual Household Members

	Gender	Racial Minorities	Persons with Disabilities	Franco-phones	Abori-ginal people	Gays or lesbians	English as 2nd language
# of Adults =65	39F 26M	12	3	3	6	5	8
# of children =67		17	1	3	5		

Chart 1: Who's Better Off?

Household	Income level	What changed?
Sara and Anand	Moved higher within high-income range	He got a promotion, she found a permanent job and grandparents provide free child care
Angie	Moved higher in medium-income range	Worked extra hours, began relationship with Travis, who has well-paid job and a home
Barbara	Moved higher in medium-income range	Began relationship with Adam, who has well-paid job and a home
Carl	Moved higher in medium-income range	Found full-time work. He and partner separated
Janet and Christopher	Hers was low, his medium; both are now medium	Moved in together. He works more than full-time hours, she cleans more houses
Monica and Randy	Was low; moved into medium-income range	Moved into her mother's home. She started paid in-home child-care business, he began receiving Workers' Compensation benefits and training and is able to do some work
Jessie and Mark	Was low; moved into medium-income range	She left social assistance for full-time job and consulting, he started and lost small business
Richard and Henry	Moved up a bit in lower-income range	Started receiving dietary supplement under Ontario Disability Support Program, family gives Richard money
Patrick	Moved up a bit in lower-income range	Found low-paid part-time retail job and left social assistance
James	Moved up in low-income range	Was homeless, now receiving full social assistance, augments this by selling crafts and doing cleaning, has more stable housing
Rosa	Moved up a bit in lower-income range	Left social assistance for low-paid clerical job, receives child support and Canada Child Tax Benefit

Chart 2: Who's Doing the Same?

Household	Income level	What has life been like between 1995 and 1999?
Gary and one teenager	Medium	Self-employment fluctuated and earnings went down while his wife was dying because he periodically took time off
Christine, Dwight and one teenager	Medium	Her in-home child-care business fluctuated, his job remained low-paying and his small business generates no income
Victoria and one teenager	Medium	Was downsized and then placed in a similar job
Frank and Michael	Medium	Both changed contract jobs and one returned to school, got a large grant, bought a house
Rosie and Bob	Medium	He started receiving Old Age Security and Canada Pension Plan benefits, she gained and lost part-time job
Cheryl, Paul and two children	Medium	He has steady job, she worked briefly at a few short-term jobs
Josie, married daughter and husband, and four children	Medium	Her job became permanent full-time, she adopted grand-children, family members moved in and out
Lisa, Ray and two children	Medium	He has a steady job, she is not in the labour market
Jerry and one child	Medium	He was in university, then had a child and got married, now has permanent job and is living rent-free in parents' home
Denzel	Medium	He was in university, then received welfare, found and lost two jobs, received Employment Insurance and is now working full-time but has large Ontario Student Assistance debt
Aida, Xavier and one adult daughter	Medium	She works more hours, his business earns less, son's medication is very expensive, they are paying Employment Insurance overpayment and back taxes
Melanie,	Medium	All three moved in together, Melanie's

Heather and Ron		hours have been cut, Ron has got full-time job, Heather's full-time job ended and she has worked at intermittent contracts but is ineligible for Employment Insurance
Natalie, Antonio and two children	Low	Moved from social assistance augmented by his cash employment to college to low-paid work for both, they have large Ontario Student Assistance Program debt

Chart 3: Who's Falling Behind?

Household	Income level	Why are they worse off?
Pamela, Bert and one teenager	Still medium, but lower	She retired from a position about to be eliminated, he chose to retire, helping son with university tuition
Maria and Leo	Still medium, but lower	She took early retirement from teaching, his work is now seasonal
Liz	Still medium, but lower	Was working half-time after taking early retirement, now earning a bit less working nearly full-time
Denise, Rick and three teenagers	Still medium, but lower	Her full-time hours were cut back, now patches together part-time or temporary jobs. He no longer is eligible for overtime
Sabrina and Elizabeth	Still medium, but lower	Sabrina was laid off, drew Employment Insurance, received welfare, patched together jobs and now combines several into full-time work, Elizabeth has received steady raises
Julie	Fell from medium to low	Moved from permanent job to government job that was eliminated. Now working part-time
Michelle and two children	Was low, now lower	Has been working a variety of contract and part-time jobs, no longer has supplementary health benefits, social assistance says she owes $70,000 in overpayment
Jackie and three children	Was low, now lower	Family is larger, she is working part-time
Ashley	Was low, now lower	Laid off, patched together income from Employment Insurance and part-time

		jobs, moved to small town and collected social assistance, now receiving assistance from the Employment Insurance self-employment program
Amy and three children	Was low, now lower	Separated, went from income from husband's job and welfare top-up to social assistance, to Ontario Student Assistance Program-supported college. Has large student debt and no supplementary health benefits
Anne and four children	Was low, now lower	Separated and lost part-time job as a result, began receiving social assistance and is now working part-time
Veronica and two children	Was low, now lower	Separated, moved, lost part-time job, now combines social assistance and new part-time job
Jenny and four children	Was low, now lower	Social assistance rates were cut
Teresa	Was low, now lower	Her social assistance for persons with disabilities took small cut, rent went up, Vocational Rehabilitation Services eliminated
Sadan and five children	Was low, now lower	Social assistance rates were cut, was shifted to General Welfare Assistance because husband returned home briefly
Kate and two children	Was low, now lower	Social assistance rates were cut, started some cash employment, cut off social assistance, partner left
Samantha, Nathan and two children	Was low, now lower	Both were in school and living at home with parents, now live together with children and receive social assistance

Chart 4: Household Income

HOUSEHOLD CHARACTERISTICS & INCOME in 2000				
Name, profile, size & ages	Location	Household Income	Individual Employment Status and Job	Percentage of Income Spent on Housing
Jenny (30) Lone-parent family of 5 – mother and 4 children, children are 11, 8, 4, & 3 mos.	Mid-size southeast Ontario city	Low $16K - 49% below LICO	Not in labour market but wants to work	29% - Rental housing, subsidy, town house $4.6K/yr $383/month
Anne (29) Lone-parent family of 5 – mother and 4 children, children are 10, 9, 6, 4	Mid-size southeast Ontario city	Low $19K - 39% below LICO	Employed: retail (pt)	23%- Rental housing, subsidy, town house $4.4Kyr $367/month
Ashley (59) Single – boyfriend joins her on weekends	Small southeast Ontario town	Low $13K - 6% below LICO)	Self-employed: hospitality (pt)	33% - Own house, no mortgage $4.3K/yr $358/month
Rosa (35) Lone-parent family of 2 – mother and 1 child; daughter is 5	Toronto	Low $20K - 8% below LICO	Employed: clerical (ft)	42% - Rental housing, market rent, apartment $8.4K/yr $700/month
Gary (38) Lone-parent family of 2 - father and 1 child; daughter is 16	Greater Toronto Area (GTA)	Middle $32K -73% above LICO	Self-employed: painter (ft)	36% - Rental housing, market rent, house $11.4K/yr $950/month
Denise & Rick (41 & 46) Blended family of 5 – mother and father with 3 teens (+2 away); children are 19, 17, 16	GTA	Middle $43K -37% above LICO	Employed: retail, service (pt x2) Employed: labourer (ft)	34% - Rental housing, market rent, house $14.7K/yr $1,225/month

Family	Location	Income / LICO	Employment	Housing
Christine & Dwight (mid-30s & 36, 2-parent family of 3 – mother, father & child, son is 14	Small southwest Ontario town	Middle $48K -124% above LICO	Self-employed: child care (ft) Employed: journalist (ft)	27% - Own house, mortgage $12.8K/yr $1,067/month
Victoria (49) Lone-parent family of 2 – mother, 1 child (+1 away), daughter is 21	Eastern Ontario city	Middle $60K -175% above LICO	Employed: social worker (ft)	10% - Own house, no mortgage $5.8K/month $483/month
Patrick (35) Single – lives alone	Toronto	Low $12K- 31% below LICO	Employed: retail (pt)	50% - Rental housing, market rent, bsmt apt. $6.0K/yr $500/month
Veronica (31) Lone-parent family of 3 – mother and 2 children; children are 9 and 6	GTA	Low $18K- 33% below LICO	Employed: school bus driver (pt)	70% - Rental housing, market rent, sep.unit in house $12.6K/yr $1,050/month
Frank & Michael (39 & 41) Couple – no children	Toronto	Middle $103K -372% above LICO	Student (ft) and research assistant Employed: counsellor (ft)	21% - Own house, mortgage $21.8K/yr $1,817/month
Natalia & Antonio (42 & 38) 2-parent family of 4 – mother, father and 2 children +1 lives away; children are 13, 9	Toronto	Low $21K- 36% below LICO	Employed: clerical (pt) Employed: courier (ft)	46% - Rental housing, market rent, apt. $9.6K/yr $800/month
Teresa (33) Single – lives alone	Toronto	Low $8K- 54% below LICO	Not in labour market	30% - Rental housing, subsidized rent, apt. $2.4K/yr $200/month
Angie & Travis (36 & mid 40s) Blended family of 5 –	Eastern Ontario city	Middle $115K -214%	Employed: building mgr.(ft)	9% - Own house, mortgage $9.8K/yr

Household	City	Income	Employment	Housing
mother, new partner, her 2 and his 1 children (+ 1 lives away); her sons are 16 and 14; his is 22		above LICO	Employed: tradesperson (ft)	$817/month
Sadan (42) Lone-parent family of 6 – mother and 4 children (+ 1 who lives away); children are 21, 16, 14, 9, 2	Toronto	Low $19K - 53% below LICO	Not in labour market	24% - Rental housing, subsidized rent, apt. $4.5K/yr $375/month
Richard & Henry (52 & 44) Couple	Toronto	Low $18K - 17% below LICO	Unable to work/ill Employed: construction (pt)	60% - Rental housing, market rent, apt. $10.8K/yr $900/month
Amy (29) Lone-parent family of 4 – mother, 3 children; children are 14, 8, 6	Toronto	Low $22K - 33% below LICO	Not in labour market; attending college ft	56% - Rental housing, market rent, apt. $12.4K/yr $1,033/month
Kate (30) Now 1-parent family of 3 – mother and 2 children +1 lives away, rents house with sister; children are 9, 4	Toronto	Low $13K - 52% below LICO	Now unemployed; was receptionist (pt)	65% - Rental housing, market rent, house $8.4K/yr $700/month
Carl (36) Now single – rents apartment with brother	Toronto	Medium $40K -130% above LICO	Employed: outreach worker (ft)	13% - Rental housing, market rent, apt. $5.1K/yr $425/month
Liz (56) Single – lives alone	Toronto	Medium $29K- 67% above LICO	Retired: now working retail (pt)	23% - Own house, mortgage, $6.7K/yr $559/month
Michelle (43) Lone-parent family of 3 – mother and 2 children; children are 10 and	Toronto	Low $18.5K -31% below LICO	Unemployed; seeking work; was doing clerical work (pt)	48% - Rental housing, market rent, apt. $8.8K/yr $733/month

8				
Rosie & Bob (62 & 68) Couple (+adult son who pays rent)	Toronto	Medium $23.5K -8% above LICO	Employed: crossing guard (pt, seasonal) Retired	18% - Own house, no mortgage $4.3K/yr $358/month
Denzel (28) Single	GTA	Medium $23K -32% above LICO	Employed: call centre supervisor (ft)	20% - Rental housing, market rent, apt. $4.6K/yr $383/month
Jackie (36) Lone-parent family of 4 – mother and 3 children; children are 17 and 3, 2 mos	Mid-size southeast Ontario city	Low $22K - 22% below LICO	Employed: on maternity leave from community development worker (pt)	25% - Rental housing, rents part house from mother, $5.4K/yr $450/month
Cheryl & Paul (49 & 51) 2-parent family of 4 – mother, father and 2 children; sons are 17 and 14	Small southwest Ontario city	Middle $72K -157% above LICO	Seeking work Employed: teacher (ft)	18% - Own house, mortgage $13K/yr $1,083/month
Josie, Rebecca & Frazer (50, 26 & late 20s) 3-generation family of 7 – mother, daughter and partner, 4 children; children are 8, 6, 4, 4 mos	GTA	Middle $45K Low $11K Middle $22K	Employed: health care aid (ft) Not in labour market: maternity Employed: (ft)	30% - Rental housing, partial subsidy in co-op, townhouse $14.2K/yr; moving to rental market housing $1,183/month
Maria & Leo (53 & 54) 2-parent family of 3 – mother, father and 1 son (+ 1 away); son is 25	GTA	Middle $56K -141% above LICO	Retired: teacher Employed: textile worker (ft, seasonal)	28% - Own house, mortgage $15.6K/yr $1,300/month
Sabrina & Elizabeth (34 & 36) House mates – no children	Toronto	Middle $72K -230% above LICO	Employed: caregiver (ptx2) Employed: social	17% - Rental housing, market rent, share a house with others

Family	Location	Income / LICO	Employment	Housing
			worker (ft)	$12K/yr $1,000/month
Jessie & Mark (34 & 33) Couple – no children	Mid-size northern Ontario city	Middle $27K -46% above LICO	Employed: coordinator (ptx2) Unemployed: small business failed	36% - Live in house owned by parents, pay mortgage $9.6K/yr $800/month
Monica & Randy (35 & 33) Blended family of 5 – mother, father and 3 children; children are 16,10, 8	Small southern Ontario city	Middle $37K -18% above LICO	Employment($20K)/ Self-employed: child care (ft) Self-employed: landscape architecture (seasonal); garage (pt)	16% - Rental housing, rent part of house from parent $6K/yr $500/month
Lisa & Ray (46 & 40) 2-parent family of 4 – mother, father and 2 children; sons are 16 and 13	Mid-size northern Ontario city	Middle $36K -29% above LICO	Employed: cash jobs (pt) Employed: community worker (ft)	23% - Rental housing, market rent, apt. in a house/duplex. $8.4K/yr $700/month
Janet & Christoher (42 & 49) Blended family of 5 - mother, father and 3 children (+2 more on weekends +2 away); children are 19, 17, 14	Mid-size southeast Ontario city	Middle $63K -102% above LICO	Self employed: small service business (ft) Employed: nurse (pt x2)	19% - Own house, mortgage $11.9K/yr $992/month
James (29) Single – staying with a friend	Toronto	Low $11K - 37% below LICO	Self employed: squeegeeing, crafts (pt)	38% - Rental housing, market rent, paying friend to stay in her apt, $4.2K/yr $350/month
Pamela & Bert (late 40s & early 50s) 2-parent family of 3 - mother, father and 1 child	Mid-size northern Ontario city	Middle $50K -117% above LICO	Semi-retired: was in managment, now does consulting (pt)	22% - Own house, mortgage $11.2K/yr $933/month

			Retired: primary industry	
(+1 away at university); sons are 28 and 18				
Aida & Xavier (49 & 45) 2-parent family of 3 – mother, father and 1 daughter (+2 away); daughters are 26, 28, son is 21	Toronto	Middle $41K -25% above LICO	Employed: community worker (ptx2) Employed: construction labourer (ft, seasonal)	51% - Own house, mortgage $21K/yr $1,750/month
Barbara & Adam (30s & 40s) Family of 4 – lone parent with 2 children and new partner; daughters are 18 and 17	Small northern town	Middle $87K -235% above LICO	Employed: office administration (ft) Employed: primary industry (ft)	Unknown - Own house, small mortgage
Melanie, Heather & Ron (53, 31 & 29) 2-generation family of 3 – mother, daughter and daughter's partner	Toronto	Middle $102K -277% above LICO	Employed: teacher (seasonal) (ft) Unemployed: clerical(ft) Employed: computer support (ft)	Unknown - Own house, mortgage, daughter and son pay mother rent
Sara & Anand (38 & 39) 2-parent family of 4 – mother, father and 2 children; children are 5, 8	Toronto	High $250K -657% above LICO	Employed: researcher(ft) Employed: head of college department (ft) & Self-employed: researcher (pt)	24% - Own house, mortgage $60K/yr $5,000/month
Julie Single (37)– lives alone	Toronto	Low $15K- 14% below LICO	Employed: researcher (pt)	88% - Own condominium, mortgage $13.2K/yr $1,100/month
Samantha & Nathan (17 &	Toronto	Low $14K-	Not in labour market	26% - Rental housing,

20) 2-parent family of 4 - mother, father and 2 children; children are 3 and 1.5 years		57% below LICO	Seeking work	subsidized rent, apt. $3.6K/yr $300/month
Jerry (26) Lone-parent family of 2; daughter is 4	Eastern Ontario city	Middle $26K -19% above LICO	Employed: office administration (ft)	Rent-free housing, bsmt apt in parent's home

Characteristic	Term	Definition
Household Income	LICO	Low Income Cut-Offs (used by Statistics Canada to determine whether families fit into a "low income" category)
Individual Employment Status & Job	ft	job is full time
Individual Employment Status & Job	pt	job is part time

Please note: there are three households for whom information about housing expenditures and individual responsibilities within households for overall expenditures was incomplete and therefore no calculations were made about LICOs or about percentage of income spent on housing.